PERFORMANCE AND EVOLUTION IN THE AGE OF DARWIN

Performance and Evolution in the Age of Darwin reveals the ways in which the major themes of evolution were taken up in the performing arts during Darwin's adult lifetime and in the generation after his death.

The period 1830–1900 was the formative period for evolutionary ideas. While scientists and theorists investigated the law and order of nature, show business was more concerned with what was out of the natural order. Missing links and throwbacks, freak taxonomies and exotic races were favourite subject matter for the burgeoning variety theatre movement. Focusing on popular theatre forms in London, New York and Paris, Jane Goodall shows how they were interwoven with the developing debate about human evolution.

With this book, Goodall contributes an important new angle to the debates surrounding the history of evolution. She reveals that, far from creating widespread culture shock, Darwinian theory tapped into some of the long-standing themes of popular performance and was a source for diverse and sometimes hilarious explorations.

Jane R. Goodall is currently Director of Research in the College of Arts, Education and Social Sciences at the University of Western Sydney where she specialises in the development of cross-disciplinary research. She is the author of *Artaud and the Gnostic Drama* (1994).

PERFORMANCE AND EVOLUTION IN THE AGE OF DARWIN

Out of the natural order

Jane R. Goodall

London and New York

First published 2002
by Routledge
11 New Fetter Lane, London EC4P 4EE

Simultaneously published in the USA and Canada
by Routledge
29 West 35th Street, New York, NY 10001

Routledge is an imprint of the Taylor & Francis Group

© 2002 Jane R. Goodall

Typeset in Garamond by
Florence Production Ltd, Stoodleigh, Devon
Printed and bound in Great Britain by
TJ International Ltd, Padstow, Cornwall

British Library Cataloguing in Publication Data
A catalogue record for this book is available
from the British Library

Library of Congress Cataloging in Publication Data
A caatalog record for this book has been requested

ISBN 0–415–24377–7 (hbk)
ISBN 0–415–24378–5 (pbk)

FOR ROSE

CONTENTS

ILLUSTRATIONS

ACKNOWLEDGEMENTS

I began work on this book in Aberystwyth in Wales, where the Centre for Performance Research afforded me access to their library, and helped spark ideas with the kind of generous and energised engagement for which they are renowned. It was finished in Canberra, on a visiting fellowship with the Humanities Research Centre, which enabled me to spend concentrated time writing, again surrounded by scholars with sympathetic interests. This was made possible through a study leave allocation from the University of Western Sydney, where I have enjoyed the support and collective genius of a unique group of colleagues who continue to maintain a stalwart commitment to scholarship and research in the midst of intense pressures. I am deeply grateful to all of them, not least Peter Hutchings, who took over from me as Head of School during a difficult restructure. I have had specific advice on chapter drafts from Ruth Barcan, Chris Fleming, Peta Tait, Steven Maras and Katrina Schlunke. Other colleagues and friends who have helped with inspiration, suggestions, exploratory conversations and not a few bottles of wine include Lesley Stern, Helen Grace, Nick Haeffner, Mark Haeffner, Wendy Holland, Fran Dyson, Douglas Kahn, Kathy Robinson and Zoe Sofoulis. Jim Davis and Victor Emeljanow gave generous advice on some of the historical material. Talia Rogers at Routledge is an inspiration to talk to about any book in the performance studies area, and her encouragement has been vital, as has the expertise of Rosie Waters in the submission stages. Linda Barcan was an exceptionally skilled last-minute research assistant. Any errors in the book are my own.

The experience of conducting historical research gives one a sharp appreciation of the importance of a good archive, and of the invaluable role played by the specialist librarians who manage them. I have benefited especially from the expert assistance of Annette Fern at the

Harvard Theatre Collection and Julie Anne Lambert at the John Johnson Collection in the Bodleian Library. I would also like to express my gratitude for permission to access the collections at the Theatre Museum in London, the British Library, the Westminster City Archives, the New York Public Library, the New York Historical Society, Fisher Library at Sydney University, the State Library of New South Wales, the Hancock and Menzies Libraries of the Australian National University and the Australian National Library in Canberra.

Every effort has been made to obtain permission to reproduce copyright material. If any acknowledgement has not been made, we would invite copyright holders to inform us of the oversight.

On a personal note, my father Paul Haeffner has been a wonderful support in every way and, with his sixth sense about all things theatrical, has found some of the most valuable references. Susan Murphy has given wise council about the strange by-ways of the mind road, always with her uniquely anarchic humour. Peter Goodall is a companion in all things. Besides listening to the litany of anxieties, answering weird factual questions with unfailing accuracy and applying his eagle eye for style to doubtful paragraphs, he has managed to keep some kind of domestic order in our lives during a year when we were both trying to finish books. Jon Goodall lifts the spirits with his cool sense of irony, and just goes on evolving.

Some parts of Chapter 3 were originally published in 'Acting Savage' in Peta Tait (ed.), *Body Show/s*, Amsterdam, Rodopi, 2001. I would like to thank the publishers for permission to reprint this material.

ABBREVIATIONS

ANL   Australian National Library
HTC   Harvard Theatre Collection
JJC   John Johnson Collection, Bodleian Library
NYCL   New York City Library (Billy Rose Collection)
NYHS   New York Historical Society
TML   Theatre Museum, London
WCA   Westminster City Archives

INTRODUCTION

A *Punch* cartoon of 1849 shows a mother and small child walking along the street, and passing a performing monkey dressed in a hat and coat. 'Mamma!' says the child, 'Look! Dere, dere Papa!'[1] This 'awful instance of perception of character in an infant prodigy' (as the caption runs) precedes the Darwin-inspired debate on ape ancestry by ten years, but the equivalence of monkeys and humans had been a commonplace joke in street performances and fairgrounds for centuries. The performing arts linked with fairground tradition provide overwhelming evidence of general curiosity about the relationship between humans and other species, but also about the human as species. 'The question of questions for mankind,' said Thomas Henry Huxley, ' – the problem which underlies all others, and is more deeply interesting than any other – is the ascertainment of the place which Man occupies in nature and of his relations to the universe of things.'[2]

This book is concerned with the ways in which the major themes of evolution were taken up in the performing arts during Charles Darwin's lifetime (1809–1882), though particularly from the time of his early adulthood in the 1830s, and in the generation after his death. Thus I have concentrated the focus on the decades between 1830 and 1900. This was the formative period for evolutionary ideas, when questions about human origins and ancestry, about the status of humans as a species among others and about the diversification of life forms were matters for popular speculation as well as specialist research.

The animal nature of man was one of the most ancient themes of the drama, and it was to the fore in non-dramatic performances such as acrobatics, clowning acts and monster shows, where humans and animals often worked together. Aping and mimicry had been synonymous since the seventeenth century. While fossil hunters

1

AWFUL INSTANCE OF PERCEPTION OF CHARACTER IN AN
INFANT PRODIGY.

Prodigy. " Mamma ! Look ! dere, dere Papa ! "

Figure 0.1 'Awful instance of perception on the part of an infant prodigy',
cartoon, *Punch*, Vol. 17 (1849), p. 242

Source: State Library of New South Wales (GRL Ref: DQ 050/P984)

sought in vain for the crucial missing evidence of transitional forms,
showmen were making claims that the missing link was to be seen
alive and well for a small fee, together with a whole programme of
complementary entertainment.

This is not to suggest that such entertainments were theory
driven, but rather that they reveal how popular curiosity often operates in the same areas as scientific study. Exhibition was the public
medium through which the science of natural history was conducted
but, as Richard Altick has shown in his landmark study *The Shows
of London*, exhibition and performed entertainment were both forms
of show business, and the boundaries between them were not always
clear.[3] Where museum displays concentrated on portrayals of the
natural order, the entertainment side of their business began to

exploit a counter-fascination with what might be 'out of the natural order': freak shows in which extreme differences of bulk and stature, form and feature were the staple ingredients. In variety theatre, racial diversity and gender difference were explored through character sketches and burlesque impersonations. 'Species' was a term rich in comic associations, and in the popular imagination there was always something intrinsically ludicrous about an evolutionary view of natural life.

The mid- to late nineteenth-century was a period in which Europe and North America developed an acute consciousness of themselves as the modernising nations, the leaders of the industrial revolution and therefore the generators of progress for mankind in general. The rise of evolutionary thinking was a shaping influence on this self-conscious sense of modernity and progress. The period may be called 'the age of Darwin', in that he became the figurehead of its scientific advancement and, through the wider application of his theories, its social and cultural advancement too. However, although the shift to evolutionary interpretations of nature occurred decisively during Darwin's lifetime, and in the name of Darwin, he was not the only or the first evolutionist.

A reader of the Darwin debates in popular science writing of the 1990s might easily be deceived into thinking that 'the' theory of evolution arrived on the scene in a blinding flash in 1859, but cultural historians of evolution offer a different view. Peter J. Bowler has emphasised that the Darwinian Revolution was 'not such a one-man show' as is commonly implied, and that even the term 'Darwinian Revolution' may be misleading, given the relatively minor influence of the theory of natural selection in Darwin's own time.[4] The idea that the natural order was not stable, and more specifically that organic forms were subject to change through interaction with their environment, dated back at least to the eighteenth century, when its exponents included Denis Diderot, Erasmus Darwin and Jean-Baptiste Lamarck, whose views were in conflict with those of his more conservatively minded senior colleague, Georges Cuvier. Lamarck's interpretations were further developed by Geoffroy Saint-Hilaire, who was influential in spreading the notion of 'transformism' among medical professionals from the 1820s, but fierce opposition from Richard Owen, who came to prominence as Britain's leading anatomist in the 1830s, served to escalate the controversy, and so to widen the public debate.

According to Michael Ruse, it was in the 1840s that this debate really 'blew open'. Robert Chambers's *Vestiges of the Natural History of Creation* (1844) drew a huge general readership, running to ten editions within a decade and selling over 20,000 copies. Herbert Spencer, who coined the phrase 'survival of the fittest', developed his own theory of social evolution in a succession of publications from the early 1850s. The story of how remarkably similar theories of descent with modification were developed simultaneously by Darwin and Alfred Russell Wallace is well known. Following the publication of Darwin's *The Origin of Species* in 1859, the debate intensified further and a new generation of thinkers began to develop a school of thought that has become known as 'social Darwinism'. Many of their ideas fed back into Darwin's *The Descent of Man* (1871); thus any account of the evolution debate during the age of Darwin needs to encompass a range of contributors and directions. The ideas put forward in *The Origin of Species* and *The Descent of Man*, Darwin's most widely influential books, draw on the work of many of his contemporaries and reflect the cultural ethos of his times. Michael Ruse suggests that 'the whole success of the industrial revolution worked its way into the organic origins debate, turning people toward evolution'.[5]

While a society straining under the demands of accelerating industrial growth inspired ruthless pronouncements about the survival of the fittest, performers who embodied the types of the throwback, the harlot and the wilful degenerate enjoyed particular success in the competitive world of show business. Performative reflections of new ideas about species formation, social evolution and the place of the human in the natural order ranged from the wildly facetious to the deeply ambivalent. The earnestness of scientific speculation inspired anarchic parodies, but performers also attempted shrewd ironic engagements with new forms of analysis and their implications.

The influence of the debate among the general public is a complex area of study which needs to be approached from a number of angles. Alvar Ellegård's *Darwin and the General Reader* provides a detailed account of the reception of Darwin's ideas in magazines and newspapers, but acknowledges that the readership of these did not constitute a representative cross-section of the community, since the upper classes contained a higher proportion of readers.[6] In an essay on satire and science in Victorian culture, James G. Paradis focuses on *Punch* as 'a comic theatre of ideas' in which natural history and evolution came in for particularly vivid lampooning.[7] This, suggests Paradis, was a form of dissent from the rigidities of scientific reduction, and part of 'a cultural struggle to construct . . . humorous contrasts between closed and open ideologies'.[8] The virtual theatre of *Punch* was in continual dialogue with the actual theatre, where the satire continued by other means.

Since theatre and performance not only provided entertainment for the widest spectrum of the public during this period, but were also a major form of general communication about topical issues, they are important indicators of the reception of evolutionary ideas. Audiences themselves are not the focus for my study, but rather what was presented to them, though the icons and genre crazes of the popular stage are evidence of the paths in which general curiosity was working. Fashions for particular kinds of performance, such as monkey man pantomimes, protean impersonations or blond burlesque, can be indicators of topical issues. As importantly, they tell us much about the spirit in which certain themes were treated. What does it mean that the ape ancestor could be treated as a common joke, or white gentlemen playing primitives should generate screaming hilarity, or a presentation of Lilliputian Aztecs be taken seriously?

The theatrical commerce in ideas, attitudes and interpretations thus cannot be studied with the precision Ellegård brings to his analysis of opinion in print media. A different kind of approach is needed, and one that is based on different premises. The study of performance, as distinct from dramatic literature, as a medium for the exploration of ideas poses special challenges. Performance is not only or even primarily a verbal medium and it does not necessarily engage with ideas through discursive articulation. Communication occurs as much through imagery, movement and expression, all of which leave only partial and secondary traces in the archive. It is a rich archive, nevertheless. Where there is no extant script for an entertainment, there may be reviews and handbills indicating its content (sometimes in considerable detail) with a sense of the style or mood in which it was performed. Thus an enquiry into how performed entertainments played with and upon the themes of evolution will not bring out patterns of argument and opinion, but can reveal some of the fertile associative games that were played with ideas which captured the imagination of the general public.

Joseph Roach has pointed out that, in spite of the fact that 'theatre exists at the center of civilized life', there is a dearth of studies focusing on the role of theatre and performance in intellectual history.[9] Here too, though, the correlation between the development of ideas in intellectual circles and the treatment of them in performance is not straightforward. Entertainers in the nineteenth-century were free of the intellectual responsibilities that weighed on those who represented educational, scientific, religious or political institutions. Where the latter controlled the parameters of enquiry in order to stabilise a model of knowledge, popular discourses could engage in explorations without a map, exercising the freedom to invent as well as observe.

The dialogic relationship between the popular stage and the world of ideas was mischievous, yet it was often insightful. Entertainments established their own forms of ironic distance from the views generated by the opinion-making classes (who were, of course, also among their audiences), and from the long-term cultural and economic investments with which these views were underpinned. In the worlds of show business, investment of any kind was usually short-lived: performers and their promoters took up polemical positions rather as they took up personae, retaining their capacity for quick change as the vital essence of their art. There was a sense in which performers literally tried ideas on, testing them out through enactment.

Bram Dijkstra complains about stereotypical views of the nineteenth century that 'often delineate romantic images of embattled progressively minded scientists struggling mightily against reactionary prejudice to discover "truth"'.[10] A study of popular theatre and performance allows no such story to be told. Rather than evidence of shock, what emerges is a picture of eager – even over-eager – receptiveness to new ideas from the realms of science, a fascination with their implications and an alertness to changing directions of speculation, albeit with a cavalier attitude to comprehension. Shock and denial, the responses so often claimed for 'the Victorians' by some proponents of Darwinism in our own day, are not much in evidence. Bishop Wilberforce may not have been happy at the concept of ape ancestry, but his was hardly the voice of the people. The child in *Punch*'s cartoon who, without the aid of Darwin, recognises the performing monkey as his father has a broad grin on his face. In this era of abandoned waifs, miserable boarding-school boys and domestic neglect by severe and distant parents, many children would have been only too glad to acknowledge a monkey or a member of any other friendly species as a father.

In the paradigm shift narrative that now frames most writings on Darwinian evolution, scientific revolution is the actor, and the consciousness of the public is that which is acted upon. Performative interpretations show that the cultural struggle with new views of natural law and order was no simple matter of scientific insight versus resistant ignorance. If there was resistance, it took the forms of alert scepticism, a sense of the ludicrous, a desire to play the game of knowledge-making too, but under the anarchic rules of humbug. Show business intervened in the world of ideas with its own forms of expertise: in passing things off and in stretching the parameters of curiosity. P. T. Barnum's career, which ran parallel with Darwin's (they were born within a year of each other) and continually crossed between the worlds of show business and scientific natural history, demonstrates this abundantly.

In this study, I have chosen to focus on performers rather than dramatists as interpreters of the themes and issues associated with human evolution. Some writers – Zola, Wedekind and Wilde – feature prominently in the later chapters because the figure of the performer is central to their vision, and they offer important perspectives on the evolutionary significance of the performer him- or herself. An evolutionary view of the human was one that foregrounded embodiment, and the performing arts have in common the body as their primary instrument of communication, so that physiognomy, sexuality, energy, expression and mobility – important theoretical concerns for the evolutionist – are integral components of the performer's work. The experimentalism of minstrel entertainers, actors, acrobats and dancers often mirrors that of natural scientists in its exploration of the limits and modalities of the human body, but it tends to be a burlesque mirroring.

Most of the performers and genres considered here have an element of the burlesque about them in that they engage in forms of drollery, mock gravity or grotesque exaggeration. James Paradis's description of *Punch* as engaged in a cultural struggle to create humorous contrasts between closed and open world views transfers well to the whole area of burlesque performance. Unburdened by the need for moral seriousness, performers were more promiscuously hypothetical than any self-respecting scientist could afford to be. They did not have to take the issues seriously, or to get the ideas right, or to be consistent in their approach. What they did have to do was appeal to their audiences, and here the imagery and narratives of evolution provided them with abundant material.

My first four chapters are concerned with popular genres – freak shows, circus acts, ethnological shows, variety impersonations, Wild West shows and minstrel burlesques – in which the drollery was overt, as were the references to the scientific cultures of natural history and evolutionary interpretation. The relationship between the two cultures of science and performance was dialectical, interdependent, but also adversarial. The final two chapters show how the burlesque acquired melancholic underpinnings and over-tones of hysteria as the *fin-de-siècle* mood swung towards more pessimistic views of social and cultural evolution. The performer, besides being a commentator, was also commented on. The body on stage became the focus for issues that were of critical concern to social Darwinists: sexual selection, degeneration, madness and wild-ness, natural vigour. But even as the most stringent forms of social Darwinism took hold, the theatres of decadence and the Grand Guignol retained a facetious edge and a capacity to dissent from the hierarchies of value that were generating so much anxiety among those who feared the degenerative turn.

Burlesque enactments have some of the qualities of the carnival-esque, especially in their focus on the body as a site of contention. Robert C. Allen emphasises the significance of burlesque genres as enabling contestations of vertical hierarchy and cultural worth in nineteenth-century American culture, but suggests that Bakhtin's model of the carnival needs to be adapted rather than adopted in its application to the burlesque.[11] The carnivalesque depends upon sharply defined polarities – classical/grotesque, high/low, privileged/oppressed – which are switched to create reversals of established hierarchies. Even when these polarities are seen to be superimposed in 'a mobile conflictual fusion', as in Peter Stallybrass and Allon White's sophisticated reading of the carnivalesque, the term still implies dichotomous political tensions that are not necessarily present in burlesque.[12] During the nineteenth century, there was a concerted movement among theatre managers and entrepreneurs to rescue their businesses from the taint of association with older style fairground shows. 'Popular' does not necessarily equate with 'low' when it is applied to theatre and performance, since the most popular shows were those marketed to appeal to the widest social spectrum, which often meant that the middle classes comprised the vital core of their audience. Popular theatre was whatever theatre gave its audiences the best time. Its grounds of appeal were spectacle, humour, variety, eroticism and surprise. Certainly the traditional tensions between the classical and the grotesque body were there, but they were crossed with other kinds of dynamics. In many burlesque performances the threat (or promise) of an inverted natural order was less at issue than a fascination with its warps and inter-stices. The sliding scale of evolution also created new kinds of cultural tensions, about the direction and pace of movement through the hierarchy, rather than about relative placements within it.

In exploring the impact of the radically revised interpretations of the natural order inspired by Darwin and other evolutionists, it may be better to speak of cultural anxiety than of culture shock. One of the most widely quoted examples of the culture shock narrative is Freud's pronouncement on the sequence of 'great blows to the naïve self love of men' which the human ego has suffered from the discoveries of science. Copernicus delivered the first of these blows, says Freud, and the second fell 'when biological research destroyed man's supposedly privileged place in creation and proved his descent from the animal kingdom and his ineradicable animal nature'.[13] Where the notion of culture shock tends to generate images of great blows delivered by science upon the thick skulls and naïve sensibilities of the intellectually backward, that of cultural anxiety allows for a more complex and multi-directional picture of human reactions. The anxiety has not, as recent Darwinists have been keen to suggest, been all one sided.[14] Darwin, his peers and his predecessors in the debate put themselves on the line intellectually. Potential turns in the evidence that could prove 'fatal' to his theory are a concern throughout the later editions of *The Origin of Species*, which Darwin revised and expanded to address the main objections to his reasoning. Faction groups in the debates were trying on roles and meanings, setting up rhetorical antagonisms, positing identity models for themselves and others. In doing so they were creating investments that had to be fought for and protected.

There were serious issues at stake for all sectors of society. The Church had to deal with a central doctrinal challenge; the principles of education and social welfare were in question; new interpretations of industrial progress were being promoted; the role of the nation could be redefined in evolutionary terms, as could the project of colonisation. Evolutionary theories generated a hotbed of speculation in which interpretations crossed from the natural to the social world and vice versa. It has become almost conventional to equate modernity with anxiety, and the explosion of interest in evolutionary narratives may be seen as a core factor in this equation, but anxiety here should not simply be equated with worry, nor does it necessarily carry connotations of a depressive or pessimistic outlook. Anxieties are psychical energies which can manifest in many ways. These energies, generated in a culture whose self-image was undergoing a critical process of redefinition, lent themselves readily to dramatic and performative exploration.

During the period that saw the rise of evolutionary approaches to science and social science, show business enjoyed unprecedented economic success and was undergoing intensive expansion and diversification. The circus, the cabaret, the music-hall and the theatrical ballet grew to reach a zenith of popularity through the later decades of the nineteenth century. Shows toured rural towns, and played to packed metropolitan houses. Mass publicity created an escalating scale of national and international celebrity for the most successful artists and companies. In this study, I have focused on the metropolises of London, New York and Paris. In the early and mid-nineteenth century, these were the major generative centres for popular performance, and the most successful entertainers travelled between them, so that there were strong lines of influence and cross-fertilisation. Evolutionary views of the natural order were pioneered in Paris, and spread to London and then to New York, so the relationship between evolution and performance can be seen most clearly in these centres. In making a study of this kind, one is continually aware of what has been left out. German and Italian influences in both areas became increasingly important as the century progressed, but it would not be possible to treat these adequately without extending the length and range of the study beyond the scope of a single book.

Any writer engaging with nineteenth-century European and American culture has to deal with sharp differences in the protocols of language, and this is especially the case in areas of ethnology and racial representation. Language that is racially derogatory – such as the terms 'savage', 'native' and 'primitive' – is pervasive in the performance events I am discussing and in the accounts surrounding them. In order to avoid strewing the text with inverted commas, I have left the reader to assume that these terms refer to roles and images belonging to the European imaginary. Emphases in quotations are according to the original in all cases, as are punctuation and variants in spelling.

1

OUT OF NATURAL HISTORY

I remember the Museum of Natural History. It was full of still bodies, staring at you with glass eyes on which a light coating of dust was sometimes visible. Here, the wild species of the world – eagle, polecat, rat, fox, kangaroo, zebra, penguin, deer – had been upholstered, like the armchairs of suburbia. There was no sign of death having done its work on them, either by violence or decomposition; death comes to the living, and it was hard to believe these creatures had ever been alive, though here and there a special effort had been made to suggest as much. A badger half emerged from a replica of what might have been its hole, constructed from materials which fairly imitated dried mud and grass. Tall jars filled with brown liquid contained lizards, snakes and frogs, their stomachs and the vulnerable undersides of their feet exposed against the glass. The suffocating quiet emanating from these creatures gave the place something of the muffled atmosphere of suburban sitting-rooms.

My grandfather was an entomologist, but as a child I was never drawn to the study of natural life. The museum had given such study an image of fustiness and perhaps an edge of fear, though not the dramatic fear of some threatening agency; rather the dull fear of confinement and suspended animation. There is an obvious perversity about this association of naturalism with suspended animation, a perversity that hinges on the exclusion of the element of performance. I first visited the theatre and the circus at the age of 6, and to these I was irresistibly drawn. They seemed like the antithesis of the museum, as in obvious ways they were, but it never occurred to me then that these institutions were radically bound up with each other in their histories.

When in 1675 the philosopher Leibnitz envisaged a new Academy of Sciences that would be 'a theatre of nature and of art', there was nothing radically unconventional about his idea. Such an academy, he suggested, would attract 'holiday spectators' to learn about new advances in science by presenting displays such as rope-dancing, conjuring tricks, Italian and French clowns, an English fire-eater, dancing horses, Pygmies, shadow plays, fiery dragons and Turkish comedy performances together with demonstrations of scientific instruments, anatomy displays and collections of shells, plants and minerals.[1] Leibnitz published this idea under the title 'An Odd Thought Concerning a New Sort of Exhibition'. What was odd and new was not the mixture of performative and academic elements, but the scale of the enterprise and its design to appeal to a popular audience in order to make money. Here, Leibnitz anticipated P. T. Barnum and was perhaps ahead of his time, but in combining science with performance he was following tradition. These two domains were not easily separable in the medieval and early modern periods. Exhibition and display were inherently performative, and those who accumulated private collections as an expression of their curiosity about the natural world often included in them living marvels such as a dwarf, a giant or a menagerie of exotic beasts. Cabinets of curiosity were theatres of nature, where portents of strange and dramatic natural events made prize possessions.

Yet there is some irony in the timing of Leibnitz's idea of combining human and animal performances with exhibitions of new scientific technology. The academies of science founded in Europe in the later seventeenth century approached the study of nature in technical and experimental ways that were not conducive to the culture of wonders, with all its performative dimensions. When Fellows of the Royal Society toured the showground areas of Bartholomew Fair seeking to study the prodigies and monstrosities assembled there amidst the jugglers and rope-dancers, they did so in a spirit of enquiry that was becoming sharply alienated from the spirit in which these monstrosities were displayed. In accordance with principles of study defined by Francis Bacon, the new scientists distanced themselves from popular attraction towards prodigies as 'frivolous impostures for pleasure and strangeness', in order to make 'a substantial and severe collection of the heteroclites or irregulars of nature'.[2]

As changing interpretations of nature in the domains of science saw the demise of the culture of wonder in favour of a practice of 'substantial and severe collection', how did this impact upon the realms of performance and on performative interpretations of the natural order?[3] My purpose in reviewing the historical relationship between performative and scientific traditions of display is to identify the forms of co-dependency operating between them, and to notice the tensions arising from this mutual dependence. These tensions surfaced during the scientific revolution of the late seventeenth century but they did not become critical until the middle decades of the nineteenth century, when evolutionary inter-pretations of nature began to take hold with a relentless programme of demystification. Versions of evolutionary theory arose in connec-tion with anatomical research conducted in Paris by Lamarck and Geoffroy Saint-Hilaire early in the nineteenth century, and became the subject of widespread debate in scientific circles a generation before Darwin published *The Origin of Species*. By 1840 these theo-ries were being taught at the major medical schools in Edinburgh and London.

At this time, there was a risk that a continuing adherence to wonders, marvels and monsters would relegate popular performance forms to the backwater of a folk culture that was coming to be seen as vulgar and moribund. There was also the alternative prospect that scientific modernisers might lose their battle against the supersti-tious ideas that had such a strong hold on the popular imagination. But these agonistic tensions did not settle into a set of simple dichotomies: modernity versus tradition, rationality versus supersti-tion, natural order versus an outlandish theatre of wonders. What makes the history interesting is the breakdown of these dichotomies, as through the nineteenth century a responsive movement of re-interpretation takes place in popular performance, a movement that refuses to abandon monsters and marvels, but gives them a new lease of life. In the Victorian era, scientific views of natural history presented threats to the imaginative freedom of show business, but also opportunities for parody and performative elaboration. If prodigies and monsters of the fairground tradition were supposed to be 'out of the natural order', their modernised descendants in the circuses and freak shows were out of the natural order in another sense: that they emerged from the order of nature as it was modelled in the scientific museums and anatomy theatres, looming out of its interstices, filling its gaps and relentlessly evolving on their own terms.

Monstrosity in crisis

In 1840, an act permanently banning all forms of theatrical enter-tainment from Bartholomew Fair in London was implemented for the first time. Henceforth, the stage-players, rope-dancers, jugglers, puppeteers and all who 'made show of motions and strange sights' were excluded from the grounds near the gate of St Bartholomew's Hospital where for seven centuries they had congregated. The most celebrated monster show in Europe had come to an end.

In the same year, the radical journal *The Lancet* published the texts of two lectures on monstrosity recently delivered to medical students of Middlesex Hospital. The lecturer, John North, was a specialist in obstetrics and his declared aim was to acquaint his students with recent research in an area where 'a great blank in medical science' had for too long been filled by 'gross superstition and credulity'. In particular, North paid tribute to the pioneering work of Parisian anatomist Geoffroy Saint-Hilaire, who a generation previously had demonstrated that 'monstrosity is not, as was once believed, a disorder arising from the blind freaks of Nature, but that it is governed by constant and precise laws, and is capable of being submitted to a regular and scientific classification'.[4] Saint-Hilaire's interest in monsters was an extension of his concern with the progressive development of biological forms. What were tradition- ally called monsters, freaks or prodigies of nature were, he thought, symptoms of regression to an earlier organic type. A human born with a tail, or any mammal born with its limbs in an embryonic state, were ready examples. For the latter instance, North cited the case of a Miss Biffin, who toured the fairs for nearly twenty years and became celebrated for her ability to paint miniatures with a brush in her mouth or attached to her shoulder. Such anatomical anomalies were evidence to support a view of the natural order as engaged in a perpetual process of progressive organic change or 'transformism'. Transformism was Saint-Hilaire's word for evolu- tion, a term which did not begin to gain general currency in scientific circles until the 1830s. The view of monstrosity as an occasional side effect of natural change was one that restricted the scope of conjecture so that, as North put it, 'whimsical and absurd hypotheses' could no longer hold sway.[5] Even the most extreme anomalies were subject to the laws that governed all organic forms. John North's students might expect to encounter Siamese twins, giants, six-legged cows or humans with tails during the course of their professional lives, but they need not expect to see flying horses, mermaids or satyrs.

North's argument was not altogether new. As Lorraine Daston and Katherine Park point out in their book *Wonders and the Order of Nature*, historical research soon gives the lie to any linear story about monsters disappearing to be replaced by naturalised objects. Attacks on wonders and marvels go back many centuries in European culture: in the thirteenth century Albertus Magnus saw it as the task of wise men 'to make wonders cease'. To the philosopher, Daston and Park comment, 'monstrous births or the rare meteorological and topographical particulars that so amaze the layperson appear only as the necessary (if unforeseeable) effects of similar and universal causes'.[6] By 1840, though, scientists were getting closer to the causes, so that North was not mounting a philosophical argument on principles but rather an explicit line of evidence-based interpretation. The threat to make wonders cease was becoming more immediate and more general.

The kind of popular credulity that was being discredited through new developments in anatomical research was typified in the culture of monstrosity at Bartholomew Fair. For centuries in Europe, monster displays were a major ingredient of popular show business. No fairground would have been complete without some kind of exhibition of monsters, whether real or faked, and such exhibitions played a major role in cultivating notions of monstrosity in the popular imagination. Monsters were most successfully exhibited as part of a show rather than as isolated spectacles, and they went especially well with displays of conjuring or acrobatics. A 1641 tract describing the activities of Bartholomew Fair gave some sense of the cumulative effect:

> Here a Knave in a Fool's Coat, with a trumpet sounding, or on a drum beating, invites you and would fain persuade you to see his puppets; there a Rogue like a Wild Woodman, or in an antick shape like an Incubus, desires your company to view his motion; on the other side Hocus Pocus with three yards of tape or ribbon in's hand, showing his art of Legerdemain to the admiration and astonishment of a company of cockaloaches.[7]

Dwarfs, giants, fire-eaters, three-legged hens, jugglers, Siamese twins, dancing dogs, philosophical pigs and contortionists were alike prodigies, and the line between prodigies of nature and prodigies of enactment was always confused in the fairground.

Henry Morley, who published the first history of Bartholomew Fair in 1859, was concerned to explain why the term 'monster', in its original meaning, encapsulated something essential to the culture of the Fair: 'A monster, according to the derivation of the word, means in the first sense a show, a thing to be pointed at, and in that first sense it was then used in Bartholomew Fair with a tie of the word to living wonders, such as the dog Toby, the dogs that dance the morrice, the eagle, the black wolf, the bull with five legs . . .'[8] Shows worked their chemistry on audiences more or less successfully depending on the mix of acts they had managed to assemble. Monstrosity was an essential ingredient. Without it, a certain edge of strangeness was missing. Bizarre skills could amaze and surprise, but bizarre embodiments gave a sense that the body itself was a theatre of surprises. The earliest forms of English drama used monsters as catalytic presences: the dragon in the mummers' plays; the hobby-horse in the pageants; the devil in the mystery plays. The devil was a favourite character in the play booths and puppet plays at Bartholomew Fair, where he was typically given the full monster treatment as a human/animal hybrid, with horns and a tail, a humped back and a capacity to generate ferocious energies. In the clash between the perspective of the modern anatomist and that of the popular performance tradition, much was at stake on both sides. John North's matter-of-fact concept of 'anatomical anomaly' had the potential to dispel the powerful mystique attached to fairground monsters and prodigies. Anatomical anomalies could not play the same role as monstrosities and, besides, the explanations that accompanied them were a threat to the whole ethos of popular shows, for which 'whimsical and absurd hypotheses' such as John North condemned were a kind of life-support system.

A performative display of strange embodiments was an invitation to the game of imagined possibilities, as, for example, with the case of 'Bold Grimace Spaniard', a successful act that played on the semi-mythical stories of exploration and discovery in vogue at the beginning of the eighteenth century. Bold Grimace, it was claimed,

> lived 15 years among wild creatures in the Mountains, and is reasonably supos'd to have been taken out of his cradle, an Infant, by some savage Beast, and wonderfully preserved, 'till some Comedians accidentally pass'd through those parts, and perceiving him to be of human Race, pursued him to his Cave, where they caught him in a Net. They found something wonderful in his Nature, and took him with them on their Travels.

The promotional description in this handbill is an essential preparation for the audience, evoking as it does the coalescence of mismatched organic forms:

> He performs the following surprising Grimaces, viz.: He
> lolls out his tongue a foot long, turns his eyes in and out at
> the same time; contracts his face as small as an Apple;
> extends his mouth six Inches, and turns it into the shape of
> a Bird's Beak, his eyes like to an Owl's . . . licks his nose
> with his tongue like a Cow.

This was clearly an example of monstrosity by enactment, and the
display of hybridity included mixing genres of performance. After
his contortionary excesses, the Bold Grimacer would 'sing wonder-
fully fine', accompanying himself on the lute.[9]

Prodigies could be faked to suit an imagined preconception, but
the prodigy status of actual exotic species could also be enhanced
through imaginative construction. A cassowary exhibited at around
the same time as the wild Spaniard was promoted as 'the strangest
creature in the Universe, being half a Bird and Beast . . . his head
is like a Bird, and so is his Feet . . . his Body is like to the Body of
a Deer; instead of feathers, his fore-part is covered with Hair like an
Ox, his hinder part with a double feather of one Quill; he eats Iron,
Steel or Stones'.[10] As a way of imaging the cassowary, this involves
a fertile sense of hypothesis. Exotic animals with body forms never
seen before in Europe were potential evidence that the most bizarre
and wonderful combinations of animal types could indeed occur in
the natural world.

After all, even the most sceptical scientists sometimes found
themselves profoundly challenged by new discoveries brought back
from expeditions to distant continents. George Shaw, keeper of the
Natural History Department of the British Museum, received
the body of a platypus from Australia in the 1790s, and described
it in terms that would have graced a fairground handbill. It was, he
pronounced, 'of all the Mammalia yet known . . . the most extraordinary in its conformation; exhibiting the perfect resemblance of the
beak of a Duck engrafted on the head of a quadruped'.[11] Shaw had
put himself in an awkward position by establishing a reputation for
hard-line orthodoxy in classification. He refused to believe in the
Dodo, and declared that what was not in Linnaeus did not exist.[12]
When it came to the problem of the platypus, he commented that
it was impossible 'not to entertain some doubts as to the genuine
nature of the animal, and to surmise that there might have been
practised some arts of deception in its structure'.[13] On the other side
of the fence, those who practised such artifice as a way of earning a
living were significantly advantaged by the confusion that genuine

cases were able to cause. Such cases helped to create a reception for fairground presentations like the 'strange monstrous creature brought from the Coast of Brazil, having a head like a Child, legs and Arms very wonderful, with a long tail like a serpent, wherewith he feeds himself, as an elephant doth with his trunk'.[14] The reader in our own times can only speculate as to where nature ended, artifice began, performance embellished and inventive description took over in the composition of this creature.

By 1840, though, the monster tradition appeared to be finally on its way out. A new generation of students was being taught that even monsters were subject to 'the general laws and principles of organization', of which the first and foremost was 'that of the unity of organic composition'.[15] While the life sciences were establishing firm limits to the potential for heterogeneity in nature, a rich and long-standing culture of heterogeneity was to be quashed. Since the Restoration, theatrical booths at Bartholomew Fair had been subject to annual licence, which had intermittently been refused (always to great popular indignation), but the category exclusion after 1839 was permanent and sweeping. It was clear from the decisions made about individual acts in 1840 that the term 'theatrical entertainments' was taken to include performance of any kind. Specific refusals are recorded for an equestrian, a gymnast, and 'Mr. Lakey's Living Curiosities', which comprised a giantess, a dwarf, serpents and a crocodile.[16]

A reactionary craze for monster exhibits flared up in the commercial museums and showplaces of London, with *Punch* satirising 'Deformito-mania' in an 1847 cartoon showing crowds pressing around the doors of the Egyptian Museum in Piccadilly to see 'the Ne Plus Ultra of Hideousness', 'The Greatest Deformity in the World' and 'The Ugliest Biped'.[17] In the same year, *The Illustrated London News* (in its April Fools' Day issue) proclaimed that even Deformito-mania was on its last legs:

> In olden times, Museums were, doubtless, receptacles for freaks of imposture, and thus they may have greatly extended popular error: in these days such tricks are out of the question, and every wonder monger must dread the detective police of enlightened public opinion.[18]

This picture of old-style fraudulent spectacle under pressure from the new detective police of enlightenment gave far too simple a reading of the situation, which was not to be resolved quite so expeditiously.

Figure 1.1 'The deformito-mania', cartoon, *Punch*, Vol. 13 (1847), p. 90

Source: State Library of New South Wales (GRL Ref: DQ 050/P984)

Henry Morley characterises the spectators at Bartholomew Fair as 'a credulous multitude, easily practised upon by the grossest frauds' (p. 155), but the value of prodigies and monstrosities as entertainment often had little or nothing to do with whether they were genuine examples of what they purported to be. Did those who paid their money to see the learned pig or the 'living Fairy' (a man supposed to be 150 years old) or the boy with a tail like a trunk believe in what they saw? And if not, was this an important issue? When handbills promised 'satisfaction', this was commonly related to claims about the character or skills of the person exhibited: midgets were advertised as elegant conversationalists or good dancers; people born without arms would play the piano with their feet, or paint, or thread needles.[19] The circumstantial evidence is overwhelmingly that those who had some ability as entertainers made the most successful shows. Imposture itself was a presentational skill that could be thoroughly enjoyed for its own sake by an audience who accepted it as a convention. If spectators had demanded nature untampered with and had sought to bring the enlightenment police down on the ingenuity of the exhibitors, they would simply have spoiled their own amusement. What Coleridge termed 'the willing suspension of disbelief', a precondition for receptiveness to imaginative works, was surely operative in the fairground where spectators circulated between the play booths, the acrobatic shows and the exhibition platforms that were all part of the same milieu.[20] Different kinds of show certainly experimented with different ways of negotiating belief. The occasional exposure of a fraud may have added to the entertainment, but a visitor to the fairground who approached the sights with a determination to apply stern reality testing would have got as little enjoyment as the Puritans who were favourite targets for lampoon among players and performers.[21]

The changing cultural and intellectual environment that threatened the survival of monster shows contained tensions far more deep-rooted and complex than those concerning authenticity and credulity. The issue of monstrosity was crucial to the modernisation of knowledge about nature: as John North's lectures made clear, the questions concerning monstrosity were questions about the natural order as a whole. An eighteenth-century definition of 'monstrous' as 'deviating from the natural order; unnatural' goes together with Henry Morley's gloss on the word 'monster' as a show or spectacle, and indicates how monstrosity might be part of the core business of popular performance. Credulity itself was no simple matter in this performance tradition, which continually played on an extended sense of possibility. Deviance from the laws of nature was one of the defining qualities of fairground shows. Conjurers defied the laws of matter with vanishing acts and the apparently magical transportation of objects from one place to another; acrobats defied the laws of gravity; monsters were examples of counter-natural creation. Anthropomorphic animal acts breached the natural limits of species and confused the human/animal divide. John Evelyn left this description of a performance by monkeys at St Margaret's Fair in Southwark:

> they were gallantly clad à la mode, went upright, saluted the company, bowing and pulling off their hatts; they saluted one another with a good grace, as if instructed by a dancing master. They turned heels over heads with a basket having eggs in it, without breaking any; also with lighted candles in their hands and on their heads, without extinguishing them, and with vessels of water, without spilling a drop.[22]

A performative view of nature was one that was intellectually permissive, encouraging all manner of hypotheses and maintaining a wide scope for caprice and surprise. A scientific view restricted the parameters of interpretation. Nature as a theatre of mysteries was not compatible with nature as an order whose rules could be learned and whose ways could therefore be anticipated. While assiduous efforts were made in the realms of science to consolidate and clarify an understanding of the natural order, the popular performing arts came up with endlessly resourceful strategic challenges to this enterprise, though not always in the form of outright resistance.

Shrewd entrepreneurs soon learned to shift the terms of their pitch to audiences so as to claim validity according to newer forms of scientific knowledge, and no one was more skilled at this than P. T. Barnum. Barnum's rapid ascendancy in the early 1840s – not in Europe but in the burgeoning commercial world of America – marked a turning point in the relations between science and performance. Just at what may have looked like the moment for the demise of popular shows based on fantastic ideas about the natural world, Barnum gave them a new lease of life by setting out to modernise performative engagements with science.

In a long and wide-ranging career contemporary with that of Charles Darwin, Barnum was constantly alert to developments in the science and culture of natural history. By the end of 1840 he had completed negotiations which put him in charge of the American Museum in New York and it opened under his management early in 1841. The title of his previous enterprise, 'Barnum's Grand Scientific and Musical Theatre', was a clear indication of what he had in mind for his new venue. He began, though, with the old fairground formula, offering educated dogs and fleas, automatons, jugglers, ventriloquists, giants, dwarfs and rope-dancers. He was shamelessly on the look-out for 'all that is monstrous, scaley, strange and queer'.[23] He corresponded with Moses Kimball, owner of the Boston Museum, about strategies for diversifying their enterprises to raise the level of public interest, and this reciprocity soon led to the exchange of 'attractions'. It was Kimball who came upon the first potentially high-profile exhibit, one that had actually been shown at Bartholomew Fair in 1825. This item was most certainly monstrous, scaley, strange and queer and had exchanged hands a few times over the previous twenty years for considerable sums of money, on the claim that it was a mermaid.

It had first been exhibited in 1822, when the press reported its success in attracting paying visitors, in spite of its failure to impress the professional anatomist who was asked to evaluate it. This was William Clift, who was curator of the prestigious Hunterian natural history collection at the Royal College of Surgeons and therefore something of a connoisseur when it came to detecting the authenticity or otherwise of a specimen. He instantly proclaimed this one a fake, and made a drawing of the cobbled-together arte-fact, annotated to the effect that the tail was that of a salmon and the torso was orang-utan. Refinements included 'jaws and teeth to a Baboon . . . arms have been shortened – Nails made of quill – Eyes artificial'.[24] The public exhibition was nevertheless so successful that it inspired something of a vogue for manufactured mermaids. Mermaids were an important debating point in natural history, with most taxonomists, from Linnaeus onwards, taking the view that there could be no such hybrid. As anatomical knowledge became more sophisticated, theories such as those taught by John North made mermaids a definitive impossibility.

Why, then, should so shrewd and resourceful a showman as Barnum choose to risk the reputation of his new museum on the promotion of an obviously fake example of a creature few people still believed in, especially as it led him straight into the trap identified by *The Illustrated London News*? Was he, perhaps, issuing a deliberate challenge to the detective police of enlightened opinion? Since Kimball had acquired the mermaid in the first place, Barnum's agreed role was to devise an effective promotional approach that would make its exhibition profitable. He began with quite a subtle strategy for arousing the interest of the press, by organising a series of letters to be sent to the New York newspapers from various places around the country, giving local news and mentioning the recent visit of a London naturalist Dr Griffin, who was touring America on his way back to Britain, having travelled the world and picked up along the way certain remarkable exotic specimens and curiosities.[25] The mermaid was mentioned, but only, at this stage, in passing. Eventually, Dr Griffin arrived in New York and invited some of the newspaper editors to a private viewing of his curiosity collection. By this time the mermaid was clearly the focus of interest, and the idea of a public exhibition was being raised, though not, let it be said, by Dr Griffin, who cultivated the impression that he was quite resis-tant to the suggestion. It was only after considerable urging from one of New York's most persuasive entrepreneurs – P. T. Barnum – that he agreed to put his specimen on show. In August 1842, Barnum duly announced that he had acquired the rights to exhibit an astonishing phenomenon made available to him by a naturalist from the Lyceum of Natural History in London. He had thus compounded the fraud of the mermaid itself with an elaborately concocted story to invent scientific credentials for it. This is where the performative element, as his own particular form of expertise, came in. Dr Griffin was a role played by Levi Lyman, who had worked for Barnum before and shown considerable skills in adopting the persona of the expert, improvising just the right pseudo-facts and details to support the claims made for an exhibit.

In his autobiography, Barnum also brings another naturalist into the story. This is Emile Guillaudeu, who had been the resident taxidermist at the American Museum for thirty years under its former owners. It may have been out of simple generosity that Barnum kept him on the payroll when his own attitude to the museum's renowned taxidermy collections was to dismiss them as 'stuffed monkey and gander skins' and when his interests tended decisively towards livestock. Yet judging from Guillaudeu's prominence in Barnum's various narratives, he had a vital role to play. Barnum recounts numerous dialogues between them, as, for example, on the occasion when he consulted Guillaudeu about a pair of pigeons he had just acquired from a chemist experimenting with gold dyes for fur and feathers:

> When he saw the 'golden pigeons from California' he was considerably astonished. He examined them with great delight for half an hour . . . and said:
> 'Mr. Barnum, these golden pigeons are superb, but they cannot be from California. Audubon mentions no such bird in his work upon American Ornithology.' The next day, the old naturalist called at my office and remarked: 'Mr. Barnum, those pigeons are a more rare bird than you imagine. They are not mentioned by Linnaeus, Cuvier, Goldsmith or any other writer on Natural History, so far as I have been able to discover. I expect they must come from some unexplored portion of Australia.'[26]

On the matter of the mermaid, Guillaudeu conspicuously failed the test that William Clift had passed so easily twenty years previously. He 'could not conceive how it could have been manufactured, for he never saw a monkey with such peculiar teeth, arms, hands etc., and he never saw a fish with such peculiar fins'. He was careful, though, to show his theoretical correctness with the proviso that he 'did not believe in mermaids'.[27] Earnest, gullible, elderly and French – but with academic credentials – Guillaudeu made perfect casting in the role of scientist as stooge.

To 'startle the naturalists and wake up the whole scientific world' was an important part of Barnum's agenda from the outset.[28] To begin with, this was largely attempted in the spirit of hoax and humbug, but his interest in measuring his own establishments against those of institutionalised science became a serious attempt at rivalry as his career developed. The high-profile marketing campaign for the 'Fejee Mermaid: the most stupendous curiosity ever submitted to the public for inspection' may be seen as a calculated challenge to the scientific world. Although there was indeed a risk of the fraud being detected at some stage, the pay-off would be the gratification of demonstrating that the public were just as likely to be taken in by fake scientists as by fake monsters, and that the game of imposture and exposure could be played both ways. It was all a matter of performance, in the social theatre of bluff and counter-bluff which Barnum excelled at, and was pleased to call 'humbug'.

In due course, the bluff was called on the Fejee mermaid, which was on tour in South Carolina in early 1843 when an amateur naturalist recognised how the specimen was constructed and, more significantly, decided, together with some of his peers, to make an issue of the fraud. They wrote to the *Charleston Mercury*:

> Regarding as we do the exhibition of such deformity, an injury to natural science – as calculated to perpetuate on the minds of the ignorant an absurd fable, and to extract money from the public under false pretenses, we feel it our duty to expose this vile deception.[29]

As a damaging local campaign gathered, Barnum ordered the mermaid's return to New York, and set about deciding the best counter-strategy. Should he raise the stakes and start a lawsuit for slander against the Charleston naturalist? This would have been risky indeed and, in the event, he hedged his bets, took a step back from the line on which he had put himself, and devised a way to capitalise on the attack. The mermaid was advertised to New Yorkers as the subject of a controversy among 'doctors', a phenomenon 'implicitly believed by many scientific persons, while it is pronounced by other scientific persons to be an artificial production'. Audiences were invited to inspect it and judge for themselves. This is an example of how authentication itself became something of a theatrical game for Barnum, one in which the scientist had a vital role to play, but strictly as either the back-up or foil to the starring role of the showman as he demonstrated charismatically that knowledge of nature could always be trumped by knowledge of human nature, and fact would always be subject to manipulation. 'The naturalist' was the favourite witness in these games.

In a letter to Kimball, Barnum reported a contribution to the controversy from another kind of doctor. This was the Reverend Dr Edwin H. Chapin, a Universalist minister, whose close friendship with Barnum was based on a shared love of hoaxes and practical jokes, and a shared understanding that the art of popular influence was the art of role-play. At the time of the mermaid's return from South Carolina, Chapin gave a sermon in New York in which he proclaimed that 'it is not only an arrogant but a shallow philosophy that says "the existence of this or that is impossible, it is contrary to the laws of nature"'.[30] He dwelt on the topic of the unfathomable mysteries of creation, using the miracle of the common wild flower as his example. If this was a fraudulent sermon, it was no doubt a fine performance; but Chapin may have been serving his friend's interests while expressing views he genuinely held. For churchmen as for performers, there were vested interests in maintaining a space for mystery and strangeness in nature. There was also a very long-standing theological tradition to back him. Katherine Park and Lorraine Daston's summary of a view commonly held among medieval theologians accords closely with the message of his sermon: 'Some Christian writers, especially those most influenced by Augustine, saw skepticism concerning wonders as the hall-mark of the narrow minded and suspicious peasant, trapped in the bubble of his limited experience, while belief characterized the pious, the learned and the theologically informed.'[31]

Controversies on the question of the mermaid linked up with the controversy over monstrosity in general, and by 1840, when John North gave his lectures, this controversy was by no means settled even among scientists. *The Lancet* published only one response to the lectures, from a correspondent who challenged North's explanations and insisted, 'the cause of monstrosities is at present involved in mystery'.[32] A few months previously, the journal had published a report on some recent cases of monstrosity from a member of the Royal College of Surgeons who also took the view that 'with all our sophistry, we must yet own that there are many things in heaven and earth, that are not dreamt in our philosophy'. Theoretical systems like those of Geoffroy Saint-Hilaire gained no credence with this writer. In 'professing to unravel the hidden mystery', he said, such systems 'have been satisfactory alone to the minds of their founders'.[33] Thus some of the views expressed in the pages of the most forward-thinking medical journal were not so different from those expressed by Reverend Chapin from his pulpit. As debate over the interpretation of nature gained intensity, the lines of allegiance were by no means drawn up straightforwardly, with science on one side and theology and popular culture on the other. It was this confusion of allegiances that Barnum participated in and exploited, and in so doing he played a major role in modernising the tradition of 'monstrous' performance. Some historical consideration of the interrelationship between science and performance through traditions of exhibition and collection may help to set this role in context.

Theatricality and collection

Science and show business shared an involvement in the culture of exhibition, and since the time of the foundation of the Royal Society in 1660, this had produced adversarial tensions that were intensified through the co-dependency from which neither side could extricate itself. The character and purpose of any exhibition derives from the principles of assemblage on which it is based, and it was here that theatricality and science began to diverge at the time of the scientific revolution.

The precursor of the modern scientific collection was the cabinet of curiosities or *Wunderkammer*. These collections were often referred to as 'theatres of nature'. The word 'theatre' is derived from the Greek τηεατρον or 'place for viewing', so its application to places in which collections were housed is straightforward, but in the Renaissance it acquired connotations of assembly: assembly of spectators and also of things to be viewed.[34] Paula Findlen sees a clear inflection towards the dramatic:

> In the eyes of early modern naturalists, nature was drama personified. Inviting them into her midst, she lured them with her seemingly infinite possibilities and the potential for heroic adventure. When collectors brought nature into the museum . . . they attempted to recapture not only the totality of nature but also the excitement, conflicts and expectations that their initial voyages in the vast 'natural' theatre had produced.[35]

Cabinets of curiosity typically combined large accumulations of natural objects – for example, shells, plants, fish skeletons, birds' eggs and minerals – with objects to which some special or portentous significance was attributed.

Ulisse Aldrovandi, known as 'Master of Portents, indeed of Monsters', assembled one of the most celebrated collections at

Bologna in Italy in the later sixteenth century. His most prized item was a 'dragon' that appeared on the outskirts of Bologna in 1572 and was considered 'an omen of terrible times to come'.[36] English collections were strong on portents. The museum created by John Tradescant in Lambeth in the early eighteenth century was celebrated as 'a world of wonders in one closet shut'.[37] Among its rarities was listed 'blood that rained in the Isle of Wight'. Even the museum attached to the anatomy school in Oxford at this time had in its collection

> A Mermaid's hand; Two horns which grew out of the head of a woman in Tuttle Street, Westminster; The Teat of a Witch; A monstrous lamb, with one head and two intire bodies; A Moor's ears cut off; Two small worm-eaten loaves of the time of the Siege of Oxford.[38]

Ralph Thoresby's collection in Leeds was scholarly and systematic, but here too the portent had special privilege. A common or garden fly was sent to Thoresby in 1699

> with this remarkable Account, That in May the same Year, at Kerton in Lincolnshire, the Sky seemed to darken North-Westward . . . as though it had been with a Shower of Hailstones or Snow; but when it came near the Town it appeared to be a prodigious Swarm of these Flies, which went with such a force towards the South-East, that persons were forced to turn their backs of them, to the wonder of those that were abroad and saw them.[39]

The fly was an amazing paradox: it was the most ordinary of things, exhibited as the sign of a spectacular disturbance in the natural order. All these collections were brought together by people who made extensive and minute study of ordinary natural phenomena, but wonder remained the dominant principle in them. The material traces of portents and marvels that were displayed among the other objects were reminders that nature was essentially theatrical, given to making extravagant gestures, staging spectacles and offering sudden revelations.

The Royal Society condemned 'this wild amuzing men's minds, with Prodigies, and conceits of providences . . . of which our country has long been the Theatre'.[40] In its place they promoted a culture of 'sceptical doubting' in which hypothesis was kept within the bounds of 'solid speculation' and tested through experiment. Marvels and monsters were to be studied not as things out of the natural order, but as phenomena whose place within it could be understood through enquiry into their causes. One of the major resources for the advancement of this new culture of learning was the Society's Repository, which included a natural history collection that was to be arranged 'according to the exact method of the Ranks of all the species of Nature' as these were set forth in a new taxonomic system based on the principles of grammar and syntax and known as 'Universal Language'. Robert Hooke, appointed caretaker of the Repository in 1663, set out to build 'as full and compleat a collection of all varieties of natural bodies as could be obtained, where an inquirer might be able to have recourse, where he might peruse, and turn over, and spell, and read the book of nature, and observe the orthography, etymologia, syntaxia and prosodia of nature's grammer'.[41] When the principle of singularity – of the curiosity as a bizarre or wonderful object, something out of the order of known objects – was replaced by the principle of comprehensiveness, the collection became legible to scholarship in the new scientific mode practised by the Royal Society. The spectator seeking to be fascinated by an exhibit in its own right was to be superseded by the scholar who set out to read the system. Over the next two centuries, the cabinet of curiosities with its display of singularities gave way to the scientific museum as 'Classifying House',[42] and an intrinsic theatricality gradually disappeared from natural history collections.

The museums of natural history founded in the nineteenth century by major scientific institutions owed their very existence to forms of research which involved the rendition of beings as specimens and then, more particularly, as 'type specimens'. The type specimen, as the representative of its kind, was selected precisely for the absence of any exceptional features. Those who studied nature through type specimens sought to focus on the normative and the regular. Through a thoroughgoing investigation of the order of nature, the scientist promised to dispel the mystery surrounding any of its aberrations. This detheatricalisation of nature was accompanied by its deanimation. A specimen must be immobilised for convenient examination, but also treated so that every detail of its features would be preserved. In other words, it must be dead. As Michel Foucault puts it, 'the naturalist is the man concerned with the structure of the visible world and its denomination according to characters. Not with life.'[43] The work of classification and anatomical analysis advanced, quite literally and schematically, through the exclusion of vitality.

The story of the British Museum begins as a picture of the spreading realms of the dead. It was established on the bequest to the nation of Hans Sloane's private collection in 1753, one section of which was designated as natural history. The collection was accommodated at Montague House, where shortage of space meant that large numbers of items had to be relegated to the basement. Here, the museum became a mausoleum. Additional basement rooms were excavated as more storage was needed, and the underground area became known as 'the catacombs', where the vital principle took a last virulent stand in the form of microscopic parasitic life. An article in *The Edinburgh Review* described the remains of the Sloane collection 'mouldering or blackening in the crypts of Montagu House, the tomb or charnel-house of unknown treasures', where they fell prey to '*moths, ptini, dermestes* busily employed amid the splendours of exotic plumage, or roaring through the fur of animals'.[44] As better qualified curators took over, taxidermy and bottling – the two sciences of preservation – accompanied the work of specimen arrangement. Death itself had to be contained and controlled, prevented from going through its 'natural' entropic processes. Although it was the precondition for natural history display, death was never its focus. The aim was to create an order of arrested life.

Nowhere was this order more suggestively realised than in the domain known as the spirit room. Albert Gunther describes his first visit to it in April 1855 with his future employer. (He was subsequently appointed curator of this part of the collection.)

> Tuesday 10th [April 1855] Greeted by Dr Gray in most friendly fashion, and taken down to see the fishes and snakes in a subterranean 'grotto' (the spirit room), 'three humans high', which left a dismal impression.[45]

The impression seems to have been short-lived, since Gunther was to spend years of his life working up to fourteen hours a day cataloguing bottled fish and reptiles in the almost unlit, half-ventilated, half-submerged suite of rooms. When the spirit room contents were inventoried in 1882 for removal to the new purpose-built Museum of Natural History in South Kensington, there were 52,635 bottles, all fully catalogued.[46] After a free-ranging youth shooting birds in the Schwabian Alps and accumulating a collection in which the live and the dead mingled (his aviary at one stage had included a large live eagle), Gunther turned his attention to anatomy, and from there to taxonomy in a relentlessly closing sphere of operation which led to the spirit room where, he claimed, he found the most congenial work he could have wished for. For Gunther, there was no such thing as the innumerable. It seems he preferred his birds dead, his bottles numbered, in a world from which the behavioural and the performative were totally excluded.[47]

The modernised museum culture that Gunther represented, though, maintained a necessary and anxious relationship with the traditions of live display from which it tried to dissociate itself. The museum had to depend on menageries for its supply of animal carcasses, and so was inextricably linked to what were effectively show businesses. When the Zoological Society of London was founded in 1826, the decision to fund a menagerie at Regent's Park as well as a natural history museum split the membership. Professional scientists identified with the museum and sought to distance themselves quite literally from the 'raree-show' by acquiring premises for the inanimate collections somewhere closer to the library. The charter of the Zoological Society restricted its activities to 'the advancement of zoology and physiology and the introduction of new and curious subjects of the Animal Kingdom', but in 1854 the Regent's Park Zoo lost a court battle to be exempted from rates under the Scientific Societies Act, on the grounds that it was involved in entertainment: snake-charmers were employed to help attract the crowds and bands were playing to the promenaders.[48] The Zoo was no doubt pushed in this direction by its major rival, the Surrey Gardens Zoo, where the management went all-out to attract the public by staging panoramic spectacles and firework displays. In 1845 the Gardens offered a 'Sylvan fete' catering to nostalgia for the old street fairs and described in *Punch* as 'sundry ryghte stupidde freakes of ye grosseste humbugge'.[49] The Zoological Gardens at Regent's Park offered a 'high culture' animal show but could not entirely break its generic association with the vulgar show business of the commercial menagerie.

The museum of natural history, besides being engaged in the production of a classifying system, was part of one itself and, as such, was suffused with anxieties about pollution and hybridisation. As the class that was closest to it and on which it had a dependent relationship, the menagerie was its most immediate source of anxiety. The classification of the menagerie itself was unclear. It was at once a zoo, a circus and a livestock market; it also laid claim to educational status as a purveyor of natural history. Polito's menagerie toured widely in Britain in the later eighteenth century, and worked to improve the image of the animal collection by advertising 'Royal tigers' and other 'noble' animals, the 'finest ever' examples of the greater creatures and the 'most industrious' of the lesser.[50] In 1805 George Wombwell established the next significant touring menagerie and turned it into a national institution. In 1872 *The Scotsman* reviewed its long track record and concluded:

> Wombwell's collection . . . has done more to familiarise the minds of the masses of our people with the denizens of the forest than all the books of natural history ever printed during its wandering history.[51]

The menagerie, though, was also synonymous with deafening noise and chaotic activity. Touring brought one accident after another – many of them connected with animal escapes – and managers often encouraged publicity about this in order to surround their enterprise with an air of high-risk excitement. Leading menagerists realised that audiences also loved watching risks being taken, so collaborative animal–human performances were developed to cultivate the mixture of danger and flamboyant skill that was guaranteed to draw crowds. Keepers began to be trainers and co-performers, and the menagerie became the circus with all the elaborations in scale and variety that belonged to the enterprise of 'putting on a show'. Animals also developed stage personalities and became celebrities in their own right, which made them commercially valuable draw-cards. One notable example was Chunee, an elephant in the Exeter Change menagerie, who began his career in a pantomime appearance at Covent Garden in 1811. Chunee was executed by firing quad after a couple of episodes of violent behaviour, and his death was a major item in the press. He was posthumously honoured in a play performed at Sadler's Wells with the title *Chuneelah; or, The Death of the Elephant at Exeter Change*.[52]

Show business had its own principles of assemblage, and these would inevitably come into play in forms of collection that were commercial and had to market themselves as popular amusements. The fairground performance tradition resisted the classificatory approach through its adherence to monsters and prodigies, and resisted orderliness through an adherence to the principle of Bacchanalian overload. This often gave the impression that the fairgrounds were spaces in which natural law and order dissolved into chaos. William Wordsworth recalls leaving Bartholomew Fair in a state of 'blank confusion' so profound that the chaos of the fairground seems to extend itself over the whole of the city of London, whose inhabitants are

> Living amid the same perpetual flow
> Of trivial objects, melted and reduced
> To one identity of differences
> That have no law, no meaning and no end.[53]

But fairground resistance to scientific orderings of nature did not amount to a blanket commitment to disorder. An order/disorder antithesis makes for too simple a view of the tensions between scientific and performative interpretations of nature. If performers wanted to preserve a freedom to move out of the natural order, or to experiment with ideas about what might breach its limits, they also maintained their own versions of order and classification.

Successful showmen and women had always known that there were categories of appeal to common curiosity: the mysterious, the bizarre, the mischievous, the surprising, the hyperactive, the comic, the dangerous. A well-structured combination of items from these categories would generate an atmosphere of excitement sufficient to draw an audience to a particular place. Rope-dancers, tumblers and jugglers raised the energy level with fast-moving acts full of surprise and danger; plays and puppet shows provided dramatic narrative to develop the crowd's imaginative engagement; monster exhibits satisfied the spectators' visual curiosity and created an aura of strangeness, or provoked anarchic humour. The combination of human and animal was pervasive: animals mimicked humans and vice versa; sometimes they worked in partnership, and sometimes presented as monstrous hybrids. Again and again, descriptions of Bartholomew Fair take the form of inventories of its diverse performance offerings, whose cumulative effect creates the atmosphere of the place.

The impression of chaos was a tried and tested blend of particular kinds of noises, movements and sights. While institutionalised science was gradually eliminating the principle of singularity in favour of the principle of comprehensiveness in its approach to collection, commitment to the exceptional and the singular was markedly strengthened in the popular performance world during the eighteenth and early nineteenth centuries. Performances or exhibits were advertised through the use of superlative phrases such as 'the most astonishing part of the Human Species', 'the strangest creature in the Universe', 'a Miracle of Nature', 'the most famous companies in the Universe', 'the just wonder of the Age' and 'the Dwarf of the World'.[54] Yet there was a version of the type specimen in this culture. Exhibits were strongly generic. The Learned Pig, the Irish Giant, the Fairy or midget and the limbless virtuoso are all examples of well-established prototypes; each was billed as completely unique but the different versions of them were described in almost identical terms in promotional literature. If they were challenges to the natural order, they were linked together in the order of wonder that prevailed in show business like a distorted reflection of the natural world as it was portrayed in the scientific museums. Given that there were antithetical cultures in these two domains, it would seem logical for them to have simply avoided each other, but they were also necessary to each other and, if anything, their co-dependency strengthened as their principles and practices diverged.

Just as exotic animals crossed the boundary from the fairground to the museum when they died, the corpses of human prodigies were likewise keenly sought for research purposes, and were purchased by the Royal College of Surgeons for significant sums of money. In the Hunterian Museum of Comparative Anatomy – a collection started in the late eighteenth century and acquired by the Royal College of Surgeons after the death of its founder John Hunter – the skeletons of a giant and a dwarf were displayed side by side: two 'specimens' that in their lifetimes were minor celebrities in show business. Barnum would later echo this image by arranging for the giant Anna Swan to be photographed with a midget known as the Lilliputian King in the palm of her hand. The technique of showing human opposites in pairs (typically, the fat lady and the thin man, the giant and the midget) was one developed by early modern curiosity collectors and continued through to the twentieth century in the circus side-shows. A technical interest in the polar extremes of human anatomy was not, perhaps, so far removed from popular curiosity about marvels. If scientists were concerned to harden the distinction between these forms of interest, astute entrepreneurs in the entertainment business saw an advantage in confusing them.

The potential for theatricalising anatomy displays was recognised by a number of entrepreneurs in the mid-nineteenth century. Madame Tussaud was one of the first to move in this direction, with her technically meticulous wax renditions of the guillotined heads of French revolutionaries. The exhibition of human bodies subjected to violence in dramatic settings with atmospheric lighting transformed the Chamber of Horrors into a kind of theatre. In 1828 the murkier side of professional anatomy was exposed through the prosecution of Burke and Hare for robbing graveyards and even committing murders in order to supply Robert Knox with material for his lectures. At this point, as Richard Altick comments, 'the word "anatomical" suddenly turned to gold in the show business vocabulary'.[55] Exhibitors of waxworks diversified their offerings to include 'pathological' displays of dissected torsos, bottled organs and other lurid items. Public lectures or tours with commentary were often part of the entertainment programme. The purport of all this was not to promote scientific rationalism by teaching the punters about evolutionary theories of anatomy, but to create a Trojan horse in which the old lure of 'extraordinary natural wonders and curiosities' could be reintroduced in the guise of scientific education.[56] Dr Kahn's Museum combined an anatomical collection and a lecture programme with live monster shows. In 1857, Kahn advertised the presentation of The Heteradelph, 'the most extraordinary natural phenomenon ever witnessed'. The same advertisement gave notice of a lecture on brain diseases, also at the museum. Kahn's business was to sell a heavily dramatised view of nature. It was the declared object of his institution 'to combine Natural with Experimental Science, and to show the connection between the functions of the Human Body and the Great Forces of the Universe'.[57]

Although it was easy for guerrilla entrepreneurs like Kahn to gain a temporary foothold in the exhibition business, most showmen were anxious that the ban implemented at Bartholomew Fair might spread more widely. Peter Stallybrass and Allon White see the prohibition on entertainments as part of a mid-nineteenth-century anxiety about the boundary between play and economically useful activity. The fair being a site where play and trading were hybridised, 'the emergent middle classes worried away at it'.[58] Established showplaces around London, such as the Exeter Change building in the Strand and Bullock's Museum in Piccadilly, could not afford to be shunned by the middle and upper classes. In America at this time, theatres were still struggling to achieve respectable status in the face of Puritan opposition to all forms of theatrical representation, which were considered on a par with drunkenness and gambling as threats to the moral fibre of the nation. In England in the 1840s, moral and religious condemnations of the performance traditions of the fairground were being compounded by disapproval arising from new ideas about cultural and scientific progress. Show businesses were, after all, businesses, and if they were to thrive in an increasingly complex social and industrial environment, they needed to sustain an established presence. Conversely, problems arose in scientific institutions as a result of the loss of theatricality from museum collections. The commercial potential of museums that kept their displays strictly according to the dictates of science – inanimate, comprehensively classified and silent – was negligible. Those who could bridge the two cultures would be in the strongest position to give both status and commercial viability to the museum as a public institution.

The museum of everything . . .

Leibnitz's vision of an encyclopedia of items housed together with an encyclopedia of entertainments in the 'museum of everything that could be imagined' was prophetic. P. T. Barnum was to realise the concept, if not entirely in the form Leibnitz described, in an enterprise which extended from the early 1840s to the 1880s when it became the Greatest Show on Earth. What Leibnitz had not envisaged was the development of his 'new sort of exhibition' outside the scientific academy and, in some essential respects, as a counter-culture to it. As Barnum was developing the museum of everything that could be imagined, academic curators like John Gunther in London and Louis Agassiz at Harvard were making it their lifetime's work to develop the museum of everything with the imagined dimensions firmly ruled out of order. Barnum's career spans exactly the period which saw the institutionalisation of natural history in national museums, and with it the dominance of a species-based arrangement of exhibits.

His acquisition of the American Museum in 1841 was a definitive move. From this point on, he sought to make large-scale entrepreneurial connections between the performing arts and the professional establishments of the natural sciences and, in doing so, he created types of performance that were a kind of outlandish commentary on scientific interpretations of nature. Theatricality and natural history were the twin poles of his attraction and he continually used one to set off the other. The purchase of the American Museum gave him the opportunity to acquire a ready-made natural history collection within which to house a performance collection. He set out to include every known category of popular entertainment:

> educated dogs, industrious fleas, automatons, jugglers, ventriloquists, living statuary, tableaux, gipsies, Albinoes, fat boys, giants, dwarfs, rope dancers, live 'Yankees',

pantomime, instrumental music, singing and dancing in
great variety, dioramas, panoramas, models of Niagra,
Dublin, Paris and Jerusalem; Hannington's dioramas of the
Creation, the Deluge, Fairy Grotto, Storm at Sea; the first
English Punch and Judy in this country, Italian Fantoccini,
mechanical figures, fancy glass-blowing ... dissolving
views, American Indians, who enacted their warlike and
religious ceremonies on the stage.[59]

In drawing the cultures of the fairground and the museum together,
he became the primary catalyst in a show business development that
reinvented the traditions of the wondrous and the monstrous so
that they could be assimilated into the self-conscious modernity of
American and European society in the latter half of the nineteenth
century.

Having declared the traditional stock of the American Museum
to be 'as dead as a herring', Barnum exploited this image of it in
order to fend off rival bidders during the negotiations for its
purchase.[60] In a nutshell, this was why the museum had failed as a
commercial enterprise under its previous owners, the Scudder
family. It was the problem Moses Kimball also faced at the Boston
Museum. Kimball and Barnum had the same idea about revitalising
their museums, which was to introduce a full theatre repertoire into
the lecture halls, and to supplement this with highly publicised
exhibitions of whatever wonders and prodigies they could lay their
hands on. The inclusion of various kinds of entertainment was not
in itself a new departure in the museum business. Even the Scudder
family, who by Barnum's standards were woefully lacking in promotional flair, had offered variety programmes in the lecture theatre
and occasionally presented prodigies, including the Tattooed Man,
the Irish Giant, a ventriloquist and a lady magician. What was new
was the balance of priorities, which gave much greater emphasis to
entertainment and especially performed entertainment, while maintaining a prominent investment in quite large-scale formal natural
history collections. This represented a change in the concept of the
museum, not just an adjustment of its practise. If, in the words of
Francis Bacon, the museum was the storehouse of 'whatsoever singularity, chance, and the shuffle of things hath produced',[61] Barnum
made it into a place that actively produced singularity, played with
chance and shuffled things so that something unanticipated was
always being generated. He established a modernised version of the
museum *as* theatre.

Through combining the scientific with the performative approach to collection and display, he could use each to solve the commercial problems of the other. Natural history exhibitions were culturally respectable, and lent themselves readily to institutional foundation and civic recognition as museums, but they were static and inanimate and had a very limited attraction for the public, whose paying visits were often the only means of financial support. Conversely, performances were immediately attractive and could lure audiences with their energy and their promise of the unexpected, but with no passport in the civic environment they were accorded outsider status by the world of respectable commerce. When Barnum chose the title *Struggles and Triumphs* for the second edition of his autobiography, he was alluding to the special challenges confronting any American of his time whose preferred line of business was performed entertainment. Even in states where there were no formal prohibitions, organised forms of theatre could not establish themselves as sound commercial ventures when they were shunned by respectable society.[62] It was relatively easy to find a few acts that could be toured to local audiences, but if cash for curiosities was one of the oldest trades, it was also one of the lowest and least reliable. 'The itinerant amusement business is at the bottom of the ladder. I had begun there, but had no wish to stay there', he announced.[63] His struggles and triumphs were in his endeavours to make the transition from the level of the travelling showman to that of a respected businessman who could set out to build his empire, and here his sustained commitment to the natural history collections proved to be vital.

Given his habitually dismissive way of referring to the original stock of the American Museum as 'stuffed monkey and gander skins', one wonders why Barnum did not break away from the museum model altogether once he had taken advantage of the opportunity to install himself in a recognised establishment. Henry James in a memoir of his childhood recalls visiting the American Museum in its early days, when 'the weary waiting, in the dusty halls of humbug, amid bottled mermaids, "bearded ladies" and chill dioramas' was a prelude to entering 'the lecture room, the true center of the seat of joy', where plays were performed with full stage sets, singing and dancing.[64] Over the years, though, the dusty halls of humbug expanded and diversified under Barnum's management, gaining a dynamism of their own as he acquired more and more living people and animals to occupy them; and instead of relinquishing his commitment to the traditional forms of natural display, he persisted, with escalating determination, to measure himself against the ultimate in institutional orthodoxy:

> The rapid expansion of the establishment, and the immense interest excited in the public mind led me to consider a plan I had long contemplated, of taking some decided steps towards the foundation of a great free institution, which should be similar to and in some respects superior to the British Museum in London.[65]

An important step towards this goal was the acquisition of the natural history collections owned by the Peale family in a carefully managed take-over strategy that was completed in 1850 with the purchase of their major Philadelphia collection, founded by Charles Willson Peale in 1786.

The transfer of ownership was a symbolic coup for Barnum, who acquired priceless cultural capital in addition to what he paid for. Peale's intention in founding the Philadelphia museum was to create a great national institution. He addressed himself to the leading statesmen of his time and to 'the Citizens of The United States of America' in broadsides explaining his vision for 'a collection of all animated nature . . . requiring an age to enlarge it to the full consideration of a national magnitude'.[66] The status of the collection was to be ensured by its scale and comprehensiveness (friends of the museum sent specimens from Africa, India, China, the Pacific islands and all parts of America), and also by its scientific credentials. It was arranged according to the Linnaean system, and Peale drew on advice from leading scientists of his day in identifying and analysing specimens. He employed a taxidermist who had trained in state of the art techniques of preservation and lifelike modelling at the Musée d'Histoire Naturelle in Paris, and he himself worked to create advances in these techniques. The civic status of his museum was also assured. In its inaugural year, Peale was elected to the American Philosophical Society in Philadelphia as one of the 'Men of distinguished Eminence' who could assist them in 'promoting useful Knowledge'.[67] The Society's Philosophical Hall was the museum's second home between 1794 and 1802, when its prestige was further enhanced with a move to the Pennsylvania State House. P. T. Barnum's aspirations to greatness were never going to be fulfilled through the kind of cultural authority that derived from Peale's meticulous dedication to the advancement of knowledge, but he rapidly began to demonstrate that the talent for turning a profit might subsume other kinds of talent. As the new owner of Peale's heritage, he was in some sense acquiring the status of a successor, though Barnum's ambitions extended beyond being anyone's successor. He was out to supersede any forerunners, and his style was both imitative and corrective.

The contrast between Peale and Barnum as museum managers is less stark than their polarised reputations might suggest. It was part of Peale's mission to contribute to the education of the general public and a consistently high level of ticket sales was essential to the survival of his enterprise. He therefore set out to give his museum broad popular appeal, developing a range of promotional strategies that showed a distinct flair for theatricality. The Peale Museum always added to the curiosity value of its regular collections with special attractions that brought an element of sensationalism: the vast skeleton of a prehistoric mastodon; a live grizzly bear, promoted as a ferocious man-killer and 'the most formidable wild beast of the continent of America'; the orang-utan or 'wild man of the woods' depicted in advertisements as a human–animal hybrid and described as a possible ancestor of the human species; a five-legged cow reconstructed by the taxidermist in company with a two-headed calf. Peale kept a menagerie whose inhabitants were destined for the taxidermist's studio, but he also understood and exploited their attraction as live exhibits.[68] His stuffed birds and animals were arranged in lifelike scenarios and their immobility was compensated for by exhibitions of 'moving pictures with changeable effects' in the Eidophusikon, a theatre of light and moving images that was one of the specialities of the museum.[69] On one occasion Peale hired a professor of English to read accompanying dramatic texts, but this was as far as he ventured towards the presentation of acting. Quaker opposition to theatre was particularly strong in Philadelphia.

As the Peale family expanded their museum business to open premises in Baltimore and New York, they remained wary of losing their prestige through too overt a commitment to entertainment, but the matter was a source of tension between the sons Titian (who was an academic naturalist) and Rubens (who was more commercially minded). Essentially, Peale's enterprise was caught between the cultures of science and commerce, which he and his sons could not reconcile. Barnum emulated Peale's status and the standing of his institution, and also copied many of the things he did as a museum manager, but he was determined to succeed where Peale failed, and this meant an entirely different approach in style and priority. Like Peale, Barnum worked to gain a reputation for insisting on decorum in the behaviour and dress of visitors to his museum so that the middle classes would regard it as a safe and improving place of family amusement. Like Peale, Barnum employed a Paris-trained taxidermist (Guillaudeu), and collected a menagerie as an attraction in its own right. He departed from Peale's approach by prioritising the menagerie over the 'stuffed' collections and expanding it to the point where it was effectively a major zoo. By the early 1860s, the American Museum boasted the first private aquarium in America, whose most charismatic (but very temporary) tenants were a pair of white whales captured in the St Lawrence River. As the museum began to return substantial profits, Barnum was able to commission travellers to acquire specimens for him from all parts of the globe. The result was an increasingly impressive collection, in spite of his claim that he knew little about the contents. Peale, who had all the expertise Barnum lacked, made slower and more uncertain progress with his collection. 'My finances are such,' he complained, 'that I cannot leave my family to go after any article of curiosity however valuable and easily obtained.'[70]

It was the practice of the major scientific museums to count the specimens in their collections and make tables summarising the thousands upon thousands of items they had catalogued, as when Gunther claimed to have labelled and identified 52,635 bottled specimens, or Peale inventoried 1824 birds, 650 fishes, 135 reptiles, 250 quadrupeds and 363 bottled specimens.[71] Barnum preferred to deal in round numbers and habitually advertised '100,000 curiosities'. Six weeks after his museum burned to the ground with all its contents in 1865, he was still advertising 100,000 curiosities. In 1873, in the aftermath of a second fire, the 100,000 curiosities were again billed on his posters. He knew that in scientific circles the status of a collection depended on its scope and magnitude and, no doubt in a parodic spirit, always let it be known that he had the numbers.

Crude as these numerical claims were, they belonged to a promotional strategy based on a commitment to comprehensiveness. In applying the principle of comprehensiveness equally to his performing arts repertoire and his natural history collections, Barnum was already creating a new form of hybridity. While the performance collection overtly dominated, the museum collection was part of its life-support system, and Barnum never allowed the two to be separated. His subsequent enterprises bear witness to this in their titles: The Asiatic Caravan, Museum and Menagerie (1851), The Barnum and Van Amburgh Museum and Menagerie Company (1866), Barnum's Museum, Menagerie and Circus (1871). In the 1870s, he took up the title 'exposition' in preference to 'museum' as the trend for World's Fairs and Universal Expositions gathered momentum internationally, bringing science and performance into conjunction in their ethnographic displays. The Barnum Universal Exposition Company (1874) boasted a 'Museum of unsurpassable extent and magnificence'.[72] Advertisements emphasised the massive purchasing power behind it and the global reach of its acquisition agents.

Barnum loved rivalry, and one of his favourite preoccupations was measuring his establishment against the major science museums founded during his lifetime. These included the American Museum of Natural History that opened in New York in 1872, the Smithsonian Museum founded in 1873 and the Museum of Natural History, which separated from the British Museum and opened as a major institution in its own right in South Kensington in 1880. Barnum confidently anticipated that thousands would flock to his new premises near Broadway in the mid-1870s to see the animals trained for 'every species of circus performance' while, just across town, the American Museum of Natural History was fighting off bankruptcy after acquiring an expensive fossil collection from which the public stayed away in droves. The living, as commercial exhibitors had always known, were immeasurably more bankable than the dead. There was envy, though, in Barnum's competitive attitude towards the science museums. Their prestige was something he clearly wanted to share. He wanted, in the most literal sense, to patronise the scientific academy. As owner of 'the only exhaustive Zoological Collection in the United States', he could make highly sought-after donations to the natural history museums in the form of carcasses of rare species.[73] He also made financial gifts to the Smithsonian Museum and the American Museum of Natural History, and during the last years of his life he endowed Tufts College with $100,000 towards the foundation of the Barnum Museum of Natural History.

Sustained determination to foster connections with the highest levels of the scientific establishment had much to do with Barnum's success in giving a new lease of life to popular and 'monstrous' traditions of performance. By issuing a standing invitation to the enlightenment police, and by making it his business to know their business, he insured his enterprises against being denigrated as vulgar throwbacks to the old fairground traditions. From the mid-nineteenth century onwards, an aura of science became crucial to the commercial appeal of Barnum's shows. It was not so much that he needed to fear exposure for exploiting the credulity of the public (he had a particular flair for dealing with accusations of fraud and humbug), as that he needed to cater to a growing popular interest in science.

In 1840 John North was educating a new generation of medical practitioners about evolutionary theories of monstrosity, but by the mid-1850s evolutionary theories were being taught to general audiences in working men's clubs and public lecture halls. Thomas Henry Huxley made a personal crusade of spreading new scientific ideas among the working population. His publications were sold by the thousand as pamphlets on street corners, and when he lectured he drew capacity audiences at the working men's clubs.[74] Popular science journals targeting this kind of readership proliferated in the 1860s. Charles Dickens's *Hard Times* (1854) portrays the new influence of scientific natural history on the education of young children who are taught to 'define a horse' in the terms used by Cuvier:

> Quadruped. Gramnivorous. Forty teeth, namely twenty-four grinders, four eye-teeth, and twelve incisive. Sheds coat in spring; in marshy countries, sheds hoofs, too. Hoofs hard, but requiring to be shod with iron. Age known by marks in the mouth.[75]

This knowledge of the horse as species is counterposed to knowledge of the horse as living being and, more specifically, performing animal. The child whose father works with the horses in the circus is humiliated in the classroom for her failure to define the horse as a species and, more broadly, to grasp the brave new doctrine of 'fact'.

Barnum refused to observe the stand-off between the circus and the classifying house. In his determination to house them together, he broke through the centuries-old contradistinction and made the whole notion of species into a vast programme of entertainment. He was uniquely attuned to the new possibilities afforded by the rapidly changing profile of common knowledge in his own time, as the impact of science became immediately visible on the industrial landscape and the links between knowledge and evidence were being widely reinforced with the new moral weight accorded to 'fact'. When he advertised his entertainments, he also set about catering to the growing sense of popular responsibility for knowing about nature:

No species of human learning is so well calculated to form habits of attention and correct observation as the study of the different branches of Natural History; and none is more admirably adapted to the tastes and capacities of the young. Besides the improvement of his intellectual powers, which the examination of the structure and habits of any class of organized beings is calculated to produce . . . there is something in the study of Nature which approaches to philosophy of a higher kind – something that, while it teaches man his place in this Creation of Wonders, infallibly leads him to admire the wisdom and power and goodness displayed by its Great Author.[76]

There is, of course, a dose of humbug in this little sermon. Barnum was not trying to attract audiences to inspect fish skeletons, but rather to visit his roaring rhinoceros and his gallery of freaks.

In the 1870s and 1880s, when the major natural history collections in Paris and London were being comprehensively arranged and catalogued in accordance with evolutionary theories of the natural order, Barnum devoted himself to displays that offered a very different approach to categorisation. His freak shows were pictured in advertisements on an orderly arrangement of labelled platforms around the walls of a glass hall, as if to parody what was being presented in the science museums. Under the umbrella title 'Prodigies of Rarest Interest, and without Parallel: the Most Peculiar Creatures in all Wonderland', Barnum boasted:

The Tallest and Bulkiest Giants
The Tiniest and Prettiest Dwarfs
Phantom-Like Living Skeletons
Most Enormous Fat Folk
The Only Full-Bearded Lady
Human Obelisks; Elfin Pilgrims.[77]

There were important differences between the cultures of monstrosity and freakery, differences reflecting the vast shifts in knowledge between the early modern period and the era of industrial modernity. These are evident in the changing connotations of the word *prodigy*. Barnum's prodigies are marvellous individuals, each with his or her own distinctive stage personality and performance skills. In the promotional literature the leading members of the freak show are given a biographical and personality profile, so that their status as prodigies seems to be a kind of personal attribute. This is most vividly evident in the case of Charles Stratton or Tom Thumb, the charismatic midget who made his way to international stardom through his impersonation of Napoleon and his portrayals of the formal Victorian gentleman as a miniaturised icon of cuteness. Stratton's qualities as a child prodigy, with a born genius for improvisation and impersonation, were as significant a factor in his success as his size. The use of the term 'prodigy' to denote virtuoso ability or genius (especially childhood genius) was an eighteenth-century development. Earlier associations between prodigy and monstrosity derived from the Latin meaning of the term *prodigium*, a prophetic sign, and belonged to an interpretation of nature as the medium through which divine intention was expressed.

Changing interpretations of nature may have threatened the theatricality of the monster tradition in show business, but Barnum proved that the threat was also a rich opportunity to reinvent the tradition so that it was responsive to new scientific perspectives. The view of nature as a theatre of wonders giving rise to monsters as signs of divine wrath, where monstrous births were portentous events, could be replaced by a view of nature as unpredictable, given to capricious gestures or freaks. The latter view was quite compatible with evolutionary theories, and enabled a kind of humorous dialectic between the culture of freakery and Darwin's theory of natural selection. The Darwinian world was a world ungoverned by divine intention, given over to chance and unpredictable change, though Barnum disingenuously continued to refer to Mr Darwin and the Great Author of creation in alternate statements; he needed to please all comers. Mr Darwin created some new opportunities for the purveyor of strange species, since the Darwinian world was one in which diversity was not restricted by some primordial determination of the categories of being, but rather where differentiation was perpetually in progress. The laws of an evolving natural order were harder to determine than those that belonged to a natural order designed in perpetuity.

'No matter how you view them,' declares the Barnum and Bailey *Wonder Book of Freaks and Animals*, 'Nature's works are wonderful. Her ways of dealing with man are as strange and incomprehensible as in the development of a world, or in the adaptation of species to their surroundings.' The freaks in the 'remarkable family of strange human beings' are 'people upon whom nature has played pranks'.[78] If former traditions of show business found theatricality in the awesome and dramatic gestures of nature, Barnum found it in the quirks and humours. Nature was as fond of hoaxes as he was himself. In 1870 the freak show was titled the 'Museum Department' where it was combined with an 'Ethnological congress' (to be discussed further in Chapter 2). The standard categories of dwarf, giant and bearded lady were variously augmented with ethnological groups: Sioux Indians, Esquimaux, Zulu warriors, Aztec children and 'Fiji Cannibals'. There was a trend towards the overlapping of freak and ethnological categories.

Freakery was, among other things, taxonomic parody. Towards the turn of the century at Barnum and Bailey's *Greatest Show on Earth*, the curious onlooker could see enough in an afternoon to confound the life's labours of an Albert Gunther. As the Barnum enterprise continued to inflate its scale of operation, an anarchic explosion of species-defying diversity had occurred, including:

> JOHANNA the Educated Giantess Gorilla, Giant, Midget, Bearded Woman, Armless Wonder, Tattooed People, Moss Hair Girl, Expansionist, Sword Swallower, Cat Orchestra, Albino Dislocationist, Strong Man, Wild Men of Borneo, Barnum's Original 'What is it?', Electric Woman, Snake Charmer, Child Oracle, Musical and Card Playing Pig, Needle Eater, Legless Wonder, Lady with Horse's mane, Human Ostrich, Talking Dog, Human Pin Cushion, Jo-Jo the Dog-Faced Boy, Skeleton, Elastic Skin Man.[79]

The original list is almost twice as long. Diversity gone troppo is the nemesis of natural history, and performance operates as the dynamic factor in the proliferation, continually supplementing the prodigies of nature with prodigies of enactment.

The species question was paramount in the marketing and promotion of Barnum's freak shows. If the notion of species was hard for scientists to stabilise from the evidence of everyday life, the freak show turned it into an absurdity. 'Dog-faced' people confused the human/animal boundary while the missing link cavorted about in a cheap fringed monkey suit; bearded ladies broke through the gender divide; giants, midgets, fat ladies and skeleton men tested the limits of human scale and made nonsense of the late-nineteenth-century obsession with anthropometry. The cumulative effect of the combined freak and ethnological shows was to suggest the existence of a vast world of anomalies and exotica, a world over which Barnum ruled as emperor.

Towards the end of his life, this was a metaphor he developed consistently. Posters with his photograph in the centre, surrounded by scenes of his past triumphs, proclaimed him 'The Sun of the Amusement World'.[80] He renamed his museum the Colosseum and his circus ring the Roman Hippodrome. Here 'Nero or the Destruction of Rome' was staged as a mass spectacle for the London visit of the *Barnum and Bailey Greatest Show on Earth* in 1889, two years before Barnum's death. In the later phase of his career, his enterprises mimicked the imperialism of the World's Fairs. Just as the World's Fairs demonstrated the capacity of their host nations to own and manage the contents of colonised countries around the globe, Barnum emphasised the global catchment of his collections and promoted them as 'symbolic universes'.[81] Here, too, he was in tune with the obsessional modernity of his time. In the later nineteenth century, industrialised nations began to see themselves in Darwinian terms as highly evolved, and their sense of themselves as modern was demonstrated as a capacity to supervise the evolutionary development of peoples whom they took to represent lower stages of advancement. The culture of natural history was thoroughly bound up with colonisation. If the commitment to comprehensiveness that was integral to the enterprise of taxonomy meant going global in the search for specimens, it also meant bringing them home, to be encompassed in a single collection whose extent was a visible and material expression of the extent of the owner nation's knowledge. New specimens appearing in the major national history museums of Europe and America were the visible and tangible expression of a knowledge system whose reach extended throughout the world. Parodic as ever, though, the Barnum persona recalled the image of the Roman Emperor, whose power was demonstrated through staged spectacle. If the great science museums and scientifically oriented World's Fairs put the natural order on parade so as to demonstrate command through knowledge, Barnum filtered this knowledge through his own science of humbug so as to convert it into mass entertainment.

2

MISSING LINKS AND
LILLIPUTIANS

When the Zoological Society of London launched an incentive to
steer popular curiosity away from the traditional lures of wonder
and marvel, its stated aim was 'to substitute just ideas, drawn from
actual observation' for 'wild speculations built upon erroneous
foundations'.[1] The transition was, of course, nothing like the
straightforward matter envisaged in the Society's information
booklet, first printed in 1830. Seven centuries previously, Adelard
of Bath had warned about the kind of ignorance that 'leads into error
all who are unsure about the order of things', and by the first half
of the nineteenth century a whole culture was becoming unsure
about the order of things, not just through the kind of wilful ignorance Adelard was attacking, but through loss of confidence in
inherited ways of knowing, and doubtful adherences to new and
often clashing forms of interpretation.[2] This was a culture in search
of a new kind of consensual explanation of the laws and order of
nature well before Darwin made his bid to provide it. Among the
educated, general adherence to Biblical accounts of creation was
becoming fractured, while scientific interpretations of natural
history were in conflict with each other over such fundamental
questions as whether species were fixed in their original forms, or
whether they evolved over time.[3]

One of the contributing factors to uncertainty about the order of
things was the discovery of radically unfamiliar animals such as the
platypus, the echidna and the kangaroo in remote parts of the globe.
Conservative naturalists might be confident that whatever was not
in Linnaeus did not exist, but, in a world whose furthest reaches
were yielding their secrets to European scrutiny, such confidence was
looking premature. As Harriet Ritvo comments, 'a system that
was too rigid to make places for new discoveries, or too limited by
the state of knowledge existing when it had been devised to tolerate

occasional realignments, was a system whose time had come and gone'.[4] This was a situation ripe for exploitation by showmen seeking to encourage speculation to err on the wild side. With a little help from some carefully edited expert opinion, it was easy to suggest that nature might still be able to produce bizarre surprises. Freaks and prodigies could be reconceived as marvellous individuals, the consequence of warps in the order of nature, but popular interest could also be lured through suggestions that the natural order itself was wider in its scope and stranger in its laws than was commonly realised. Thus examples of fantastic species might be the focus for greater sensation and controversy than freaks because they widened the angle of possibility through which the very principles of natural formation might be viewed.

What was intriguing about the platypus and the kangaroo, says Ritvo, was that 'their oddity was not confined to the merely physical but extended to the level of theory or system'.[5] This was the kind of extended oddity that Barnum and other alert showmen sought to trade in, in response to the growing influence of science on the curiosity of their audiences. One of the most sensitive areas for speculation was the relation of species to each other; comparative anatomists were engaged in heated debate about whether corresponding structural patterns (homologies) in species of the same genus were evidence of common ancestry. The evidence needed to settle the argument decisively in favour of the transformists was, of course, the missing link: some creature representing the half-way point of development of a recognisable species or, more intriguing still, combining characteristics from different genera. In Barnum's parlance, such a creature was a 'nondescript'.

Where monsters were nature's mysteries, nondescripts contained the promise of revealing her missing explanations, so they could be promoted in relation to scientific debate rather than in denial of it. Although Barnum earned more ridicule and condemnation for his nondescripts than for any other form of exhibit, they were evidently a challenge he found irresistible. His advertisement for the Mermaid included the information that it was one of many intermediate species in the collection of Dr Griffin of the Lyceum of Natural History in London. Among the others were 'the Ornithorincus, from New Holland, being the connecting link between the Seal and the Duck', the mud Iguana, 'an intermediate animal between the Reptile and the Fish', and the 'Proteus Sanguitus, a subterraneous animal from a grotto in Australia'.[6] Just as notorious as the Mermaid episode was that of the 'Woolly Horse', exhibited in 1848 when the

wilds of Western America were still promising to yield as yet undiscovered species. This one, said to have been captured by Colonel
Fremont in California, was promoted as an isolated remainder of a
hybrid race:

> He is extremely complex – made up of the Elephant, Deer,
> Horse, Buffalo, Camel, and Sheep. It is the full size of a
> Horse, has the haunches of the Deer, the tail of the Elephant,
> a fine curled wool of camel's hair colour . . . . Naturalists
> assured Colonel Fremont that it was never known previous
> to his discovery. It is undoubtedly 'Nature's Last.'[7]

Human forms of the missing link or nondescript were, of course,
at the highest premium. When a discovery such as the platypus had
demonstrated that new worlds would yield new creatures, who was
to say that explorers in distant continents might not also find giants
and midgets, subterranean races, or beings situated on the borderline between human and animal species? In the 1840s, Barnum and
others began to promote the idea that among the still unknown
species of the globe were to be found strange varieties of the human.
As individuals they might look like freaks to a European or Anglo-
American, but they were said to be typical representatives of whole
races whose physical development had run on different lines. Here
entertainment entrepreneurs tapped into the newly named 'science
of ethnology'. The Ethnological Society of London was constituted
in 1843 with the declared purpose of 'inquiring into the distin-
guishing characteristics, physical and moral, of the varieties of
Mankind which inhabit, or have inhabited the Earth; and to ascer-
tain the causes of such characteristics'.[8] Paris and New York soon
followed with their own national Ethnological Societies, so that this
became a decade of particularly intense speculation about where the
outermost edges of the human species might lie, what forms they
might take, and what they might reveal about 'human nature'.

One of the founder members was James Cowles Prichard, whose
influential book *The Natural History of Man* (1843) aimed 'to furnish
for the use of general readers, a brief and popular view of all the
physical characteristics, or varieties in colour, figure, structure of
body, and likewise of the moral and intellectual peculiarities which
distinguish from each other the different races of men'.[9] Besides
forming a model for specialist ethnological research, Prichard's
work was taken up in a number of fashionable magazines and was
abstracted in the *Penny Cyclopaedia*, so it contributed to an intensified

popular interest in the significance of racial difference. His interpretive framework was founded in Quaker religious beliefs and was
soon superseded as evolutionary explanations came to predominate,
but he had triggered the ethnological debate in the public arena and
established its focus around questions of origin and species.[10]

In exhibitions created for popular entertainment, experiments
with the image of the human species depended for their success on
a mixture of science and fantasy. The showman's favourite guide-
book to ethnology was *Gulliver's Travels*, and Lilliput was the imaginary space into which some of the most successful racial creations
were projected, but those presented to the public as Missing Links
and Lilliputians were introduced as authenticated facts, living
evidence in the most important scientific debates of the era. Barnum
liked variety in his explanations as in his exhibits and he mixed and
matched freely, regardless of any fundamental conceptual clashes in
his points of reference.

Jocko and his lineage

Two hands reach for each other, their index fingers almost touching
but not quite, so that the space between them recalls for a moment
the gap between the outstretched fingers of God and Adam on the
ceiling of the Sistine Chapel. The figures in this small coloured lith-
ograph, though, belong to a whimsical scene whose philosophical
resonances are taken lightly. The hands are those of a child and a
monkey, two dancing figures depicted in their parallel roles in the
sentimental drama *Jocko or the Brazilian Ape*. Their *pas de deux* is
choreographed as a sequence of mirror images: the child prays and
the ape copies the attitude; the ape jumps around and the child does
likewise; they go through a dialogue of grimace and counter-
grimace. Jocko the ape has just rescued the child from a shipwreck,
and in the next scene will save him again, this time from the attack
of the giant serpent from which he himself was once rescued by the
child's father. Through this symmetrical and sentimental plot, *Jocko*
emphasises a fundamental equivalence between ape and human;
through its balletic and pantomimic interludes, it highlights physical and behavioural similarity.[11] Jocko has replaced Adam as the
missing link, which is no longer located in the metaphysical space
between the divine and animal kingdoms, and is now situated in the
natural world, between animal and man.

Jocko was performed in Paris in 1825, where the title role was
played by the pantomime artist Mazurier. Among the principals

Figure 2.1 Joseph Mazilier as Jocko

Source: Courtesy of the Harvard Theatre Collection

in the ballet cast was Joseph Mazilier, who a year later was cast with the young Marie Taglioni (playing Cora, a wild girl of the Brazilian forests) in a more fully balletic version of the drama choreographed by Taglioni's father, to be performed in Stuttgart. By this time, versions of *Jocko* were also playing in London and New York. It was in New York that Jocko's stage career really took off, with a series of interpreters making their own contributions to the role over the next twenty-five years, usually in heavily adapted versions. The play effectively founded a genre of monkey-man productions, with *Jack Robinson and his Monkey, The Island Ape, The Dumb Savoyard and his Monkey, Bibbo the Patagonian Ape, The Orang Outang* and *Pongo* all serving as vehicles for pantomime artists and acrobats wanting to showcase their versatility.[12] The popularity of the genre, indeed, may be attributed entirely to the success of particular performers in the monkey-man role. Among these were Master Cony of the celebrated pantomime team Cony and Blanchard, Monsieur Gouffe, the freak acrobat Hervey Leech and, above all, Monsieur Marzetti of the Ravel Troupe which arrived in New York in 1849 and dominated the bills at Niblo's Garden for most of the following decade. The secret of the monkey-man genre as a performance vehicle was a well-balanced combination of balletic grace, acrobatic spectacle, mimed pathos and grotesque comedy. This was not an easy mix, and Marzetti excelled at it, though at times his health was seriously threatened by the 'extraordinary physical exertion' demanded in the role.[13]

The popularity of charismatic perfomers like Cony and Marzetti reflected back on the monkey-man role itself. Jocko and his lineage were New York favourites; perhaps their struggle for acknowledge-ment as beings worthy of inclusion in human community reson-ated especially strongly with the citizens of a metropolis flooded with disparate migrant groups who had to establish anew their own claims to social inclusion. Since the monkey-men were at the height of their popularity during the 1840s and 1850s, in the period immediately prior to the release of Darwin's *The Origin of Species*, they were an important element in the context for the reception of his theory, with its new and radical implications about human descent. (Although *The Origin* did not directly address questions about human descent, it triggered a new wave of speculation in this area.) The human primate was no stranger to New Yorkers, and if he was an outsider he was one to whom the door had already been opened.

If in mid-nineteenth-century science the missing link was one of the most divisive topics, in entertainments it was the focus for more heterogeneous collections of meaning and association than any other role in the popular repertoire. Before Jocko, the ape-man had a long history in show business as a clownish grotesque or an acrobatic entertainer. At Bartholomew Fair, monkeys had imitated men and vice versa for centuries. On stage, the missing link was an excuse for uproarious burlesque, a figure of whimsy and sometimes of pathos. In our own time, some commentators still like to promote a picture of the Victorian ladies and gentlemen recoiling in horror from Darwin's 'dangerous idea', or trying to protect themselves from its humiliating impact by retreating to ever more trenchant forms of religious dogmatism, but this is not all the picture that emerges from the world of popular entertainment. In the case of the missing link, the overlap of new and traditional associations is so intricate as to make nonsense of the culture shock narrative. There may indeed have been a gradual and broadly based shift in views of the human as species, but judging from popular representations of the missing link, the general public took this in their stride far more easily, and with a great deal more mental agility and parodic detachment than is consistent with the culture shock narrative.

However, it must be acknowledged that there was a significant side-step between representations of Jocko, who belonged in a narrative drama with its own moral logics and world-making capacity, and portrayals of the missing link as such, designed to link in with the discourses of science. One performer who took this side-step was Hervey Leech, or (as he liked to be billed) Hervio Nano, whose physiological qualifications for the man-monkey role were exceptional. This description of him was published in *The Times* in 1847 as part of his obituary:

> The head is remarkably fine in form and the expression intelligent and benign; the chest, shoulders and arms form a perfect model of strength and beauty; the arms are exceedingly muscular, and the hands very well and strongly formed; when standing, the arms could reach the ground easily, so as to be employed in progression or leaping; in the place of the legs there are two limbs, the left about 18 inches long from the hip to the point of the toes, the right about 24 inches from the same points. The feet are natural.[14]

The account proceeds to go into some detail about how the set of the legs and the distribution of muscle gave Leech preternatural strength and agility in jumping. Leech took his monkey-man interpretations to the grotesque edge of the spectrum, where they lay adjacent to his other signature role, the Gnome-Fly, which, as the name suggests, projected an image of freakish hybridity.

In 1846, Leech contracted with Barnum to appear as the missing link – 'The Wild man of the Prairies, or "What is It?"' – at the Egyptian Hall. Although his physical characteristics made him an obvious choice in this capacity, it is clear that Leech was also appearing as an actor playing a role.[15] 'It leaps, climbs, runs, & c., with the agility of a monkey,' proclaimed the advertisement, 'it lays the cloth and sets a table with the sang-froid of a London waiter; bows, lifts its hat & c. with the grace of a master of ceremonies; distinguishes colours, remembers what is said to it, goes through with military exercises, and plays various games with an instinct and skill that would reflect honour on Hoyle himself.'[16] The staple ingredients of the minstrel show are recognisable here, but they were to be adopted with a twist. Instead of bungling the routines of laying the table, doing military drill or playing master of ceremonies, as in minstrel comedy, Leech was to execute them impeccably, but to create dramatic tension by alternating them with alarming savage outbursts and weird acrobatics. It seems that what was being attempted was some kind of cross between an ethnological exhibition and a vaudeville performance, with the leaning strongly towards the latter; but even this semi-serious imposture was vulnerable to exposure on the basis of its claim to be 'the long sought for link between Man and the Orang Outang, which naturalists have for years decided does exist, but which has hitherto been undiscovered'.[17] Leech was unlucky enough to have his bluff called by a theatrical acquaintance who recognised him instantly, and Barnum responded by distancing himself from the exhibit.[18]

On the American release of *The Origin of Species* in 1860, Barnum judged the time was right for a revival of 'What is It?', this time at the American Museum. He was taking an interesting risk here. The debacle in London could have been damaging; it was certainly damaging for Leech, and may have contributed to his early death the following year. A similar debacle on his home ground could have been disastrous for Barnum. By 1860 he was an established public figure who was at some pains to throw off the image of the tawdry showman and to associate himself with science, education and the institutions of government. He left himself no escape route, having widely identified himself with the exhibit (billed as 'Barnum's Incredible What is It?'), which was directly promoted as a provocation in the evolution debate:

> Is it a lower order of Man? Or is it a higher development of the monkey? Or is it both in combination? Nothing of the kind has ever been seen before! It is alive! And it is certainly the most marvellous creature living! . . . He possesses the countenance of a human being! He is probably ten years old; is four feet high; weighs 50 pounds; and is intelligent, docile, active and playful as a kitten.[19]

In order to claim credentials as a natural history exhibit, 'What is it?' was provided with a story explaining the circumstances of its discovery. An accompanying pamphlet made the claim that a race of strange beings 'in a perfectly nude state' had been found by a party of explorers in search of gorillas near the mouth of the river Gambia. The creatures were swinging in the branches of the trees and so were hard to capture, but the explorers managed to secure three of them, of whom the present exhibit was the only one remaining. This account presents the very traditional image of *Homo sylvestris*, the man of the woods who had been the stuff of legend in Europe for centuries and was often represented as half-ape, or cohabitant with apes. The new element in the story was a detailed physiological description of the kind ethnologists liked to record. The human/monkey overlap was attested in a pseudo-technical account of the formation of the hands and feet, placement of the ears ('set back about an inch too far for humanity, and about three fourths of an inch too high up'), musculature of the legs, the angle of the forehead and shape of the cranium.[20]

To present an exhibit as the missing link itself, rather than just to suggest proximity, was an especially bold move for the entrepreneur, but, if played effectively, it was the trump card in the profitable game of ethnological exhibition. It meant giving flesh to the phantasm upon which an entire culture of ethnological curiosity depended. Barnum, however, was almost circumspect in his introduction of 'What is It?', giving the presentation third billing after the Aztecs and Earthmen in an information pamphlet about his museum's ethnological curiosities. In general advertisements, the image of 'What is It?' was situated between that of The Learned Seal and Professor Hutchings, the Lightning Calculator. Its taxonomic position was thus between the entertainment categories of the learned animal and the human genius, but also adjacent to the fantasy-laden racial figures of the Aztecs and Earthmen. By Barnum's standards the promotional campaign for 'What is It?' was, to begin with, a pretty average beat-up, whimsical rather than proclamatory, with a text reminiscent of children's riddle books:

That mystery of mysteries, the
What is it? What is it? What is it?
That most inscrutable of things, the
What is it? What is it? What is it?
That animal which is clearly not a man, the
What is it? What is it? What is it?
And just as clearly not a Gorilla, the
What is it? What is it? What is it?[21]

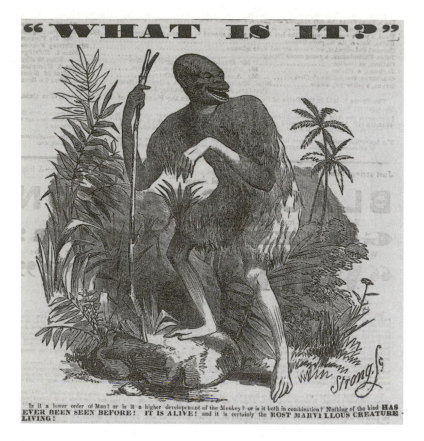

Figure 2.2 'What is It?', at the American Museum, March 1860

Source: Courtesy of the Harvard Theatre Collection

The campaign escalated in response to the success of the presentation, which had much to do with the audience appeal of its performer. 'What is It?' in his second incarnation was William Henry Johnson, a young American black from New Jersey who was microcephalic and so slightly built as to appear childlike. There was nothing about him, though, that could give support to the advertised claim that he had 'the limbs and general appearance of an orang-outang'. How could this young man in his cheap costume have withstood the scrutiny of a genuinely scientific curiosity? One deduction to be made is that Barnum never seriously intended he should do so, and took some pleasure in portraying the missing link as a casual joke at a time when the scientific world was in a furore over it. In show business, Jocko was an old friend and familiar, who might stage his return in any guise he pleased and be confident of a warm reception. The hallmark pose for 'What is It?' – leaning on a staff with smiling face and slightly bent legs and back – exactly echoed that of Marzetti as Jocko, so the genealogy of the image was instantly recognisable.

Barnum knew a great deal less about science than he pretended and a great deal more about entertainment. His ethnological exhibits always skewed towards performance, as he needed to give them high amusement value in order to keep the audiences coming. 'What is It?' must have succeeded as an exhibition almost entirely on its performance qualities, for succeed it most certainly did. Johnson, who took the stage name of Zip after Zip Coon, the favourite minstrel anti-hero, appeared in the man-monkey role for over sixty years, becoming something of a cult figure. His obituary in the *New York Times* ranked him with Jenny Lind and Tom Thumb as one of the 'aces' in Barnum's pack, and described how he 'convulsed both little children and grown-ups with his imitations of "Ajax Defying the Lightning" and "The Maiden's prayer"'. Zip's associates testified to his remarkable memory for gags and his ability at the end of his career to replay all the routines he had learned in the 1860s.[22] It was said that he was so attached to the circus life that he could not leave it and, even at the age of 84 when his health was failing, worked the whole year round, alternating seasons at Coney Island with seasons on the Barnum and Bailey circuit.

Opinion was divided over the question of Johnson's mental capacities. Did he suffer from impaired brain function and childishly follow orders for a dollar a day, co-operating in the fiction that he was almost entirely inarticulate?[23] Or was he a born performance artist who knew exactly what he was doing and enjoyed seeing the self-styled members of *Homo sapiens* being taken for a ride by one of their most earnest cultural inventions? These questions have been reconsidered in more recent critical controversy surrounding his career. Robert Bogdan acknowledges the extent to which Johnson was a professional performer who must have gained both pleasure and profit from consistent success, but at the same time he is concerned to point out that 'Johnson's presentation reveals the patterns of white America's deep disdain and contempt for the black'.[24] James W. Cook describes Barnum's 'What is It?' concept as 'perhaps the most complex, daring, and (to our eyes at least) disturbingly cruel enterprise of his long tenure as manager of the American Museum.[25]

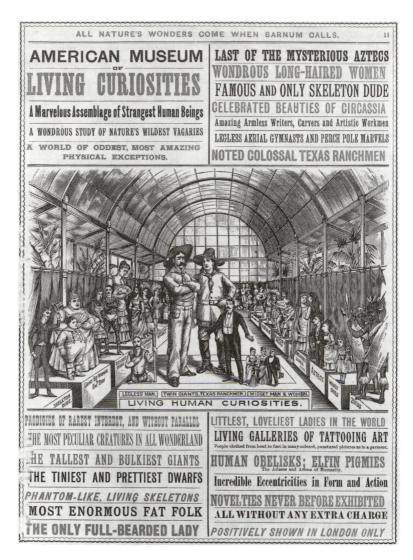

Figure 2.3 'A marvellous assemblage of strangest human beings', P. T. Barnum's *Advance Courier* (11 November 1889), p. 11

Source: Courtesy of the Harvard Theatre Collection

An equally negative reading is offered by Bluford Adams, who discusses the relationship between the presentation of the African man-monkey and the dramatic repertoire at the American Museum at a time when the abolitionist debate was raging and Barnum was trying to cater to sympathies on both sides of the fence. Boucicault's *Octoroon* was in Barnum's repertoire in an interpretation that accentuated the anti-abolitionist aspects of the play's 'craftily blurred' politics.[26] 'What is It?' was brought on for interval appearances, Adams suggests, 'to encourage cross-readings between the freak and the play's characters of colour'.[27] This may be so, and I would not be inclined to defend Barnum against the charge of craftily blurred politics, but the question is whether the effect of Johnson's appearance in this context was such as is being assumed. As Misia Landau has pointed out in an analysis of narratives of human evolution by Darwin, Huxley, Haeckel and later exponents, the role of the missing link is, in structural terms, essentially heroic. This imagined being is the very symbol of upward mobility, of triumph over the odds.[28] He/she/it is the chosen one around whom the whole story of human ascendancy revolves, so that once the figure is installed in a narrative drama it necessarily begins to grow in stature and appeal. The pantomime of *Jocko* demonstrates this. 'What is It?' was not himself a character in a drama, but he was unmistakably of Jocko's lineage.

While there is no denying that the missing link also had pejorative associations as the zero point of human evolution, and that racial groups were deprecated as the examples of humanity closest to it, the politics of ethnological shows are complicated by images and narrative associations from the entertainment world. When a slightly built young African-American with a mischievous grin was dressed up in a fringed monkey suit and mask to portray the missing link, his appearance may have done more to undermine than to reinforce the idea that Africans were like monkeys. One curious development that has not been reported in the debates surrounding Zip is that in September 1860 Barnum tried – albeit briefly – an even more bizarre ruse: an exhibition of a family group entitled 'What Can They Be?' The image shows a frog-like baby lying on a rock, watched over by a naked two-headed man with protruding teeth. The text underneath proclaims: 'Mr. Barnum will give one thousand dollars to any naturalist or any other person who will correctly classify the What Can They Be? under any species or genus laid down in Goldsmith, Cuvier, or any other published work on Natural History.'[29] The real mystery is what on earth Barnum

Figure 2.4 'What Can They Be?', at the American Museum, September 1860

Source: Courtesy of the Harvard Theatre Collection

thought he was doing with this preposterous image, and whether he ever actually presented the exhibit in question, which disappears from the advertising almost immediately. On a number of occasions the great showman could not resist the temptation to call his own bluff, and this may be one of them. Whoever had been taken in by the pseudo-scientific claims for 'What is It?' would surely have to see the joke this time.

As a concept in natural history, the missing link was safest where it originated: in the human imagination. To attempt to actualise it was to put it at risk by making it appear preposterous. A notion that in the abstract was acquiring increasing scientific credibility was vulnerable to parodic subversion by whoever was employed to embody it. Johnson evidently enjoyed his pseudo-scientific status. During the notorious trial in 1925 of John T. Scopes, the Tennessee schoolteacher who contravened the state law against teaching an evolutionary version of human origins, he offered to appear for the defence as 'Darwin's missing link'.[30] There are many indications that 'What is It?' was overtly a tongue-in-cheek presentation, an in-joke of a kind that could be made with confidence at the American Museum now that its manager's national reputation as 'the Prince of Humbugs' was established as one of the attractions of the business.

Johnson may have been fully complicit. As Bluford Adams himself records, the *New York Clipper* commented on his 'many sly manoeuvres that lets in the light on the humbug terribly'.[31] The facts that Johnson was microcephalic and black should not in themselves lead to the conclusion that he was completely disempowered, a mere exhibit designed to cater to the worst kinds of prejudice. He may have had some degree of mental disability, but we should be wary of drawing the conclusion that this prevented him from being an effective performer or from knowing what he was doing in this capacity. Like the classic circus clowns, he created the impression of being a naïve discoverer of the world by substituting gestural expressiveness for speech and cultivating a repertoire of exaggerated, ingenuous reactions.

The history of Johnson as Zip raises complex issues. His maintenance of a non-speaking role both on- and off-stage involved the development of skills in mime and mimicry, a propensity that evolutionists associated with apes and lower varieties of the human species because it was taken to be involuntary. But mimicry can also be a demonstration of wit because of its close associations with parody. When the ambiguities of mimicry are combined with the enigmatic qualities of mime, as they are in most clowning performances, an audience is presented with heavily overcoded forms of behaviour. Zip's 'What is It?' would not have been easy for audiences to read in terms of derogatory ethnological conceptions about savages: he was the missing link as eternal child, a charming Lilliputian and a virtuoso at monkeying about.

Pocket humanity

The double context of 'What is It?' in the worlds of science and entertainment meant that radically mismatched frames of reference were brought together in the marketing of the image. Perhaps only at Barnum's American Museum could 'Darwin's missing link' (the epithet adopted for Zip after the somewhat cumbersome title of 'What is It?' was dropped) be presented in the imaginary space of *Gulliver's Travels* with such an apparently seamless blend of associations. Perversely, the new science of ethnology had given a new lease of life to the racial fantasies developed in *Gulliver's Travels*, especially that of the Lilliputians. Ethnologists needed to study living 'specimens' of remote races because, according to Prichard, it would be hard to believe that there were human beings 'differing so immeasurably in their endowments and capabilities . . . if it were not manifest to our observation'.[32] How far could the idea of immeasurable differences be stretched? For those engaged in commercial exhibition, here was an incitement to naturalise some racial fantasies that had acquired archetypal status in the popular imagination.

Lilliputians were the primary choice for this exercise for a number of reasons. First, they were the most vivid and memorable creations of Gulliver's world. Second, they had child appeal, which was always at a premium in entertainments, and so could be presented as neat, clean, cute and non-threatening. Third, they had the appeal of all miniatures which, as Susan Stewart has shown, was emblematic and integrally bound up with cultures of possession and arrangement.[33]

The doyen of the 'race' of Lilliputians was of course Tom Thumb. The sales pitch surrounding him included constant assertions about his perfect formation: the symmetry of his limbs, the refinement of his features and the grace of his movements. He was the freak without a trace of monstrosity, universally appealing. It was traditional for midgets to be advertised as perfect in form and free of all deformity, but Barnum's marketing of Tom Thumb went further than this by presenting him as an aesthetic standard, the very embodiment of the laws of proportion, harmony and symmetry.

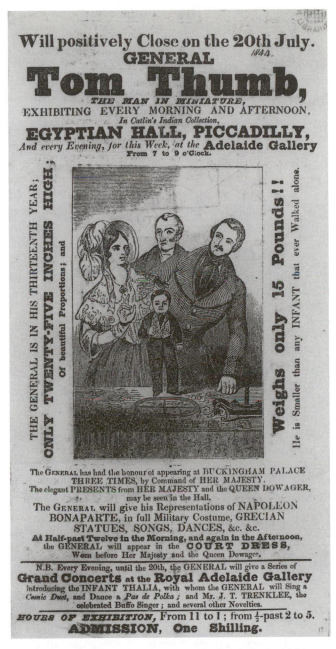

Figure 2.5 Tom Thumb at the Egyptian Hall, Piccadilly, in 1844

Source: Courtesy of Westminster City Archives

During his childhood, part of his act was a sequence of poses based on those of Greek statues, designed to display his classical physique. In the continually expanding gallery of freaks, Tom Thumb became the odd one out precisely because he was perfect. He had no single feature that was in any way remarkable: he was, in miniature, the blueprint of what the human form should be. In entertainment terms too, he was a prototype. Charles Stratton's flair for the creation of personae, his capacity for improvisation, the cuteness and charm of his manners, set the standards to which others might aspire. He had no rivals, only imitators. In every respect, he was a pattern asking to be copied. He was surely created to be the founder of a race.

In 1846 during the triumphant return season of 9-year-old Tom Thumb at the Egyptian Hall, the *Pictorial Times* speculated that 'a race of men might possibly arise of extraordinary smallness or gigantic size', and cited James Cowles Prichard as the source of theoretical authority for such a view.[34] The racialisation of Tom Thumb, though, ultimately hinged upon his capacity to produce offspring like himself. Barnum developed the image of a Lilliputian tribe first by surrounding Stratton with others built to the same scale, and then by organising these as a family group through the occasion of Tom Thumb's marriage in February 1863. His bride, Lavinia Warren, was attended by her equally diminutive 'sister' Minnie, and the best man was Barnum's newest midget star, Commodore Nutt. Aside from making a major show in its own right, the wedding was clearly intended to set up Stratton and Warren as the creators of a dynasty of midgets. If a second lineage could then be started by pairing off Minnie Warren and Commodore Nutt, it did not require a huge stretch of the imagination to speculate that a future race of midgets might ensue. In the event, the couple never did have children and the image of them with their offspring was a stage fiction; Minnie Warren and Commodore Nutt did not take to each other as Barnum hoped, and there was no second wedding.

However, the racial fantasy surrounding Tom Thumb soon found other vehicles, most notably in the figures of Maximo and Bartola the 'Aztec Lilliputians', who were first exhibited in Boston in 1850, then taken to London in 1853. Handbills advertising their appearance in the exhibition rooms at Hanover Square compared them to Tom Thumb for their diminutive perfection, and the comparison was further developed in an accompanying lecture and an information leaflet. The strategy was clearly to transpose all the prototypical characteristics to two children whose additional drawing power lay in the intriguing suggestion that they were the surviving

Figure 2.6 'The Aztec Children', cartoon, *Illustrated Magazine of Art*, Vol. 2 (1854), p. 77

Source: Mitchell Library, State Library of New South Wales (ML Ref: Q 705/31)

representatives of 'a race hitherto believed to be fabulous or extinct; a race of Pigmies about the length of a man's arm – yet most perfect in their proportions (both of their heads are less in size than Tom Thumb's.)'.[35] Perhaps it was easier to sustain the fiction of a lost ancestral race than that of a race in prospect. The children were in themselves the only evidence by which the story could be tested. Their place of origin was said to be the lost city of Iximaya, so remote and so well guarded that only one group of European explorers had ever succeeded in gaining entry to it, an endeavour that cost the lives of most of the party. As the story went, two were taken captive but managed to escape, carrying with them the prize of the two sacred children, last descendants of the ancient caste of priests who founded the city.

The performative and behavioural appeal of the Aztecs echoed that of Tom Thumb:

> Why! kind reader, you cannot witness their walk, jump or skip across the platform without laughing. You cannot behold these pocket editions of humanity without experiencing feelings such as you never before experienced.[36]

They were exhibited in company with another two children, billed as 'The Earthmen or Erdmanniges: people who burrow under the earth'. Where the Aztecs evoked images from ancient mythology, the Earthmen – also Lilliputians and, like Tom Thumb, 'distinguished by the utmost intelligence and symmetrical beauty'[37] – were given a narrative more directly in the genre of *Gulliver's Travels*. Promotional literature conjured visions of a world teeming with 'thousands of little figures', excavating the landscape with shovel-shaped toe and fingernails and creating a habitat resembling a giant rabbit warren. The joint exhibition of the Aztecs and Earthmen enabled them to reinforce each other as racial exotica. Exhibited alone, the Aztecs were easier to categorise as anatomical anomalies and the Earthmen as African 'savages'; together, they could stimulate the European imagination with ideas of extreme and fantastic racial variety. In the Aztecs especially, exotic fantasy met scientific enquiry: 'They are not dwarfs, but a new and absolutely unique race of Mankind, whose distinctive peculiarities constitute the most Extraordinary and Inexplicable Phenomena that the history of the human races has yet produced.'[38]

The images being constructed here drew on traditional European ideas of savages as child races. Eighteenth-century commentators frequently employed the 'child trope' in discussions of race, says Gustav Jahoda, typically arguing that 'as, with respect to individuals, there is a progress from infancy to maturity; so there is a similar progress in every nation from its savage state to its maturity in arts and sciences'.[39] The performing child was always a marketable prospect in the entertainment business, and as Tom Thumb had proved, this was overwhelmingly the case where performance skills were combined with cute manners and attractive looks. The child savage, though, did not necessarily have these qualities, and the prototype was accorded numerous characteristics that were distinctly unappealing. Some of these unattractive traits were just those that the Victorian English and Puritan Americans disliked in their own children: unruly behaviour, dirtiness, noise, irresponsibility and lack of competence.

Other, much more repellent traits were associated with the disturbing combination of mental childishness with physical adulthood. Jahoda traces in the literature on savages a marked shift in attitude to them as they passed the stage of puberty. Members of the child races could be intelligent and charming while they remained children physically, but as they became adult they became stupid and apelike.[40] Spontaneity became mere brutishness. Wildness carried the threat of potential violence. Adult sexuality was an alarming attribute in those who lacked self-control and social grace. The brutish savage had some curiosity value but little entertainment value, and there was a fundamental contradiction in trying to lure audiences to witness something just because it was revolting. It was therefore good business to exploit the potential of racial exoticism in a way that appealed to prevailing social and aesthetic values. One way of doing this was to invent a sanitised version of the child race.

The Aztecs, drawn standing on a gentleman's hand, or perched neatly on a small pile of books whose titles include *Cuvier* and *Ethnology*, were at once scientific specimens and toy people, to be doted on as mascots and incorporated into the drawing-room life of the upper classes. They appeared to the accompaniment of music from the crystal-ophonic as beings from a new order of wonder, supposed to have been ratified by science. The Earthmen children were depicted in posters and handbills seated on a rock with their arms around each other, their sentimental charm gaining added pathos from the rude environment of bush and scrub surrounding them. The story of the babes in the wood was a popular subject for pantomimes, and its resonances suited the ethnologists' themes: here were two innocents, set adrift through inadequate parentage, but ready to find their own way into the paths of civilisation. These images of the Aztecs and Earthmen created infinitely more marketable concepts of exotic race than those which conjured visions of ill-formed, retarded and incompetent natives behaving brutally towards each other in distant parts of the globe.

Members of the Ethnological Society were certainly ready to express their scepticism about the Aztecs, but at the same time they were compelled to give them close attention, because this was a test case for all their accepted rationales concerning the origin and development of racial difference. An article on the Aztec Children in *The Illustrated Magazine of Art* commented:

> Science has enough to do in these days to unravel the tangled threads of mysteries which surround her. Facts and fallacies jostle so unceremoniously together, and encroach with such insidious steps upon each other's domains, that to distinguish between them and refer each to its own proper empire is not an easy task.[41]

The writer reviews the successful history of fraud detection (including the episode of the Feejee Mermaid) and expresses confidence that if the Aztecs and their origin story are an imposture, the scientists of the day will be able to detect it.

If, as was claimed, the Aztec children were indeed 'average specimens of a nation until now little known to travellers', then hereditary variations of form in the human might not be so closely regulated as the new anatomists insisted.[42] Immeasurable difference between peoples was something ethnologists were pleased to contemplate when the emphasis was where James Cowles Prichard placed it: on 'endowments and capabilities'. Such contemplations endorsed the superiority complex of a colonising nation at the height of its obsession with its own progress. Endowments and capabilities would, of course, be reflected in physiological differences – stunted growth, small brains, brutish features – but physical and socio-cultural evolution were seen as being intertwined. The claims made about the Aztecs implied, however, that they were free of the physical and cultural inferiorities of the savage, yet immeasurably different in scale and feature from all other known races. Should the evidence be found truly to support such claims, then the world might indeed more resemble that of *Gulliver's Travels* than any scientific rationalist would accept.

Assessment of the evidence was therefore of the utmost importance and the Ethnological Society played a key role here. When the

Aztecs and their 'Proprietor' first arrived in London in July 1853 they were received in the house of Sir Benjamin Brodie, at that time President of the Society, who invited leading anatomists and physiologists to make their own examinations of the children. Richard Owen, Hunterian professor and conservator for the Royal College of Surgeons, made numerous measurements and recorded a detailed anatomical description of each of them, drawing the conclusion that the most striking characteristic of both was the 'abnormal arrest of development of the brain and brain-case, which gives them the character of hemi-cephalous monsters'.[43] Perhaps Owen did not give sufficient attention to entertainment circulars to notice that on poster advertising for the Aztecs and Earthmen he was quoted as saying: 'their quick perceptive faculties, their easily excited curiosity, the mild and intelligent expression of their full dark eyes cannot fail to surprise and gratify all beholders.'[44] Such polarised descriptive accounts typified the relative positions taken by the ethnologists and the promoters of the exhibition.

John Conolly, President of the Ethnological Society during the second London visit of the Aztecs and Earthmen in 1855, attacked the attempts of showmen to provoke 'unfruitful wonder' instead of encouraging interest in a 'definite sequence' in human development, and contributing to the study of 'man's unwritten history and progress'.[45] Conolly was so concerned about the distorting impressions created in popular exhibitions that he wrote a pamphlet on the subject, 'The Ethnological Exhibitions of London' (1855). This includes detailed commentary on a number of exhibited groups, and Conolly pays particular attention to the case of the Aztecs, portraying them in a way that reverses the promotional flattery almost point by point. Physiological features are described as 'unsightly', 'ill-developed', 'ill-balanced'; the children are 'idiotic in looks and actions'.[46] A proper regard for the data by which human progress should be monitored, he claimed, could only lead to the conclusion that these particular 'illustrations of ethnology' are 'very low in the scale of animal intelligence' and that their imperfections are of the kind to be associated with 'a nervous system arrested in some stage of embryo life'. Conolly is emphatic in his opinion that Maximo and Bartola are anatomical anomalies, microcephalics with dramatically reduced brain capacity who are similar but inferior to some of the worst cases of imbecility he has seen in a London asylum.

None of this seems to have halted the promotional impetus behind the Aztecs. Most of the marketing strategies used for them were based on those which Barnum employed for Tom Thumb. Maximo and Bartola were intricately costumed in such a way as to suggest aristocratic status, and illustrations of them were encouraged so that they became fashionable icons whose appealing image always preceded their actual appearance before an audience. The need to combine what was popularly engaging with what was scientifically intriguing resulted in some contradictions, though. This was especially the case with the Earthmen, who were promoted to the drawing-room status enjoyed by their partners, the precious Aztecs, but who were nevertheless supposed to be members of a savage race. In promotional literature the Earthmen are described in two ways: first as a whole race in their original environment, and second as specific individuals, Martinus and Flora. Racially, they were judged to be at the bottom of the evolutionary scale:

> 'Of the earth, earthy', they appear to live only to gratify brutish and selfish instincts. A distinct race from the Bosjeman and Kafirs, at whose approach they earth themselves with great rapidity, like mere reptiles. They desire a scanty subsistence from such of the lower animals as are easily captured.

They are said to have no language, no domestic arts apart from their 'rude and filthy cuisine', and no tools other than their shovel-shaped fingernails. In order to account for the attractiveness and accomplishment of the two specimens appearing in London, it was thus necessary to argue that they were picked out for their exceptional intelligence and capacity to learn.[47] A report in *The London Morning Post* describes the scene of their examination at Sir Benjamin Brodie's house in terms that were clearly dictated by an entrepreneur who had already promoted them rapidly from the lower rungs of the human hierarchy: 'The greatest interest was elicited by the perfect proportion of their forms; and their marked intelligence, gentleness of manners, and, gracefulness of movement, were the ruling topic of conversation.'[48] Although they did arouse great interest for a short time, in show-business terms the Earthmen were only ever a supporting act for the Aztecs.

The contradictions surrounding the Aztecs accompanied them to New York in 1854, where Nathaniel P. Willis gave an account of the Lilliputians, portraying them as a counterpoint to Kossuth 'the great Magyar', another exotic celebrity visiting the city at the time: 'At the same time that the "*greatest* specimen of humanity" was passing in triumph on one side of the Park, the *smallest* specimen of humanity was comfortably lodged upon the other.'[49] Willis acknowledges wryly that, as the humble servant of his readers, he is obliged 'to take every means to be astonished' and proceeds to play the Gulliver role with great style:

> If we had been suddenly dropped upon another planet and had rang at the first door we came to, we should not have expected to see things more peculiar. There was nothing monstrous in their appearance. They were not even miraculously small. But they were of an entirely new type – a kind of human being which we had never before seen – with physiognomies formed by descent through ages of thought and association of which we had no knowledge – moving observing and gesticulating differently from other children – and somehow, with an unexplainable look of authenticity and conscious priority, as if they were of the 'old family' of human nature, and we were the mushrooms of today.[50]

Willis's account of the children's behaviour does not accord with Conolly's view of them as 'deficient in social instincts' and lacking the physical and mental co-ordination necessary to engage in imaginative children's play. Here Conolly may have been caught up in his own distorted perspectives, seeing only what suited his paradigm. According to Willis, when he and his companions entered the room where the Aztecs were playing, 'two strange little creatures jumped up from the floor and ran to shake hands with us, then darted quickly to the washstand and seized a comb and hairbrush to give to the attendant, that they might be presentable to strangers – and, with the entire novelty of the impression, we were completely taken aback'.[51] By 1854, Maximo and Bartola had already spent four years on public show, and they could hardly have sustained their popularity for so long had they been as socially incapacitated as Conolly assumed.

In England, the Aztec debate divided into two camps, with exhibitors and their promotion campaign on the one side and the ethnologists on the other. The press tended to take sides accordingly, by declaring whether or not they were convinced by the origin story that accompanied the exhibition. In America, the clear-cut dividing lines between these points of view broke up to create a dense mixture of insights and opinions. This is reflected in the New York newspaper articles quoted at length in Willis' account. The *Evening Post* reporter had no difficulty in combining acceptance of the racial origin story with a view of the Aztecs as 'imbecile in intellect': it was suggested that the children were the last remnants of a race that had been steadily in decline since the time of their legendary glory. The same interpretation was given in the *Journal of Commerce*, though here the degeneracy was seen to be demonstrated in the 'reduced' stature of the children rather than in their intellectual impairment. The article describes their lively and playful improvisations, the 'perfect grace' of their attitudes and the easy gaiety of their social presentation. Willis agrees with this assessment, but sees in the children different layers of their racial history. The small stature and even smaller skull capacity of the children belong to their later evolution, he concludes, but they also carry in them some more impressive ancestral characteristics.

> The type of a noble breed is in the aquiline nose and soft lustrous eyes, and in the symmetrical frame and peculiar and indescribable presence . . . . You cannot but feel that the essence is still there, and the quality still recognisable and potent.[52]

What to English interpreters were completely incommensurable assessments of the evidence are here blended into a coherent point of view, though there was still plenty of scope for controversy, which Barnum set out to exploit when he took over the management of the Aztecs in 1860.

Barnum adopted one of the strategies he had used with the Feejee Mermaid, positioning himself as the Mediator in a debate over the interpretation of a particularly contentious phenomenon. The children were billed as 'these extraordinary and incomprehensible little problems of humanity'.[53] Perhaps as a small in-joke, he gave the first inspection opportunity to the learned physicians of Charlestown, South Carolina, where the initial charges of humbug had been raised against the Mermaid. The promotional literature was adjusted to make more room for sceptical points of view. Where London promoters had quoted a small favourable extract from a statement by the famous scientist-explorer Alexander von Humboldt, Barnum quoted it more extensively, to reveal the equivocal position Humboldt had taken and to include a speculation along the lines of Conolly's thinking:

> If, now, your little Aztecs are an abnormal deviation, and indeed microcephali (small heads), whilst the other parts of

72

their body are proportionate, the question presents itself, whether their parents possess the same features.[54]

Barnum was expert at positioning his audience while maintaining the pretence that he was inviting them to make up their own minds. The 'History of the Aztec Lilliputians' taken from the London information booklets was prefaced in his own literature with the comment that the origin story 'cannot be guaranteed but its apparent truthfulness, fairness and candor, coupled with the presence of these strange little beings themselves, otherwise wholly unaccounted for, will go far towards its support'.[55] At the conclusion of the story, there was a challenge to enquiring minds to encounter the puzzle that had engaged 'the profoundest philosophers and ethnologists of the age'.[56]

By the time Barnum took on the Aztecs, only one of the Earthmen children – the girl, Flora – survived, though the presentation was still advertised as 'The Earthmen'. In London, the received wisdom that was developing around the Earthmen was that it was wonderful what a few months in good society could do for a savage, especially if the individual savage concerned had qualities of character and intellect to work with. Under Barnum's management, Flora 'has become intelligent, and even graceful, and is not less remarkable as a descendent of so singular and depressed a race, than for the great improvements which her person and mind exhibit under civilised life and education'.[57] Nathaniel P. Willis saw the Aztecs as degenerate vestiges of an originally superior race; Barnum emphasised a view of Flora as the upwardly mobile offspring of a debased race.

In America, the mix of speculation surrounding the three children (now actually in their teens) was richer in theoretical possibilities than was the case in England, and Barnum's intervention had much to do with this, as he himself loved to dabble in theoretical possibilities. Were the Aztecs exemplars of a race being selected out, and the Earthmen of one beginning a steep rise in the natural order of human varieties? How much did heredity have to do with this, and could the influence of civilisation be determining in the matter?

Living proof

The influence of ethnology led to diverse forms of speculation and debate about taxonomies of the human and about the natural history of man. Darwin's work then channelled the debate more closely around questions about human descent by offering an intensively argued hypothesis. This hypothesis, said Huxley in his review of *The Origin of Species*, was as vast as it was novel, and could be summarised with a slightly adapted version of Darwin's subtitle: 'Species originated by means of natural selection, or through the preservation of favoured races in the struggle for life.' The idea of natural selection itself did not catch the general imagination, but related and implicit hypotheses about the deep history of the human species certainly did. At the mid-century, ethnological exhibits appealed to popular curiosity by emphasising the degree of possible difference between human races, and missing links were presented as radical hybrids or (as in the case of the Woolly Horse) bizarre anthologies from different genera. During the 1870s and 1880s, the emphasis had shifted towards exhibits that might demonstrate lost or recovered stages in the continuing modification of the human species. In *The Descent of Man* (1871), Darwin stated that 'the facts . . . appear to declare, in the plainest manner, that man is descended from some lower form, notwithstanding that connecting links have not hitherto been discovered'.

His theory was widely criticised for being mere speculation, unproven and perhaps unprovable, but if proof was what was wanting, it was of course what entrepreneurs in show business were going to supply. In the process of offering it, they also introduced distortions and hybridisations of the theory they purported to be confirming. Their wilful misreadings were in themselves, though, quite revealing tests of the logic underlying Darwinian speculation, and, as always, a dose of humbug was a very marketable palliative for the extreme seriousness with which scientists presented their views. 'In this mighty "war of culture", affecting as it does the whole history of the world, and in which we may deem it an honour to take part,' wrote Haeckel in 1874, 'no better ally than Anthropogeny can, it seems to me, be brought to the assistance of the struggling truth.'[58] ('Anthropogeny' was Haeckel's preferred shorthand term for 'the history of the evolution of man'.) What better response to such crusading zeal than an enthusiastic enlistment, with a few inexpertly targeted firecrackers to add to the arsenal?

Haeckel was contemptuous of those who sought vulgar proof in the form of missing links, but many other Darwinians could not resist the lure. In the early 1880s a new missing link began to claim international attention, and in ways that reflected the development of the debate in the preceding twenty years. This was Krao, a child brought from Laos by an agent working for the entrepreneur

G. A. Farini. Krao had the hereditary condition now known as hypertrichosis (profuse hair growth on the face and body, sometimes combined with atypical formations of the gums and teeth).

Krao was also double-jointed in the hands and hips. Judging from the early photographs and drawings of her, she was barely out of infancy when she was taken on by Farini, though the reports on her public appearances (beginning in 1882) said she was between 7 and 9 years old. It may be that her age was exaggerated because the size and set of a baby's limbs might be taken for monkey-like characteristics in an older child. The agent who found her was the Swedish naturalist Carl Bock who agreed to search for monkey-men on behalf of Farini while on a quest of his own for the tailed people of Sumatra.

Krao was first shown at the Aquarium in Westminster, an institution built to house exhibitions, concerts and theatrical performances and whose primary purpose was 'to stimulate the love of natural history and the acquirement of scientific knowledge'. Like the American Museum and the Egyptian Hall, the Aquarium was a place where the boundary between performance and exhibition was constantly confused. Farini claimed he had 'saturated' himself with Darwin in preparation for scientifically discerning visitors to his new exhibit, who was always advertised as 'A Living Proof of Darwin's Theory of the Descent of Man'.

> The usual argument against the Darwinian theory, that man and monkey had a common origin, has always been that no animal has hitherto been discovered in the transmission state between monkey and man. 'Krao,' a perfect specimen of the step between man and monkey, discovered in Laos by that distinguished traveller Carl Bock, will be on Exhibition in the new Lecture Room.[59]

The advertising for Krao was oriented very differently from that for Zip, in that there was a determined attempt to market her as a revelatory ethnological find, and this was where the controversy came in. A. H. Keane, a professor of ethnology, published an account of his examination of Krao in the January 1883 edition of the journal *Nature*, to which he was a regular contributor. After recounting the observations he had made during personal examination of Krao, Keane concluded firmly that this 'specimen' should be regarded as 'a "sport" or lusus naturae, possessed rather of a pathological than of an anthropological interest'.[60] This was essentially the conclusion that John Conolly had reached about the Aztecs, but Keane did make the proviso that 'her history' provided some evidence in support of the exhibitor's claims. The crucial point of her history was that she was supposed to be one of a lost tribe of hairy people still dwelling in the deep interior of Laos, whose ancestry could be traced back to ancient times. In an article that appeared virtually simultaneously with Keane's, the magazine *Bell's Life in London* provided Farini with an explicitly contrary opinion of just the kind he needed for his promotional leaflet:

> This human monkey is no *lusus naturae* such as bearded women, spotted dogs, or giantesses. She is a regular production in the regular order of Nature; the descendant of a hairy father and mother, belonging to the tribe of hairy people.[61]

Keane's article is also quoted in Farini's leaflet, but the passage is carefully selected to avoid the sceptical angle.

Farini's claims were further strengthened by Carl Bock, who published his story of Krao's origins together with a series of ethnographic sketches of everyday life among the indigenous people of Laos, supplying detailed geographic and ethnographic information that gave his account much greater credibility than the narrative that had accompanied the Aztecs. His report of 'a race of very diminutive hairy people, known as the "Krao"' (*krao* being, he asserted, the Laotian word for monkey) who had existed 'for ages' in the region may have contained only a minor tampering with the truth.[62] Krao probably was from a family of similar-looking people who may indeed have taken to living as a semi-autonomous social group. Here, too, Bock and Farini could support their story by association. Since the 1820s, information had been reaching Europe about the 'hairy family of Burma', a veritable dynasty of men, women and children with hypertrichosis.

The Aztecs would only be advertised as the surviving remnants of a dynasty, and their presentation as brother and sister (which they almost certainly were not, since they were later very publicly married) helped to create the impression that their unusual characteristics were in the family. 'Hairy people' could be presented as a tribe or dynasty much more convincingly because of the genuinely hereditary nature of their condition; they were thus a much better focus for speculation about human descent.[63] The speculations they provoked, though, were rather wayward from a strictly evolutionary view of things. The Gonzales family, a dynasty of hairy people in the sixteenth century, acquired quasi-aristocratic status as celebrities and favourites at the court of the French King Henri II, where they were dressed in the finest clothes and their children were given a classical education. When they toured the courts of Europe their status appears to have been that of visiting dignitaries, yet they were also still objects of curiosity and still considered by some to be animals, to the extent that on the marriage of 17-year-old Petrus Gonzales a cave in the royal parks was made available for his future family, lest they should pine for their natural habitat.[64] Evidently there was no consistent view of just where such people belonged both in the natural order of things and in the social hierarchy. They were hairy, but their hair was repeatedly described as fine, silky, curling and carefully dressed.

The same contradictions appear in more acute form in the case of the nineteenth-century Burmese family. When Barnum exhibited the matriarch Mah-Phoon and her son Moung-Phoset in America in 1884, he promoted them as 'a primal, distinct, astounding race of human beings, the hirsute paradoxes of all mankind' but also as 'the Royal Mascots of the Court of Mandalay' who, having been 'petted and pampered in gilded palaces', were accustomed to appearing only on great state occasions. Barnum's message was strong on the matter of their anthropological interest: 'They are not freaks or monstrosities but the incredible results of fundamental continuous natural laws.' No sooner had he made this Darwinian claim, though, than he was also pronouncing them 'lineal descendants of Esau'. Mixing his own blend of biblical and evolutionary explanation with what he called 'Hindoo tradition', Barnum created an origin story for sale to all creeds: 'the first man was a Hairy Man, from whom all the inhabitants of the earth are descended, with each succeeding generation the hair growing less and less until it will finally disappear.'[65]

While in the case of this Burmese family the hair had not disappeared, in other respects they were examplars of the most elite human qualities. The question of where heredity ended and civilisation began in the scale of human ascent was left hanging. Farini, however, wanted to address this question directly. One of his special projects at the Westminster Aquarium was a collaboration with the naturalist Frank Buckland to teach a gorilla known as 'Mr Pongo' to read and write. This was a direct challenge to claims made by ethnologists such as E. B. Tylor, who in his *Researches into the Early History of Mankind and the Development of Civilization* (1865) referred to the evolution of human language as 'this great movement, which no lower animal is known to have made or shown the least sign of making'.[66]

Krao, like the Aztecs and Earthmen, was presented as a quick and charming learner in all the ways of civilisation, including polite speech. In Dublin, where she appeared before an audience of scientists, doctors, Trinity professors and journalists, it was reported that the expert who presented her (Dr Behrend, a Baltimore physician) began by lecturing on sub-hominoids and demonstrating the sub-hominoid features of her anatomy. The presentation concluded, though, with some clear indications of upward mobility:

> Behrend outlined the steps being taken to provide the Monkey-child with a Human Education. Nurse had already taught her a few words of the English language, and when she was older she would be best sent to school. Then Krao came forward and shaking each gentleman gently by the hand pronounced the words, 'How d'you do, Sir? Good-by,' and all were amazed how prettily she spoke. At the end she bowed them out, saying distinctly, 'Hope ge'men you come again.'[67]

'She is of a frank, affectionate disposition, and shows truly feminine delight in her clothes, jewelry and ribands', wrote *The Times* reporter.[68] Krao's image as a performer followed the Lilliputian formula. She was 'not a monster but a very bright-looking and intelligent child', presentable in the strictly Victorian sense of the term. Her unusual features – especially her hairiness – carried the appeal of those attached to an exotic domestic pet. The *Land and Water* magazine described her as having 'a silky and universal covering of hair – a veritable fur coat – and evidence of soft, silky manners'.[69] It was her manners and, more specifically, her skills in self-presentation that made Krao an outstanding success. She toured the north-eastern states of America with Farini in 1884, breaking box-office records wherever she went. Krao wore the title of 'missing link' for over forty years with dignity and a certain aesthetic flair, challenging its implications through the very way she appealed to audiences. As an adult, she spoke five languages and was an accomplished pianist.

Barnum may have been prompted by Krao's success to find a new missing link of his own, and while she was making her 1884 tour he managed to locate a promising candidate. This was 'Jo-Jo the Dog faced Boy' alias Fedor Jeftichew, a Russian with long, silky hair all over his face as well as his body, who was said to have been discovered with his father living wild, with a cave as their base and using clubs and stones as tools. This story had accompanied Jeftichew and his father on their prior travels through Europe, during which they had been examined by numerous physicians and ethnologists. 'The Darwin theory established', boasted their publicity during a visit to London in 1874.[70]

Jeftichew had a long career as one of Barnum's most successful freaks, but he used his success to divest himself of the missing link role. He was one of a group of more experienced performers who in 1898 made a formal protest against the designation 'freaks' and earned the legal right to be advertised as 'prodigies' instead. In the 1898 catalogue for Barnum Bailey's Circus there is no trace of the *Homo troglodytes* story. 'Jo-Jo' has been reinvented as, unambiguously, *Homo sapiens*:

> Jo-Jo, in his travels in the United States since 1884, has learned the English language, which he speaks as fluently as he does Russian. He reads the latter, chiefly, however, and spends long hours at home with the Russian novelists and writers of stories of adventure.[71]

As was the case with Krao, Jeftichew's rapid and very public promotion up the evolutionary ladder had helped to make nonsense of the theories he had originally been brought in to 'prove'.

A photograph of the 1903 Barnum and Bailey's side-show group shows Zip, Jo-Jo and Krao all in the same assembly. Any pretence of the uniqueness of the missing link had clearly been dropped by this time. It was one more show-business role, subject to variation and development according to the capacities of the interpreter. Krao had combined it with the persona of an accomplished lady, and Jeftichew with that of a gentleman scholar, while Johnson diversified its repertoire through his skills as a vaudeville mime.

3

PERFORMING
ETHNOLOGY

Ethnologists sought to introduce the study of human races as a specialised branch of natural history. Prichard and his colleagues in the Ethnological Society of London shared a belief in monogenesis (the origin of all humans in a single creation) and therefore viewed races not as different species but as varieties of the human created through a historical process of differentiation. The natural history of man was thus seen as one of progressive or regressive modification. Some races underwent rapid forms of cultural development that ultimately enabled them to create advanced forms of civilisation corresponding with their continuing anatomical refinement. Others developed more slowly or stood still through successive generations. The 'lower' races comprised those who had regressed from the condition of 'the Adamite family' – who with their fixed dwelling place and basic practices of cultivation represented the starting point of civilisation – and degenerated towards a nomadic way of life dominated by brutish instincts.[1] As scientists, the London ethnologists studied 'the intellectual, moral and physical modifications which man appears to have undergone'.[2] As philanthropists, they saw their role as involving a duty of care towards inferior races, whose regressive slide might at least be halted through Christian education and some training in agriculture.

The gaze of the Ethnological Society was turned outwards upon the world at large, seeking knowledge of the other and measuring difference from the assumed position of its own membership as representative of mankind in its most elevated state. As explorers and scientists, Englishmen were the scrutineers of the races of the globe. *Punch*, which began publication in 1841 with the aim of identifying all forms of comedy being played in the London scene, was quick to pick up on the potential for reversing the scrutiny. The new magazine was practising reverse ethnology at a time when ethnology was a newly named science with a professional society to promote it. Mixing the genres of science and gossip seems to have been an especially pleasurable exercise for the writers. Henry Mayhew, a founding editor and often regarded as the prime mover when it came to setting the style and topic range for the magazine, had a deep interest in social taxonomies and conducted his own 'field' research in areas of London where few men of his class would ever set foot. He drew together a team of medically qualified writers, one of whom was Albert Smith, who specialised in the satirical application of natural history terminology to the portrayal of English customs and habits.[3]

In its first year, the magazine presented the English as objects for ethnological study in a range of articles and cartoons. The series 'Punch's Information for the People' was introduced with 'an account of the species *Man*, variety the *Barber* (*homo emollientissimus*)', giving details of physical structure and peculiarities, habits, reproduction, food and geographical distribution ('from Pole to Pole').[4] The next issue featured 'The Natural History of the Opera Dancer'. A series on 'The Physiology of the London Medical Student' ran through twelve instalments. A 'Geology of Society' itemised the 'different layers or strata . . . descending from the highest to the lowest', with the Primitive Formation 'distinguished by their ragged surface and shocking bad hats'.[5] The parody of scientific terminology was hardly sophisticated, but it served to create an effect of estrangement. What was really being parodied was a new kind of English pretentiousness that involved the rendition of other species of natural life and other varieties of the human as objects of knowledge. Instead, domestic habits and customs such as courtship, the quadrille and the London evening party, rendered as natural history, were thoroughly denaturalised and could be portrayed as bizarre performances on 'the stage of Punch's theatre'.[6]

There was much facetious commentary on the growing fashion for putting exotic peoples on show around the entertainment venues of London. A tour by a group of Botocudos Indians, billed as 'belonging to a Savage Tribe' though 'perfectly harmless and inoffensive', inspired an article on 'Civilisation' in the second issue.[7] *Punch* attacked '*soi-disant* civilisers' who 'appear to consider yellow ochre and peacock's feathers the climax of barbarism – marabouts and kalydor the acme of refinement. A ring through the nose calls forth their deepest pity – a diamond drop to the ear commands their highest respect.' The article was accompanied by a cartoon showing the head of a Botocudos Indian in three versions: first, 'previous to disfigurement', second, 'disfigured by chin and ear pendants' according to his own tradition, and third, 'disfigured by civilisation' with bouffant hair, a monocle in his eye and a neck-stretching cravat.[8] *Punch* was effectively suggesting that the differences between races had much to do with costume and behaviour, and that this was what turned different races and cultures into 'shows' for each other. A cartoon published in 1843 depicted a group of Africans in tribal array, sitting in the dress circle of a theatre watching English pantomime players on stage.

Ethnology provided a new and respectable pretext for the exhibition of indigenous people from various parts of the globe. As with the Lilliputian exhibits, the draw-card was the idea expressed by Prichard that no one would believe human beings could differ so immeasurably if it were not for the immediate availability of the evidence. There was a shift in emphasis, though, from physiological difference to extreme contrasts in culture, as manifested in dress, speech, behaviour, rituals and way of life. In his book, *The Races of Men*, first published in 1850, the Scottish anatomist Robert Knox commented that when 'the word race, as applied to man, is spoken of, the English mind wanders immediately to distant countries; to Negroes and Hottentots, Red Indians and savages'.[9] These were certainly the categories most sought after by show business entrepreneurs.

Savage pantomime

Lilliputians and missing links were inventions designed for a culture that could not see the facts for the tropes, but not all ethnological shows involved such strong elements of fable or were so identifiably a commercial set-up. A demand for the exhibition of indigenous races engaging in their customary behaviours and displaying their interesting physiognomies for close inspection was created by the Ethnological Society itself, so that ethnology soon came to be glossed as 'the science of savages'.[10] The savage was a paradigm in search of supporting evidence, and those imported to provide it were being co-opted into an already defined role in which behaviour had to be repeated to order, so that the slide from exhibition to performance to fully fledged pantomime was almost inevitable. An attempt to track this slide through some of the better documented cases may help to elucidate the ways in which popular shows created their own forms of commentary on the topic of human evolution.

A report on the Bushmen of South Africa given to the membership of the Ethnological Society of London in 1845 was enhanced by the presence of two children from a group of Bushmen brought to London to be put on show at the Egyptian Hall. The children stood by as 'living illustrations' while the lecturer made comments on their stature, the growth of their hair, the angle of their foreheads, the formation of their hands and feet and the set of their eyes.[11] When the children subsequently appeared at the Egyptian Hall, they were shown together with 'the Great Ursine Baboon' and 'some exceedingly rare varieties of the monkey tribe'. The implication was clearly that the Bushmen were a variety of the human species immediately adjacent to the monkey. Their status as specimens, though, was confused by the introduction of some formalised role-play and a performance structure, in which both children (a boy aged 16 and a girl of 8) played a series of adult roles. The bills advertising their appearance also included details:

1st — Bushmen Children in the Dress of their Tribe.
The Bushman will throw his Assigi (or Spear) Dance, &c.

2nd — The Bushman representing a Corporal of the Army, will go through the Manual and Platoon Exercise, with wonderful precision. The Bush Girl appearing as a Soldier's Wife.

3rd — The Bushman as a Gentleman's servant (Tiger) The Bush Girl as a Lady's Maid.[12]

Here there is evidence that the spectator is being situated somewhere ambiguously between science and entertainment. The ethnological gaze, which lingers on people as exhibited bodies, is being converted to the theatrical gaze, which follows a sequence of action and registers bodies as communicators rather than sights in themselves.

The Bushmen show had a return season at the Egyptian Hall with a different cast, this time consisting of two adult couples and an infant. A promotional notice in *The Times* displayed a Barnumesque combination of claims: this 'most extraordinary exhibition of aborigines ever seen in Europe', brought to the public at an immense outlay of capital and 'calculated to excite the greatest astonishment', would especially gratify 'the man of science and the student of zoology'.[13]

The Illustrated London News noted how strange it was to look out of the windows of the exhibition room into the busy street and 'to reflect that by a single turn of the head might be witnessed the two extremes of humanity – the lowest and the highest of the race – the wandering savage and the silken baron of civilization'. The visitor ready to glean ethnological knowledge could see 'in the benighted beings before him a fine subject for scientific investigation, as well as a scene for popular gratification, and rational curiosity'.[14]

At the same time, expectations of a performance were raised by a 'vigorous piece of scenic effect' in the form of a theatrical painted backdrop. Posters depicted a series of titled dramatic scenes including 'Killing the Puff Adders', 'Fight of the Bushmen', 'Preparing for the Dance', 'Tracing the Footsteps of the Enemy' and 'The Surprise'. According to the *Illustrated London News*, two of the group were asleep and several of the others seemed to have no interest in doing anything very watchable, so attention shifted to the one member who rose to the challenge of the situation:

> he addressed the audience very emphatically and gave a sort of pantomimic description of the taking of a lizard, whose stuffed form he held up by way of illustration. His action was vehement, and not altogether graceless; and his pantomime was very striking . . . this fellow would have made a capital melodramatic actor.[15]

Other witnesses were less complimentary. Failure to satisfy the demand for good theatre could prompt some very English forms of savagery as, for example, from Charles Dickens, who recalled 'the horrid little leader of that party in his festering bundle of hides, with his filth and his antipathy to water, and his straddled legs, and his odious eyes shaded by his brutal hand, and his cry of "Qu-u-u-u-aaa"'.[16] This is the kind of reaction which showmen set out to avoid when they invented the Lilliputian version of the ethnological show. The 'savage displayed in his native condition' might appeal to the curiosity of those who had pretensions to scientific expertise, but it went down like a lead balloon with general audiences. *The Times* referred to the group as 'a stunted family of African dwarfs' and commented:

> In appearance they are little above the monkey tribe, and scarcely better than the mere brutes of the field. They are continually crouching, warming themselves by the fire,

chattering or growling, smoking, & c. They are sullen, silent and savage – mere animals in propensity, and worse than animals in appearance.[17]

This time around, the Bushmen were not shown together with 'varieties of the monkey tribe', but rather taken as their equivalent.

The very capacity to perform was a sign of human-like qualities in an animal; the acts that animals were trained to do involved intelligence, physical control, memory and interpretation. If monkeys conventionally performed 'up' by imitating humans, what kinds of performances should be expected of the lower humans? Here was the dilemma for showmen wanting to make successful ethnological entertainments. The complaint about the Bushmen was that they acted like the next species down from them, yet from an ethnological point of view they were of interest precisely in the extent to which they resembled subhuman species. As Barbara Kirshenblatt-Gimlett points out, 'to make people going about their ordinary business objects of visual interest and available to total scrutiny is dehumanizing.'[18] But, for those who decided to take on the challenge, performance itself was an escape route in this situation, and audiences were the first to complain when it was not taken.

Stereotypes of the savage encompassed a range of contradictions. Their brutishness was supposed to manifest itself in tendencies to be lazy, sullen, stupid, dirty and graceless. These were qualities that actively disrecommended them to audiences in search of amusement, but there was a need to vary the sanitised image of the Lilliputians with something a bit more thrilling. The fully fledged savage who offered a *frisson* of threatened violence, spiced up with whoops and yells, leaps and spins, warpaint and feathers, wild dances and murderous rituals, had obvious appeal to an audience with a taste for melodrama. The challenge for show managers was to find the right recipe for wildness and persuade their savages to turn it on and off on demand. This was no easy matter, since wildness was a very European concept and the successful performance of it required some careful fashioning. Newspaper reports of ethnological shows often commented on the repetitiveness of the dances and the monotony of the noise. The performers knew none of the codes by which an audience could be invited into the dynamics of what was being enacted; thus some of the vital elements of melodrama – the familiar patterns of narrative, the stock characters, the anticipated climactic moments and thrilling denouements – were missing. The sense of disappointed expectation that so often surrounded savage pantomime is perhaps related to a problem of conflicting demands. On the one hand, audiences wanted the thrill of raw primitivism; on the other, they would only be satisfied by a display of the kinds of highly crafted dramatic action that they were used to seeing in the theatre. William Hazlitt's description of Kean evokes the savage almost explicitly:

> he is possessed with a fury, a demon that leaves him no repose, no time for thought or room of imagination . . . Mr Kean's acting is like an anarchy of the passions, in which each upstart humour or frenzy of the moment is struggling to get violent possession of some bit or corner of his fiery soul and pigmy body.[19]

Arguments about nature versus artifice in performance became twisted and contradictory when it came to judging the performance qualities of ethnological shows. The stage wildness that was sought after and admired in some of the leading actors of the mid-nineteenth century was surely something that could be expected from a good ethnological show, but somehow the formula for natural savagery remained elusive. 'An Exhibition of Native Zulu Kafirs' presented at St George's Hall in 1853 highlighted the double bind that beset all ethnological shows by attempting fully fledged theatricality, while at the same time purporting to offer 'this wild and interesting tribe of savages in their domestic habits', in accordance with the descriptions provided in the accompanying lecture.[20] *Punch* was characteristically scathing:

> It seems that a noble Caffre chieftain has entered into an agreement for himself and his tribe to howl, leap, brandish tomahawks, and indulge in other outlandish freaks, coming under the heading of 'native customs' for a year and half, during which period the howlings, tomahawkings, & c., are to be the exclusive property of an individual who has speculated on the appetite of the British public for yells and wild antics.[21]

But the appetite of the British public was deeply confused:

> And delightful it is there, to see them transacting
> Their business of marriage and murder and war;

Delightful to sit there, and know that 'tis acting,
and not the real thing – which of course, we abhor.[22]

Judging by accounts in the more earnest press, reactions to the
exhibition were on the whole towards the 'delighted' end of the spectrum. It seems that the Kafir show had finally got the formula right.
The Athenaeum commented on 'the almost perfect dramatic effect
with which these wild men play their parts', and *The Times* declared
that 'if 11 English actors could be found so completely to lose themselves in the characters they assumed, histrionic art would be in a
state truly magnificent'.[23] The performance was praised for the full-
ness and intensity of its attempt to go through 'the whole drama' of
Kafir life.[24] The programme gives evidence of a carefully crafted
dramatic structure in which music, action and dialogue were
sequenced so as to vary the pace and mood. The techniques for
building a scene draw on the conventions of the European stage:
singing is heard off-stage before the performers make their first
entrance, so as to create a low-key atmosphere of everyday domestic
activity into which more formal dramatic elements are gradually
introduced. Hunters arrive and there are 'greetings and speeches as
they exhibit the game', but the sequence ends quietly again, with a
Zulu woman feeding her child from a calabash. The scene that
follows then opens on a high note, in the midst of a quarrel, which
is resolved through a ceremonial process of settlement and followed
by a celebratory feast and dance.[25]

The adoption of European stage conventions, contrary to *Punch*'s
insistence, did not prevent spectators from being convinced that they
were seeing 'the real thing'. Most reporters were inspired to test out
their skills in ethnological observation: 'The face of these people is
less projecting than that of the Negro, and the cranium is more
vaulted. The hair is tufted, and the cheek-bones project consider-
ably.'[26] Other accounts found the 'pantomimic facility' of the Kafirs
a source of ethnological interest in itself and admired the skills of
enactment 'that could not have been expected in the first instance,
and which practise has wrought into something which may be
designated perfection'.[27]

At the other end of the spectrum of reactions, Charles Dickens,
after making some concessions for the great beauty of the scenery
(created by the well-known scene painter Charles Marshall), gave in
to abhorrence, complaining: 'it conveys no idea to my mind beyond
a general stamping, ramping and raving, remarkable (as everything

Figure 3.1 'African Exhibition at the Cosmorama, Regent Street', cartoon, *Illustrated London News* (14 September 1856), p. 236

Source: State Library of New South Wales (GRL Ref: FO 50/129)

in savage life is) for its dire uniformity.' Dickens himself becomes repetitious in his description, but his allusions to 'screeches, whistles and yells', 'epileptic convulsions, and screeching, whistling and stamping', 'demoniacal leaps', 'plunging and tearing', 'worrying the air, and gnashing out' are in themselves a very clear statement of the problem. Most observers saw craft in the wildness, but this reaction from a connoisseur of popular theatre indicates how the ethnological show presented a crisis of judgement to the show-going public. Dickens's scepticism about 'that pantomimic expression which is quite settled to be the natural gift of the noble savage' freed him to judge the performances as harshly as he judged the physiognomies displayed.[28]

Perceptual frameworks were so strong that it seems different observers saw different performances. Some thought there was too much artifice and some too little, but accounts were consistent in their focus on the issue of nature versus artifice. If ethnological shows were supposed to inform their audiences about the stages of human evolutionary development, they raised some vexed questions about performance skills and their placement in the hierarchical order of human achievement. The supposition that pantomimic expression was the natural gift of the noble savage was not consistent with a view of pantomime as a cultivated art; thus the definition of pantomime itself was in question. *The Penny Cyclopaedia* defined 'pantomime' as 'imitation of everything', and as imitation was considered to be a prominent behavioural characteristic in the higher animals, so it should not be associated with the more sophisticated capacities of humans. The ethnologist E. B. Tylor saw pantomimic behaviour as a form of gestural language which 'to the uncultured savage' served 'as a very fair substitute for his scanty vocabulary'.[29] Tylor was too cautious to subscribe explicitly to an evolutionary theory of the development of language from expressive gesture to speech and writing, but he stated that 'savage and half-civilized races accompany their talk with expressive pantomime much more than nations of higher culture'. He reported claims that the Bushmen of Southern Africa were unable to understand one another in the dark, and that one of the reasons they were 'obliged to keep up a fire' at night was 'so as to be able by its light to see the explanatory gestures of their companions'.[30]

Tylor acknowledges, though, that stage pantomime such as that performed by the 'professional' mimics in ancient Greece and Rome was an art 'brought to great perfection'.[31] Where does pantomime represent incapacity for more refined forms of communication, and where is it art? A successful portrayal of the primitive acting naturally involved a complex of skills related to sophisticated forms of intentionality; these skills included role definition and interpretation, analysis and manipulation of audience expectations, choice and refinement of techniques, and the calculation of effects. Ironic and parodic elements were surely as significant here as they were in all stage pantomime. Performance skills in themselves were crucially situated on the savage/civilised borderline, so that a too-skilled presentation of savagery might paradoxically fail in its objectives, while too natural a display would frustrate the expectations of an audience who wanted to see a certain kind of mental image realised in performance.

The Athenaeum tried to wrestle with the problem of theatrical expectations in its report on a group of Ojibbeway Indians shown in 1844:

> These dusky savages are here more to instruct than to amuse us. They are not actors, representing dead or distant heroes, but the originals themselves. They are what they seem, and we have no standard to try them by, but what they wish to

set up. Mr. Rankin, under whose charge they have come
over, has done right in refusing all overtures from theatrical
managers for their stage exhibition. They are not adapted
for that arena; they are too real – too natural.[32]

The context of the Ojibbeway presentation, though, was such as to
deepen the confusion between authenticity and theatricality that
characterised most ethnological shows. The group had been brought
over to England by Arthur Rankin and were shown on a few occasions as a separate act before being introduced to George Catlin as
potential inclusions in his already well-established Indian Gallery
at the Egyptian Hall.

Catlin's interest in Indian ritual was serious: as a painter, he had
spent eight years living among the tribes in the Western Missouri
region, with the purpose of documenting the 'manners, customs,
rites and ceremonies' of a people whom he was convinced were
heading towards extinction. A pictorial record of more than 500
paintings, combined with extensive notes giving eyewitness descriptions of ceremonies never before witnessed by a white man, led to
his being acclaimed as a pioneer ethnologist. It has been said that
'American ethnology begins with Catlin'.[33] His approach, though,
was very different from that of later self-styled ethnologists, in that
he showed little interest in identifying generic character traits exem-
plary of uncivilised races but rather devoted his attention to the
portrayal of individual personae and the rendition of scenes of action.

When he transported his Indian Gallery from New York to seek
wider audiences for it in England and France, Catlin was taking a
significant financial risk, which was heightened by the cost of the
rooms he had hired for his exhibition in the Egyptian Hall. The
most commercially successful shows at the Egyptian Hall were
undoubtedly those involving live – and preferably human – exhibits.
(Barnum's Tom Thumb was the most successful of all.) Conversely,
those most at risk of making a loss were straightforward painting
exhibitions. If the Indian Gallery was going to pay its way it would
have to be a fully fledged show, but this did not necessarily conflict
with the aims that had prompted its creation. Catlin was something
of a showman and an admirer of the exhibition techniques used at
Charles Wilson Peale's museum in his home town of Philadelphia.
A sense of spectacle was clearly one of the things that attracted
him to the study of Indian customs in the first place, and his portraits of ceremonially dressed Chiefs, Braves, Squaws and Medicine

Men celebrate the charismatic personae cultivated in tribal society. In his descriptions of dances and ceremonies, Catlin conveys their dramatic structure, their emotional range and their powerful climactic moments. Without resorting to dramatisation and impersonation, the Indian Gallery could not hope to convey the impact of the scenes recorded in the paintings or the customs described in the accompanying lectures.

Catlin set up the Indian Gallery as an installation, with an imposing Crow Tipi erected in the middle of the space, surrounded by costumes and artefacts. The most popular attraction, though, was his *Tableaux Vivants*. These were composed not by Indians, but by a group of rather miscellaneous Londoners, 'arrayed in beautiful Indian Costumes, fully armed and equipped', who stood by as illustrations to his lecture on the manners and customs of North American Indians. They then acted out a sequence of dramatic episodes telling the story of a war between 'two hostile tribes', which culminated in the Scalp Dance and finished with the Pipe of Peace Dance. The pantomime sequence was summarised in the programme. For example, the opening scene was to depict a banquet hosted by the chief, with finely arrayed warriors and braves reclining around a fire. 'In the midst of their banquet the chief enters, in full dress; the pipe is extended to him – he smokes it in sadness, and then breaks up the party by announcing that an enemy is at hand, and they must prepare for war.'[34] The show was an anthology of some of the more spectacular customs and ceremonies Catlin had seen in his travels among the Plains Indians, and the rituals portrayed belonged to a number of different tribal traditions. The scenes in both programmes were chosen to correspond with those in the paintings displayed in the Gallery.

When the Ojibbeway joined Catlin's show, they were effectively taking over as the cast of what had been a structured and detailed performance, and at this point the ethnological status of the exhibition became something of a conundrum. When English players impersonated Indians and demonstrated the actions involved in rituals from various tribes, this was patently fake (Catlin was sometimes compared to Barnum and called a humbug); yet it was within the conventions of theatrical representation. As illustration for Catlin's lectures and as supplement to the eyewitness portrayals offered in his sketches, it might also be claimed as a legitimate form of ethnological demonstration. For the Ojibbeway to have played out the ceremonies of rival or even enemy tribes, however, would have involved the violation of important cultural codes. Questions of authenticity took on a different cast with the claim that these Indians were demonstrating their own customs and ways of life. There is evidence that substantial changes were made to the performance. The programme gave less detail of the schedule of scenes, and the dramatic impact was suggested partly through the cast list for the group, which included chiefs and braves whose names were translated as 'Mighty Rock', 'Great Hero', 'Hail Storm' and 'King of the Loons'. In descriptions of the performance, the stress was on immediacy and authenticity rather than (as was the case with the *Tableaux Vivants*) dramatic narrative. Highlights were a display of archery in which the Chief was to 'Shoot an Apple off a Boy's Head', 'A Fac-Simile of the Operation of Scalping: Never before attempted in this Country', and 'The War Dance, in which the Indians will give a true Specimen of the furious Rage with which their feelings are aroused against their adversary at an approaching Conflict'.

The mock scalping and the trick archery indicate that the performers understood and were consciously catering to an appetite for thrilling moments of action, perhaps drawing on their own repertoire of crowd-pleasing exploits. Catlin records that among some tribes there was a tradition of sham ceremony, often performed by children as part of their training for serious ritual events. In his *Letters and Notes on the Manners, Customs, and Condition of the North American Indians*, he gives an account of the sham scalp-dance performed by Mandan boys whose teachers direct them through the motions and incite them to a climactic display, 'jumping and yelling, brandishing their scalps, and reciting their sanguinary deeds to the great astonishment of their tender-aged sweethearts'.[35] If the Indians themselves distinguished clearly between the proper enactment of a ritual and its mock performance, this might help to explain the spirit with which they took part in Catlin's shows, but *Punch* blamed them for ruining their innate dignity and making themselves 'miserable montebanks'.[36]

Punch insisted on seeing all ethnological shows as a form of commerce (something showmen tried to hide behind their claims of contributing to the advancement of science). True commerce, though, involved exchange not just between the showman and the audience, but also between the performers and both of these parties. Indians had been involved in trading relationships with European settlers since the early seventeenth century, and there are indications that their own view of show business was essentially

commercial. The indications are, further, that their sense of trans-
action was sophisticated and strategic. The group of Iowa Indians
who succeeded the Ojibbeway in Catlin's show had previously
been in Barnum's employ, where they had caused considerable frus-
tration.

The capacity for exploiting what the other party does not or
cannot see was Barnum's hallmark strategy, but the Iowa had bested
him in his own game in a way he seems unable to recognise even as
he tells the story:

> They had never seen a railroad or steamboat until they saw
> them on the route from Iowa to New York. Of course they
> were wild and had but faint ideas of civilisation. The party
> comprised large and noble specimens of the untutored
> savage, as well as very beautiful squaws, with two or three
> interesting 'papooses'. They lived and lodged in a large
> room on the top floor of the museum and cooked their own
> victuals in their own way. They gave their war dances on
> the stage in the lecture room with great vigour and enthus-
> iasm, much to the satisfaction of the audiences. But these
> wild Indians seemed to consider their dances as realities.[37]

One of the dances which in Barnum's view they unfortunately
seemed to consider as a reality was a war dance that finished with
the Indians flourishing their tomahawks and setting out on a hunt
for enemies beyond the boundaries of the stage. This created rather
more immediate excitement than the audience had bargained for, so
Barnum decided to replace the war dance with the wedding dance,
for which the props were much safer. Principal among these was
a red wool ceremonial blanket to be presented as a gift to the
father of the bride. Problems occurred again: they demanded a new
blanket to be provided for each performance of the dance and this
was claimed as a permanent possession. Barnum made his calculations. 'As we gave two performances per day, I was out of pocket
$120 for twelve "wedding blankets" that week.'[38] Is there a hint of
recognition here that the Indians might also be tacticians: that in
the first instance they might have found some entertainment for
themselves in scaring the wits out of an audience by wielding tomahawks and pretending they saw enemies all around them, and that
in the second they might have enjoyed the contest of wits with their
profiteering manager? What was supposedly being presented was the

performance of a culture, but perhaps what took place was more in the nature of an intercultural encounter.

By the time the Iowa joined Catlin's Gallery, they were experienced performers and were generally agreed to be better entertainers than the Ojibbeway. Besides appearing at the American Museum, they had presented large-scale outdoor shows of their own devising at Hoboken and attracted 26,000 New Yorkers from across the river to see them.[39] Under Catlin's management they offered a cross between an ethnological exhibition and an action show, but with a more developed sense of commercial spectacle than was demonstrated by the Ojibbeway. Their presentation, which included equestrian exercises and an archery competition, came into its own in a special outdoor performance at the London Vauxhall Gardens. Here, the group pitched their tents to create a model village, where they performed the Wild Horse Dance and the Eagle Dance before simulating a battle as mounted warriors. Catlin has been frequently referred to as the inventor of the Wild West Show, but the Vauxhall Gardens performance was much closer to the Wild West genre than the indoor performances that Catlin devised for his Indian Gallery. The fully fledged action show with feats of archery and an equestrian spectacle was more likely to have been of the Iowa's own devising.

Although the performance included enactments of customs and ceremonies, the focus was on forms of display that themselves belonged to traditions of spectacle within the performers' own culture, so that they could be adapted for European or white American audiences without cultivating any illusion of privileged insight into the lives of human 'specimens'. In this sense the ethnological dimension was submerged. Exhibitionism took over from exhibition, and the performers were flamboyant on their own terms. Since the displays were designed to impress spectators with the powerful and dangerous capacities of those performing them, they did not encourage attitudes of patronage. As *The Illustrated London News* commented, the Iowa 'possess great muscular power . . . and when roused we should say could perform extraordinary feats of strength and agility'.[40] The outdoor spectacle was a significant new development in ethnological entertainment which may also be seen as a move away from savage pantomime. In the action show, feats of extraordinary skill became a focus in themselves, and the action produced narrative opportunities based on an immediate display of unfolding events rather than on voyeuristic engagement with the lives of the exotic other.

AN INTERESTING ADDITION TO PUNCH'S SHOW.

Figure 3.2 'An interesting addition to Punch's show', cartoon, *Punch*, Vol. 8 (1845), p. 258

Source: State Library of New South Wales (GRL Ref: DQ 050/P984)

Savage pantomime, however diversified and hybridised, was an ethnological game that could be reversed so that the scrutiny fell upon those with the need to create images of savages. *Punch* followed the succession of exotic visitors to London with a stream of satirical narratives and cartoons, remaining unenchanted but intrigued by the displays in which they featured. Mr Punch, the magazine's editorial persona, was himself a showman and, having been banned from Bartholomew Fair (an injustice of which readers were reminded intermittently), proposed to get in on the game of ethnological shows with one of his own:

> It is his desire to communicate to his fellow-citizens some idea of their uncivilised ancestors. By these, he does not mean the woad-painted aborigines, but their rouged descendants, a kind of later Picts, the somewhat less ancient Britons of a century ago.

He would present a lecture informing the public about 'what a degraded race of beings were their said forefathers' in the 'gaudy and ludicrous' fashions of the mid-eighteenth century, with their underdeveloped brains hidden by strange wigs and their torsos distended by corsetry. He would then 'make the creatures execute their ungainly minuets and other dances in all the richness of solemn burlesque; and besides, dice, gamble and otherwise enact their rude pastimes and amusements.' Transition from the condition of higher animal, to the lower or 'savage' human, to that of the *soi-disant* representative of civilisation may be considered a matter of deep history among scientists, but in the world of Mr Punch it was merely a short caper across a few generations:

> Finally, he will moralise for the edification of his company, and tell them how humble they ought to feel when they reflect on their descent from such a set of monkeys as their ancestors of the reign of George the Second.[41]

With the development of evolutionary theories of human history, the fashion for ethnological shows could backfire on its audiences in just this way. Savage pantomime continued to feature in popular entertainments, but in more overtly vaudeville forms with little or no pretension to scientific value. Studies of human evolution, such as those made by Huxley and Tylor, called for a more comparative and thus comprehensive approach to the study of racial variety.

Congresses and wild shows

In the later decades of the nineteenth century, the ethnological show was reinvented on a larger scale in two distinct forms. One of these was the wild action show, a development of the kind of outdoor spectacle offered by the Iowa at the Vauxhall Gardens, and epitomised in Buffalo Bill's Wild West Shows. The other was the ethnological congress, which became one of the most talked-about features of the World's Fairs in Chicago, Paris and St Louis. This bifurcation is easy to read in terms of a sharpening distinction between scientific and entertainment values in ethnological shows, but such an impression is superficial. The two forms continued to become intertwined, with Cody's Congress of Rough Riders of the World appearing at the World's Fairs, and major show business entrepreneurs – notably Barnum, Farini, Cody and Forepaugh – creating their own versions of the ethnological congress.

P. T. Barnum claimed to be the first to conceive of a 'Congress of Nations', recording in his autobiography that the idea had come to him as early as 1849. 'I meant to secure a man and a woman, as perfect as could be procured, from every accessible people, civilized and barbarous, on the face of the globe.'[42] In 1861 he made a move towards this goal by exhibiting five Africans, claimed to represent five major racial groups: a Hottentot, a Kaffir, a Zulu and a Fingo. 'The student of natural history' was strongly encouraged to attend.[43] Barnum's plan was not fully realised until 1884, when his 'Ethnological Congress of Savage and Barbarous Tribes', also billed as a 'Grand Ethnological Congress of Nations', was presented as a major addition to the *Greatest Show on Earth*. By this time, the ethnological congress was an element starting to be associated with the World's Fairs, but Barnum was ahead of them. The assemblage of ethnological villages in Paris in 1889 and the even larger, more comprehensive display of nations and tribes in Chicago in 1893 revoked the pageant of human variety as Barnum had first conceived it.

With his natural history and freak collections, Barnum had already demonstrated his commitment to the principle of comprehensiveness, so the ethnological congress, as a comprehensive collection of the races of man, was a logical extension of his operations. In promotional articles about his congress, he claimed to be completing the work of scientists by providing the collected examples they required to properly illustrate the findings of their research into the natural history of man. Civilisation could only be thoroughly understood when studied in its entire range, Tylor insisted.[44] Charles Rau, a prominent ethnologist at the Smithsonian Institute, emphasised the need for an overview of civilisation as a sliding scale:

> the extreme lowness of our remote ancestors cannot be a source of humiliation; on the contrary, we should glory in our having advanced so far above them, and recognise the great truth that progress is the law that governs the development of mankind.[45]

As Darwin's influence took hold in ethnology, interest shifted from the study of lowness *per se*, to a concern with charting progress and development through the identification of the intermediary stages in the natural history of man. This involved comparative study, and therefore set up a demand for occasions in which diverse groups could be together.

An extended feature on the Ethnological Congress in *Barnum's Advance Courier* promised:

100 Rude and savage representatives!
Fanatical and pagan idolaters!
Bestial and fierce human beings!
Ignorant and warlike barbarians!

This unprecedented assemblage of 'barbarous, unschooled, savage and heathenish human beings', it was proclaimed, 'appeals directly to the intelligence of public and the educated of all classes'.[46] The feature indicates that Barnum was highly alert to the matter of appeal, since he was clearly aware that the attraction alone of feeling superior was unlikely to bring large crowds to see rude and igno-rant people behaving in savage and bestial ways. This was the classic problem with ethnological shows, and Barnum was taking a risk by steering directly towards the terrain of 'science', where the demand was for displays of those who represented the degree zero of civili-sation, so that those at the other end of the developmental spectrum could contemplate the whole vista of human progress of which they were the culminating point. While the appeal to vanity here was obvious (and Barnum exploited it for what it was worth), an enter-tainment had to base its appeal on much more dynamic principles.

These emerge through the profiles created for each group in the pages of the *Courier*, where elements of thrill are promised with a distinct flavour of melodrama. Fully armed and fierce Afghan warriors from the guerrilla tribes who once defeated a fully organ-ised army of 26,000 British soldiers will enact 'a dreadful story of blood and death'. 'Their deeply bronzed features, hair black as the raven's wing, and blazing eyes, tell that they know no fear and tremble at no danger.' The thrill factor is boosted by the insistence that here the melodrama seeks to burst across the threshold between actors and audience. The Afghans 'are as difficult to control as a lot of imprisoned bandits or caged wild beasts'. They are paired with Cetawayo's Zulu Braves, who are 'symmetrical and graceful' but 'terrible and fierce in battle . . . literal demons in carnage'.[47]

To vary the mode, there are high- and low-caste Hindoos, whose religious history is the stuff of 'delightful romance and bewitching legend'. Among them are snake-charmers, jugglers and conjurers, but the edge of danger is still present, because these representatives of a once powerful culture are 'fanatical to a degree bordering on insanity'. Their once glorious nation 'is now a dream of the past before the aggressive stride of civilization'. Here the text picks up on the view held by many ethnologists that human history was a

pattern of progress and decline, in which inferior forms of civilisation gave way before those of higher races. The dream of the past
theme continues with a group of Aztecs, sun worshippers, who at
the height of their empire, sacrifice 20,000 human beings a year.
The only element of erotic *frisson* in the congress seems to have been
the Nautsch dancing girls, who are drawn performing sinuous movements in short, midriff-bearing costumes.

Over the next few years, whirling Dervishes, Australian boom-
erang-throwers and Cossack-riders were added to the mix, so that
the balance between action show and ethnological display was clearly
on the side of the former. Some of the groups originally introduced
as examples of the lowest strata of human development, such as the
Fijians and the Australian Aborigines, gradually made the transition
to action performance.[48] Dances and races were clearly the crowd-
pulling ingredients, and Barnum developed the latter as his own
special brand of pun: if, as evolutionists were suggesting, the races
of the world were engaged in a competitive race for survival, why
not stage the races of the races – including the animal species of the
world – as a great spectacular event? One of the programmes for the
Greatest Show on Earth in 1884 details this event as including
Roman chariot races, Asiatic dromedary races with mounted
Nubians, jockey races, hurdle races, grand female pedestrian races,
camel, elephant and ostrich races, Sioux Indian horse races and 'the
picturesque Indian chase for a wife'.[49]

In the context of the World's Fairs, the ethnological congress was
promoted with fuller and more earnest focus on its supposed evolutionary significance. Its definitive form was set with the Midway
display at the Chicago World's Fair in 1893. The Midway exhibition drew equally on Barnum's model and on a tradition of more
sober ethnological display that went back to the Crystal Palace
Exhibition of 1851, where the Natural History Department
included thirteen life-size model groups of savage races. The whole
of the Crystal Palace Exhibition was conceived as a congress of
nations, in that its pavilions were allocated to the progressive nations
of the world as display spaces for their cultural and economic
achievements. Savage peoples, being considered stationary rather
than progressive, did not qualify for such presentation and their
rendition as inanimate models had a certain logic to it. The Crystal
Palace exhibition, as the first of the World's Fairs, concentrated
on the representation of national achievement through the display
of tools, artefacts and inventions. The story of progress was thus told

mainly through objects. For industrialists who read the story of progress in a forward direction, the primary interest was in the most 'advanced' displays typically associated with manufacturing innovations; for the ethnologist, the direction of reading was reversed and there was a concern to identify stages of development backward to the most primitive forms of human society.

This historical perspective opened on to a wider social curiosity about artefacts as indicators of how lives were lived and tasks performed, and from there to a concern with the evolution of human capabilities. This ultimately meant presenting the other, and especially the lower other nations, 'live' so that everything about them – their physiognomy, their behaviour, their dwellings, their customs and the tasks of their daily lives – could be observed and assessed for its relative backwardness.

At the World's Fairs the symbolism of progress was paramount and the whole organisational approach was designed to demonstrate the triumph of industrial civilisation, with the exhibiting nations ranged according to their allocated places in a hierarchy of human achievement. At the Paris Exposition of 1889, encampments of living people became the core of the ethnological presentation, and were themselves arrayed to create the progress narrative. There was effectively an attempt to stage the cultural environment of peoples from all areas of the globe. The countries of Latin America, including Mexico, Uruguay, Brazil, Argentina and Chile, created the New World pavilions from their own resources, to demonstrate their capacity as producers. There was a Cairo Street, a facsimile of the Angkor Temple and a Tunisian village with bazaars and minarets. Those peoples without the resources to present their cultures on their own terms were sought out for the 'museum of ethnology in action'. This was a display of simulated 'villages' in which people from various parts of Africa, Asia and the islands of the South Pacific were to be observed ostensibly living in their customary fashion in recon-structions of their domestic environment.[50]

American ethnologists and anthropologists who visited the Paris Exposition brought back ideas for the Chicago World's Columbian Exposition of 1893. Here the theme of progress acquired a new rhetorical urgency, not least because an industrial depression was sweeping America at the time. *The Book of the Fair* proclaimed:

> Little more than seventy years have elapsed since this city was rescued from savage men and beasts . . . yet in this brief

period she has risen to prominent rank among the commercial, industrial and social cities of either hemisphere. Most fitting it is that an Exposition which is to represent the progress of the world in science, industry, and art, should be held amid this the most progressive of all our new world communities.[51]

Viewed in historical long-shot, progress was a grand imperial theme, a sweeping account of the inevitable growth and glorious improvement of great nations. Viewed more locally and in the shorter term, it was a drama of competitive survival techniques, with more immediately Darwinian connotations. The Columbian Exposition offered both perspectives, and its concentration on ethnological displays made the words *progress* and *evolution* almost synonymous.

Its Department of Ethnology and Archaeology, under the direction of Frederick Ward Putnam (director of the Peabody Museum of Ethnology and Archaeology at Harvard), organised displays to illustrate the stages of development of mankind in the Americas. Putnam's conceptual time frame was the 400 years since the landing of Columbus, and he argued that 'the great object lesson' of human progress could not be learned without the means of comparison. He saw the presentation of 'the remnant of native tribes' as a matter of urgency:

These peoples, as great nations, have about vanished into history, and now is the last opportunity for the world to see them and to realize what their condition, their life, their customs, their arts were four centuries ago.[52]

It was a convention by this time for the subjects of any ethnological exhibition to be presented as remnants or last survivors of dying races, but the comparative perspective invited spectators to identify in customs, arts and living conditions the causes behind the different destinies of races who had come to share the same land.

In the Anthropological Building, displays of tools and artefacts were accompanied by wax effigies of the peoples whose cultures they represented. 'The man who enters there,' according to the *Chicago Herald*, 'leaves fun behind' and finds himself in 'the most serious place on the face of the earth'. Readers were warned that if they wished to engage in the study of anthropology they must learn physiology, geology, zoology and many other subjects; they must prepare themselves to be fascinated by the history of a piece of flint or any other disinterred fragment.[53] But this rather dry exercise in deep history was offset by an alternative mode of study among the living exhibits camped outdoors in the Midway, the wide avenue in which the pleasure activities of the Fair were concentrated.

The Midway was described as 'a jumble of foreignness' and – in contrast to the austerity of the Anthropological Building – 'gorgeous with colour, pulsating with excitement'.[54] Sol Bloom, a young entrepreneur who was charged with the responsibility of finding exotic displays for the Midway, aimed to replicate the experience he had had at the Paris Exposition of 1889 where, as he said, 'a kind of natural selection' worked among the rival claims to the spectator's attention. A hierarchy of capabilities was in constant and dynamic evolution, he observed, so that the impact of a performance by a group of Bedouin acrobats exceeded that of a medieval tapestry and 'a tall, skinny chap from Arabia with a talent for swallowing swords expressed a culture . . . on a higher plane than one demonstrated by a group of earnest Swiss peasants who passed their days making cheese and milk chocolate'.[55] That Bloom valued the skills of entertainers over those of material producers offers a telling insight. Economic production might in theory be the primary indicator of human progress, but when it came to competing for the immediate attention of those called to witness the progress story, entertainers were going to emerge as the winners.

Popular entertainments were vital to the commercial success of the Chicago Fair, and they were included in the area under Putnam's management, which included ethnology, archaeology, progress of labour and invention. The ethnological components tied in with the theme of the progress of labour and invention since they were supposed to demonstrate primitive forms of labour in societies where progress had not been radically accelerated by human invention, and thus had failed to join the evolutionary fast track created in industrialised countries. Putnam had evidently not considered the potential for this message to be overturned through the immediate impact of skilful performance. The Midway was a zone of convergence that quickly escaped the conceptual management of its curators. A wide, straight avenue overlooked by the giant Ferris wheel, it attracted everyone who was looking for diversion from the more serious exhibits in the major buildings. Those who were brought in to be part of ethnological displays thus found themselves in a situation where there was an overwhelming demand for amusement.

On the Midway, it was almost impossible not to become theatre, and most groups seem to have assumed the entertainer role with enthusiasm, sometimes spontaneously taking advantage of circumstances for improvised performances, as when a fire broke out in the kitchen in the Dahomey village:

> The African method of fire fighting was shown gratis, and a thrilling and exhilarating exhibition it was . . . . In their bare feet they danced on the burning reeds. Some tried to tear them off with their hands. When they would not yield, Akile and other amazons just put their teeth to the reed shingles, some of which were in flames, and pulled them off. In a minute the fire had been crushed and not a man or woman complained of being burned after the fight with the flames . . . . That's the way they fight fire in Africa. They tear burning structures to pieces with their hands and teeth as readily as a Chicago hook and ladder company wreaks destruction with ladders and other appliances. The visitors applauded the work of the negro fire fighters, and were rewarded with a wild fire dance.[56]

Almost all the ethnological displays were skewed towards performance; indeed, the presentation of culture through performance emerged as a strong convention. War dances were everywhere: 'given daily' by the group of Oglala Indians who performed a dramatic show around Sitting Bull's Cabin; re-created by Zulus to lead up to the climactic display of spear-throwing; performed to the beat of the tom-tom by Samoan warriors dressed in sea grass and feathers as the main attraction in the South Sea Islands Theatre.[57] Since the war dance was by its nature a crafted, stylised exhibition designed precisely for impressing enemies and strangers with what the performers wanted them to see, it was an especially effective means of transforming the dynamics of spectatorship in an ethnological display.

The Midway attractions included theatres running what amounted to variety programmes. Some of the acts were drawn from what were traditionally display activities – such as acrobatics, whip-cracking, belly-dancing and spear-throwing – but others involved the conversion of customs or ceremonies into generic spectacles. The Algerian village, which Sol Bloom had taken particular trouble to acquire after seeing it in Paris, included a theatre which offered transgressive and thrilling acts. The *Chicago Tribune* described the reactions of audiences being presented for the first time with displays of Oriental extremism that clearly surpassed anything which their own stereotypical imaginings might have led them to anticipate:

> Incense was burning and tom toms were beating. The visitors watched the operations of the fakirs of the East with a great deal of interest, many young women who were of the crowd showing much more composure than the men when Kabash stuck an ice pick through his tongue and twisted that organ around until it was taut as a rope. They were rather edified indeed by a wiry young man who first danced himself into a fit until his eyes rolled wildly, and then devoured a live coal and several items of glassware. When Swewek feasted on live scorpions their enjoyment increased, and went beyond all bounds when Da Boufik allowed a long green adder to fasten its fangs into the end of his nose, in which position he carried it around the stage several times. When another of the performers inserted a long keen sword into his system several men repented of their attendance, but they only got as far as the door and came back because someone near the entrance told them that the next performer would stick himself full of daggers and wander around on hot iron plates.[58]

This was hardly a demonstration of everyday life in Algeria and it was a highly effective means of turning the knowing gaze of the evolutionary interpreter into another form of spectatorship altogether.

Competition between cultures took on new dimensions when it was staged as a spectator sport. Among the popular attractions in Chicago running concurrently with the Fair were Bill Cody's *Wild West Show*, Adam Forepaugh's mass spectacle *1776 – The American Revolution*, Imre Kiralfy's allegorical pantomime *America* and the Tattersall's military shows. All these shows purported to celebrate the triumph of European civilisation in a new world order where progress meant the demise of all 'inferior' races. All included ingredients of the ethnological action show, where the involvement of the wilder races served to raise the energy levels and create an aura of physical danger and unpredictability. Those who came out on top in performance terms were not always those allocated the winning roles in the great evolutionary drama of human progress, to which direct allusions were made in the promotional literature. Adam Forepaugh gave the requisite ideological line in describing the Indians as 'a race destined by a strange fatality to a slow but sure extinction . . . in the drama of civilization' but he added a note of ambiguity, hinting that the outcome of the drama was yet to be determined. 'The denouement is far in the future. The solution of the problem will be found, no doubt, in the theory of the survival of the fittest.'[59]

Forepaugh's spectacle *1776 – The American Revolution* was an obvious imitation of Cody's *Wild West Show* formula and a somewhat too obvious attempt to outdo him at his own game. Both Cody and Forepaugh were featuring Cossack riders, and both were claiming to have the 'first and only' genuine Cossacks from the Caucasus in their employ. Whatever the truth of this situation, the Cossack team were outstanding performers and it is evident that they had special kudos. They became the main attraction in Forepaugh's show, even though they were only an interval act in his 'grand pantomimic military drama' of the American Revolution. In spite of the boasted cast of thousands and acres of scenery telling 'the glorious story of the birth of American Freedom' in a drama that, it was claimed, 'upholds American superiority and challenges comparison with all the world', it was the Cossacks who won the audience.

The Tattersall's military display was built around restaged scenes from the most intense phase of the Zulu wars in 1879, and featured soldiers and horses from Britain – 'the pick of England's mighty army' – brought over specially for the display.[60] The cast of the Zulu contingent was less well authenticated and local African-Americans were no doubt employed to swell the ranks, but a core group of genuine Zulus provided the climactic display of fighting skills. This featured repeated demonstrations of 'the wild charge', in which the enemy is rushed with blood-curdling yells and acrobatic leaps as a prelude to the throwing of spears or *assegais*. In comparison with this, the Life Guards' 'musical ride and sword drill' was less than completely thrilling. The value of Zulus as contributors to spectacular shows was by this time well established. Farini had acquired a group of Zulus shortly after the 1879 crisis and presented them in numerous entertainment programmes over the next few years. Publicity for their appearances at the Aquarium placed heavy emphasis on the thrill factor:

The manner in which they illustrate the method of killing their war victims is in itself enough to strike terror into the stoutest heart. The fiendish reality of their war dances and songs is marvellous in its true and horrible intensity.[61]

Subsequently marketed as 'Farini's Friendly Zulus', this troupe developed an act which could be incorporated into anything from a music-hall variety show to a major circus spectacle. The throwing of the *assegais*, as the climax of their performance, became something of a *tour de force* and was a major success in their guest appearances with Barnum's *Greatest Show on Earth* in 1880. 'Ferocious Zulus' became a staple in Barnum's shows after this, and they were always near the top of the bill for his Great Ethnological Congress. Here, though, it was clear that the ethnological interest invited in the enactments of 'their strange customs' and 'brutal festivities' was subordinated to the appeal of the warrior role that came with its own terms.

> The Warriors of the Tribe are strong, agile and daring to desperation; and their native dress of wild beast skins and gorgeous feathers, in which they are always exhibited, displays their sinewy forms to best advantage. They are, moreover, exceedingly fleet of foot. They appear at each performance costumed in the spoils of the chase, armed with the deadly Assegai.[62]

Ten years on from this, the Zulus in Chicago proved that they could lose a staged battle while maintaining their own terms in the competition of cultures.

Kiralfy, perhaps mindful of the tendency of savages to steal the show, scripted *America* so as to confine the American Indian performers to a bland and subservient role. He laid on the ideology more strongly than any of his rival showmen in Chicago at the time, framing the action in an allegorical dialogue between Progress and Perseverence. At various moments in the pageant these two figures are surrounded by other personifications, including Civilisation, Liberty, Commerce, Industry, Wealth, Prosperity, Knowledge and Reason. The main drama begins with the landing of Columbus amidst 'Songs of Exultation'. At this point, Indians appear 'but run off in fright at the sight of the Spanish Caravels. They fall on their faces at the sound of the canon.' In the next scene, the Indians slowly venture from their hiding places and Columbus's men bring them 'toys, trinkets and bells, the sound of which so pleases them that they act like delighted children'. When it comes to confrontation as the Pioneers push their way westward, the Indians attempt ambush but quickly lose the 'grotesque battle' that follows.[63] In the finale, set against a backdrop showing the Administration Building of the Columbian Exposition, all the nations of the Earth congregate to celebrate the triumph of Columbia and do homage to American Genius.

Kiralfy's approach to the spectacle makes an interesting contrast with the action show. Narrative was a means of controlling the roles played by those representing what were supposed to be backward, uncivilised races. It was when Bill Cody dropped narrative drama in favour of strings of often unrelated action scenes that his Indian performers came into their own. In performances by Cody's first company in the early 1880s, a 'Genuine Band of Indians' were billed almost as an afterthought, to perform Wild and Weird Songs and Realistic War Dances in the third act of a mystery drama culminating in a 'terrible plot' to create a death-trap for the great scout. Cody readily admitted that his own plots were terrible, and that he often performed these early shows with the acts in miscellaneous order, much to the perplexity of critics who were determined to try and figure out the story-line. His favourite activities as a performer were shooting and riding; the *Wild West Show* proper developed when he moved his company outdoors and began to organise the whole performance around these activities, with Indians as featured participants. This resulted in the *Rocky Mountain and Prairie Exhibition* which was premiered in 1883 with Indians in six of its twelve episodes. Posting bills promised 'Mexicans, Cow-boys, Sioux and Pawnees struggling for prize and honour in familiar sports'.[64] At a time when struggle and competition were acquiring particular meaning from Darwin's theory of natural selection, Cody made a speciality of devising new forms of action competition for his performers.

Cody's *Congress of Rough Riders of the World* may have been titled and conceived as a multinational show partly to trade on the fashionable concept of the Ethnological Congress (indeed, it was sometimes billed as an Ethnological Congress), but it cut right across the theme of socio-cultural evolution. Instead of portraying a hierarchy of cultures supposed to represent different stages in the development of human civilisation, the *Congress of Rough Riders* came closer to presenting a free-for-all, in which troupes from various parts of the globe sought to outdo each other in feats of horsemanship displaying spectacular techniques developed in specific cultural contexts. It was an all-star cast of 'the world's greatest horsemen', including Mexican Vaqueros, Cossacks, Arabs, European Cavalry, South American Gauchos, Hungarian Chicos, Cowboys and Indians.

The element of free and immediate competition in the *Wild West Shows* may also have undermined the declared message of some of the productions. In 1887 Cody and his company apparently identified themselves with the prevailing ideology of progressive evolution when they presented *The Drama of Civilization* in five acts. In accordance with ethnological convention, Indians were featured living according to their traditional ways in the first two acts: The Primeval Forest and The Prairie. However, Buffalo Bill was not about to phase out his most exciting performers quietly, so the third, fourth and fifth acts, instead of demonstrating the demise of the savages and the ultimate and inevitable triumph of the forces of civilisation, became increasingly turbulent and conflictual. In the third act, the Indians were featured in The Attack on a Settler's Cabin; in the fourth they attacked the Deadwood Stage Coach; and in the fifth they defeated General Custer, with Cody in the final tableau, famously arriving too late.[65] Cody was accused of contradicting his own title and presenting 'The Drama of Savagery'. Much of the spectacle in the performances was generated by the intensity of the rivalry between Indian and white performers. History and ideology decreed that the whites must ultimately emerge as the winners, but the *Wild West Show* did not owe its success to the symbolic formality of foregone conclusions. Rather it traded on the urgent tensions of a struggle whose outcome could be in doubt.

In his recent study of American Indians in Wild West Shows, L. G. Moses sets out the need for a revision of prevailing assumptions that the show Indians were 'artless victims'. The result of such a view, he claims, is that they 'have remained merely caricatures, as wooden and artificial as supposedly were the images they created'.[66] The commercial factor cuts both ways, in that entrepreneurs 'quickly learned that Indians could work "Old World" crowds with as much facility as they could work "New World" mines'.[67] Cody himself was keen to point out that his Indians had a belief in their own superiority which mirrored that of the Europeans: 'They have a keen sense of the humorous and deep down in their hearts think white folks are the greatest lot of monkeys on the top of the earth.'[68] The leading Indian performers in his shows were given their tribal designation and status, rather than being billed as generalised Indian savages;

they also came to be featured as rivals and counterparts of the white American stars. Even the style of advertising promoted this impression, with symmetrical designs and parallel illustrations of cowboy and Indian groups. Cody as the star of the show liked to be billed with an Indian counterpart whose personal charisma could balance his own and whose image was built up accordingly. Sitting Bull was the first to create this role. He joined the *Wild West Show* in 1885 and remained with it for only one season, but Red Shirt, who made his name in the 1887 season when the show played in London, became equally celebrated as a dignitary and star in his own right.

Cody of course retained top billing and held to the convention of always heading the winning team at the end of the show, but, by presenting the Indians and their leaders as immediate rivals and near equals, he made nonsense of the ethnological hierarchy that placed 'savages' and Caucasians at vast distances from each other in capability. When Cody made pronouncements about how participation in his show helped the Indians to recognise that their world had been well and truly replaced by the modernising culture of an Anglo-American nation, he was being tactical. He had to win the confidence of the Bureau of Indian Affairs in order to obtain permission to employ large numbers of Indian performers from the reservations. On the principle that 'savage and civilized life cannot coexist on the same ground', the Bureau was responsible for implementing the necessary measures to domesticate the savages and teach them how to be settled and reliable citizens of a civilisation that was prepared to adopt them if they chose to co-operate with it and change their ways.[69] Cody's *Wild West Show*, together with the many imitation shows it spawned, was in many respects a threat to this agenda. Instead of fostering a settled lifestyle, its itinerant programme allowed Indians to renew their taste for nomadic ways; instead of training them in industrious and productive occupations, it promoted wild riding, war-dancing and fighting skills, together with an ostentatious display of traditional costume and decorations.

In 1889 a new Commissioner for Indian Affairs, Thomas Jefferson Morgan, took the view that the policy of reform was not working firmly enough, and decided to crack down on the employment of Indians in shows on the grounds that show business fostered 'a distaste for steady occupation'. He issued a circular asserting the need to impress upon Indians the importance of 'cultivating farms, building houses, and acquiring thrifty, industrious habits and surrounding themselves with the comforts of a worthy type of civilization'.[70] But a worthy type of civilisation was something that did not suit all of the people all of the time; a preference for a wild and action-packed way of life over steady occupation and thrifty, industrious habits was something to which many Anglo-Americans were not immune. Buffalo Bill's show gave its performers permission to go wild, and its audiences permission to enjoy wildness vicariously from the safety of the covered grandstand. Cody's ideological pronouncements about the inevitability of progress suited his image as the great American hero who played a leading role in 'the winning of the West', but as a showman-adventurer, his commitment to the values of 'civilisation' as it was being defined by gentlemen scientists and politicians was no doubt rather ambivalent.

The directors of the Chicago Exposition turned down Cody's application for performance space within the precincts on the grounds that the *Wild West Show* was lacking in serious educational value. So Cody stationed himself strategically on the outskirts near the entrance with a covered grandstand that accommodated 18,000 spectators. Here he did a roaring trade in all weathers. His exclusion could be seen as a resurgence of the long-standing tensions between science and show business that were typically played out over the contested ground of exhibition space. But more particularly, his performances were a source of anxiety for the science of ethnology. The study of ethnology depended fundamentally on a range of essentialist presuppositions: that physiognomy and body type were a key to character and mental capacity; that race was a defining factor in human capability; that people of lower races were what they seemed and that their behaviour was a transparent set of facts about them, just as was their physiognomy.

Performance in itself was a threat to these suppositions, and, from the point of view of those studied, it was a means of giving the slip to the conceptual grid through which they were being regarded. Cody's whole enterprise was a sophisticated exercise in the manufacture of personae, his own and those of all his co-stars. He used dramatic representation not to invent scenes and characters, but to restage those among which he found himself in life. The *Wild West Show* is generally acknowledged to be the prototype of a certain style of spectacular entertainment, but it was also the prototype for a form of autobiographical performance in which reality and representation were constantly folded back on each other. (It is said that when Cody fought his celebrated duel with the Cheyenne chief Yellow Hand, he prepared for the occasion by dressing in his full Buffalo Bill stage outfit. A re-enactment of the duel subsequently became a set piece in the show.) Autobiographical performance is self-presentation at one remove, without the candour and unconsciousness that was an assumed quality of those who were objects of ethnological study. From the point of view of those on show, autobiographical performance was a way of creating distance between themselves and their observers and, more significantly, of using this distance to manipulate perspectives.

It would be naïve to claim that showmen like Cody and Barnum were fundamentally at odds with the ideology of their times when it came to notions of white superiority. Popular, commercial show business has rarely been fertile ground for political correctness, and it certainly was not so in the nineteenth century. Yet, perhaps for the same reasons, it was also not conducive to the furthering of ideological agendas. It was a feral world in which the values of civilisation had little control, and were constantly being reflected back in distorted ways. It was a world that traded in variety and diversity but also in mobility, and could therefore have little investment in any programmatic attempt to stabilise human difference in a taxonomic grid.

4

VARIETIES

Darwin's account of the origin of species restored drama to the natural order by shifting the focus from lifeless specimens to the incessantly shifting balance of life in motion. Struggle, conflict and competition were the dynamics of his theory of natural selection, which portrayed the differences between species as relative and unstable, so that organic forms were always in a process of becoming: 'Each formation, on this view, does not mark a new and complete act of creation, but only an occasional scene, taken almost at hazard, in a slowly changing drama.'[1] The suggestion that there was something theatrical in the diversification of natural forms echoes Chambers's habit of referring to 'theatres of life', but it may have been more than a casual rhetorical gesture.

Since the species could not be considered 'a complete act', fully and finally set in a great work of creation, the drama itself tended to lose its monolithic character, ceasing to present itself as a classically authored piece and breaking down into 'occasional scenes'. It was these occasional scenes that Darwin most wanted to watch. *The Origin of Species* cast the meaning of the term 'species' into doubt, transferring attention from species to variety, and from there to the very point of difference that might lead to divergence. Darwin's lifelong obsession with variety led him to cultivate fifty-four breeds of gooseberry, collect 1500 varieties of beetle and every breed of pigeon he could obtain.[2] As his autobiographical stories testify, his curiosity was drawn less to forms in themselves than to their slippage and diversification. During his student years at Cambridge, he recorded, the discovery of new beetle specimens was a 'passion' which gave him more pleasure than any other pursuit. The determination to miss no variety led to some bizarre moments:

one day, on tearing off some old bark, I saw two rare beetles and seized one in each hand; then I saw a third and new kind, which I could not bear to lose, so I popped the one which I held in my right hand into my mouth. Alas! it ejected some intensely acrid fluid, which burnt my tongue so that I was forced to spit the beetle out.[3]

This story (whether or not it is true) betrays a touch of the showman that appears now and again in the autobiography. 'As a little boy,' he admits, 'I was much given to inventing deliberate falsehoods, and this was always done for the sake of causing excitement.'[4]

Even Darwin, it seems, was not above an occasional experiment in humbug. His precocious interest in the variability of plants at the age of 8 led him to indulge a 'monstrous fable': 'I told another little boy . . . that I could produce variously coloured polyanthuses and primroses by watering them with certain coloured fluids.'[5] It is interesting to compare this with Barnum's story of the painted pigeons, sold to him by a chemist who had devised a formula that would give them 'any hue desired, and yet retain a natural gloss on the feathers, which gave every shade the appearance of reality'.[6] Both men were acutely aware of the potential for causing excitement by the production of dramatically various natural forms.

There is a curious difference in the focus of the deception in the two stories. Darwin's humbug lay in the claims made for his technique of producing variety; he sought to amaze with the magic of a simple and instantaneous means of control over natural diversity. It was Barnum's way to conceal techniques of manipulation in order to make exaggerated claims for the forms of variety to be found in nature. Yet it was Darwin who made his life's work testifying to the marvels of variety in its natural forms, and Barnum who made his career encouraging and intensifying variety through the marvels of human artifice. An enduring fascination with variety was something the two men had in common and central to the kinds of work they chose for themselves.

Darwin's theory made *varieties* a keyword in the study of natural history. His childish idea of finding an instant formula for producing plant colours matured into an adult fascination with the principle of selection. In the hands of the experienced breeder, selection could be 'the magician's wand, by means of which he may summon into life whatever form and mould he pleases'.[7] Darwin's theoretical concern was with the causes of variety, but, in his own breeding experiments, 'wonderful difference' was evidently an endless fascination in itself. The pleasures of creating variety in animal and plant species through controlled breeding programmes were augmented by the exercise of comparing the 'immeasurably superior' effects of natural selection.[8] Beyond the control sphere of the breeder's precinct, the effects of competition between and within species created constant pressures to specialise and diversify. These processes of differentiation in the natural world were driven by a simple equation: 'the more diversified the descendants from any one species become . . . by so much will they be better enabled to seize on many and widely diversified places in the polity of nature.'[9]

Besides being referred to as a polity, nature in Darwin's writing is frequently characterised as an economy. The economic behaviours of animals and plants in what he referred to as a 'fully stocked' environment mimicked the economic behaviours of human beings in overcrowded cities but he was not the first to hint at this analogy. Ten years before *The Origin of Species* was published, *Punch* offered its own image of the fully stocked environment in the form of 'The Wonders of the London Water Drop', examined under Mr Punch's microscope:

> Creatures – who shall name them? Things in human shape – in all appearance London citizens – aldermen, deputies, common council men . . . disporting in the liquid dirt as in their native element. Behold them, fiercely hustling each other in competition for atomic garbage. What pushing, poking, fighting, kicking, scrambling! There goes an unfortunate wretch fast as if for dear life, with a hook-nosed homunculus – evidently a genuine water-bailiff – darting after him. Here a cheap slop seller has caught a smaller individual of the same species by the head, and is trying to bolt him.[10]

A growing consciousness of diversification and variety in mid-nineteenth-century Europe and America reflected the changing conditions created by the industrial revolution. In 1871, Darwin reflected this consciousness in his statement that 'as organisms have become slowly adapted by means of natural selection for diversified lines of life, their parts will have become, from the advantage gained by the division of physiological labour, more and more differentiated and specialised for various functions'.[11]

Show-business entrepreneurs may claim precedence over natural scientists in the conscious recognition of variation as the generative core of successful activity. In May 1840, Barnum leased the Vauxhall Gardens in New York for 'variety shows' that included acrobatics, Negro minstrelsy and comic impersonations. Such programmes of mixed entertainment were further developed at the American Museum and pointed the way to a new genre of popular entertainment. The variety entertainment programme was an obvious formula for success in an urban environment characterised by the rapid mobility of wealth and work, and the cohabitation of mixed cultures and classes resulting from strong patterns of immigration.[12] The best strategy for appealing to an audience with disparate and to an extent incompatible tastes was providing something for everybody in it: middle-class couples, children, rowdy youths, working men and women. Variety in show business was on one level analogous to what was going on in every other business: it was part of the process of commercial adaptation to social diversity. On another level the development of variety entertainments was directly bound up with popular curiosity about natural variety. Varieties of the human, a proven draw-card in freak shows and ethnological show business, could be explored in many more ways.

Delineations

George Odell claims that variety theatre 'got itself born' in the season of 1842–3, with the Peale and Barnum programmes leading the way by defining a generic repertoire of comedy sketches, song, dance, acrobatics and magic acts.[13] A relatively small group of 'headline' artists were the mainstay of this repertoire, and these were variety artists in a more particular sense. They were 'drollerists' or 'delineators', who specialised in the comic impersonation of social types from different classes, nationalities and races.

William Valentine was a skilled social taxonomist and a favourite with Barnum, who describes his habit of standing by the entrance to the Museum to study the characters of the visitors, then panicking if he thought they were 'country bumpkins' who would fail to respond to the diversity of his repertoire. Valentine's forte was the comic lecture with instant personality changes:

> Under [his] table, on little shelves and hooks, were placed caps, hats, coats, wigs, moustaches, curls, cravats, and shirt collars, and all sorts of gear for changing the appearance of the upper portion of the person. ... Dr Valentine would seat himself behind the table, and addressing his audience,

would state his intention to represent different peculiar characters, male and female, including the Yankee tin peddler; 'Tabitha Twist,' a maiden lady; 'Sam Slick Jr.,' the precocious author; 'Solomon Jenkins,' a crusty old bachelor.[14]

Winchell, who alternated with Valentine between the Peale and Barnum museums, specialised in cultural caricatures that reflected the changing demographics of New York at the mid-century. Besides an assortment of 'Yankee delineations', he created Irish, Scottish, Dutch, French, German and Negro characters. W. H. Williams, another comic delineator, advertised his performances as 'observations drawn from real life on Men, Manners and Things as they are'.[15] Sometimes the range of a delineator's repertoire itself stretched credibility, as in the case of George Handel Hill, of whom Odell writes, 'I wonder if there ever were as many kinds of Yankees as were now exhibited in Hill's museum'.[16]

From one point of view, the New York drollerists may be seen as part of the advance guard for a craze in popular entertainment that was to prevail from the early 1840s for over a century under the label 'variety theatre'; from another, they were linked with a tradition of comic acting that went back to the Smithfield and Bartholomew fairgrounds, where the term *droll* referred to many types of grotesque comic performance including puppet shows, farces, displays of buffoonery and caricature acts such as that of Bold Grimace Spaniard.

The Grimacing Spaniard, whose facial contortions went beyond evoking varieties of the human to produce likenesses of an apple, an owl and a cow, was an exemplar of the kind of fairground extremism that sought variety through stretching the bounds of the natural order. By the later eighteenth century, this vulgar mode of comic performance was widely disparaged by many commentators, and theatre actors were condemned for being tainted by its influence, but they continued to draw on physiognomic typology as a basis for character definition, especially in comedy. Lavater's *Essays on Physiognomy* (1789–98) were studied by actors looking for a scientific account of how character was evident in facial expression and other physical qualities. It was Lavater's view that 'material man must become the subject of observation'. Lavater's contemporary Charles Macklin encouraged actors in training to adopt an approach that involved identifying the 'genus and species' of a character, then studying to imitate the looks, tones and gestures by which the type would be recognised. Macklin related this advice to long inventories of social groups, listing professions, trades and offices belonging to different social strata as the means by which a role might be categorised ready for physiognomic analysis.[17]

In an important study of the comic actor in the eighteenth century, Shearer West argues that the quest for 'infinite variety' in acting was in tension with the taxonomic study encouraged by followers of Lavater, since a categoric approach tended towards the creation of stock character types.[18] However, from a Darwinian point of view there was no conflict between taxonomy and infinite variety, since the theory of evolution by natural selection saw all species as breaking down into varieties which were endlessly branching and proliferating. Darwin influenced a shift in perspective so that the natural order came to be seen in terms of processes rather than states; thus the emphasis moved from species to speciation, variety to variation. The best nineteenth-century comic impersonators reflected this shift, specialising in the rendition of numerous types in rapid succession, with minimal changes in costume and make-up so that the focus was on the transitions themselves, and the protean virtuosity they demonstrated.

The vogue for protean acting lasted for over fifty years and was especially strong in New York across the mid-century, with Valentine and Winchell as its leading exponents, though it was an English actor of the previous generation who established the genre, and against whom all proteans were measured. This was Charles Mathews (the elder), whose genius was commemorated in an epithet from Dryden:

A man so various, that he seemed to be
Not one, but all mankind's epitome.[19]

Mathews began his career as an actor in a stock company touring Northern England, Scotland and Ireland, but what he learned off-stage during these tours became as significant as his experience on it. He began to study regional types – their modes of speech, accents, manners, social attitudes and physiognomy – in order to create a collection of comic impersonations. In 1808 he devised an entertainment around these types, a one-man variety show in which he transformed himself into over two dozen characters during the course of a three-hour performance. Bartholomew Fair was a prominent reference point, the subject of a sequence beginning with a descriptive song and developing as a series of impersonations including the Irish giant, Mr Punch and the wild beast man. In parodying these

Figure 4.1
Charles Mathews in *A Trip to America*, 1824

Source: Courtesy of the Theatre Museum, London, and the Victoria and Albert Museum

figures Mathews also distanced himself from them, defending his own style as 'widely different' from theirs: 'I know not why the exhibition of an imitator of manners should be classed with the mere grimaces of a buffoon.'[20]

His impersonations of foreigners, servants, women, children and animals reversed the hierarchical dynamics of aping, so that imitation became a form of critical analysis demonstrating the superiority of the imitator over the imitated. One commentator on Mathews's work explicitly differentiated his approach to imitation from the 'very mean attainment' of savages who were given to copying the manners of strangers. There were two schools of mimicry, it was suggested, and Mathews was 'a professor of the superior school', which promoted study of the causal factors underlying behavioural characteristics and of 'the mental associations that either produce singularity of character or spring out of it'.[21] *Blackwoods Magazine* praised his 'plastic bodily powers working under the direction of a mind possessed of a fine talent for general observation, and an exquisite tact for discrimination between that which is common and essential to a class, and that which is peculiar to a particular individual of that class'.[22]

Mathews's interest in the general principles of human typology was given free reign in the new solo performance style that he continued to develop for over two decades under the generic title *Mathews At Home.* The staple ingredients were comic songs, dialogues and a short farce billed as the 'Monopolylogue' in which he played all the characters. With a new theme and new set of characters each year, the *At Home* became an established feature of the London theatre scene, where it was also advertised as 'Mr Mathews' Annual Course of lectures on Character, Manners, and Peculiarities'. Mathews at once demonstrated and parodied fashionable methods of analysis by delivering his lectures in character. The 1819 *At Home*, thematised as 'A Trip to Paris', featured a talk on physiognomy by a French widow, an account of the new science of craniology by Doctor von Dunderdonk von Hoaxburg, and a lecture on England and the English language by a French gentleman traveller. A dash of reverse ethnology was an essential ingredient in the Mathews mix.

Matthews was experimenting with a performative approach to social analysis that paralleled the work of biological taxonomists in following the principles of comprehensiveness, systematicity and conscious method. His theme for the 1822 *At Home* was his own life story, which he interpreted strictly from the time of his birth, recalling the ages 'from nothing to an hour and a quarter', then from infancy to the age of 10, and on through school and apprenticeship to his early career as an actor.[23] It is as though he sought to extend his techniques of 'delineation' into every compartment of human society – and occasionally beyond into the animal world. (A yelping puppy and 'poultry in the hold' of a cross-channel passenger vessel were part of his repertoire in the early 1820s.) For Mathews, the taxonomic approach never meant gravitation towards a set of stock types, but rather led to multiplying categories of persona. While he undoubtedly drew on stereotypes in creating his Irishmen, Frenchmen, English spinsters and cockney adventurers, the effect of his treatment was to lay any stock character type wide open by multiplying it into a plethora of sub-types, further differentiated through age, occupation, class and temperament. He may thus be seen as an important transitional figure in character acting, preparing the way for the delineators of the mid- and later nineteenth century whose acts were among the key elements of variety theatre.

While naturalists were beginning to focus their attention on geographical distribution, Mathews was discovering human variety through tourism. The travelling vehicle was a central concept for the *At Home*, since it enabled him to gather together types from miscellaneous social and national groups. There were sketches presenting the collected passengers in the Yorkshire Mail coach, the Dover Mail, a Parisian diligence, the 'Polly Packet' (a passenger boat), an American stage-coach and a steamboat. This afforded the pretext for capturing a random collection of people drawn from geographically dispersed locations into a shared situation. Scenes were also set in hotels, boarding-houses and among groups on walking tours. When audiences joined Mathews *At Home*, they were taken through a sequence of heterotopias in which the experience of being foreign was the paramount source of amusement.[24] Mathews was making effective topical comedy out of the social heterogeneity arising from population shifts in the early nineteenth century. An invitation to tour America in 1822 presented an opportunity to add a completely fresh dimension to the repertoire. The cosmopolitan environment of New York at this time was grist to the Mathews mill: by the mid-1820s, one-fifth of the city's population was foreign-born, and the rapid proliferation of trades and professions in the metropolis produced a veritable explosion of diversity.[25]

As one of the first systematic observers of social diversity *per se*, Mathews was also widely influential in demonstrating how the actor was uniquely placed to explore what Herbert Spencer was later to characterise as 'advancing differentiation'. Spencer's theory of social evolution was based on the premise that 'advance from lower to higher is characterised by increasing multiformity', though what he had in mind here was the multiplication of social roles in a diversifying economy, not ethnological diversity, which was something that few nineteenth-century Englishmen would have associated with advancement.[26] Mathews, with his ready assumptions that his own class and nation represented the superior forms that others might aspire to, was no exception, though his expressed opinions on this were undercut by his very fascination with ethnological difference, and his determination to learn how to embody it with the highest degree of accuracy. *A Trip to New York*, the show he devised as a vehicle for his American characters, included especially memorable Negro delineations which, to judge from the script, pandered to some typical attitudes towards African-Americans. He played a blundering waiter who mishandles a soup tureen, a 'fiddling negro' met on the road, and a slave not worth his sixty-dollar price since he 'possesses many bad qualities, and is not only fat but addicted to laziness'.[27] Such descriptions give no indication of the kind of exact study that Mathews insisted was the basis of his art but, however prejudiced his impressions, there is evidence that he went out of his way to observe African-Americans and their culture.

His most successful sketch was inspired by a visit to the African Theatre in the Bowery, where, under the management of William Henry Brown (a West Indian), black actors offered a mix of Shakespeare, pantomime and comic songs and dances for audiences from the African-American community who were debarred or at least segregated in most of the existing New York theatres. At the African Theatre, these audiences were safely partitioned from white spectators who might not know 'how to conduct themselves at entertainments for ladies and gentlemen of colour'.[28] By Mathews's account of it, audiences and performers combined to offer a spectacle of grotesque exuberance:

> [Mr Mathews] . . . beholds a black tragedian in the character of Hamlet, and just enters as he is proceeding with the speech, 'To be or not to be? That is the question: whether it is nobler in de mind to suffer, or tak'up arms against a sea of trouble, and by oppossum end 'em.' No sooner was the word oppossum out of his mouth, than the audience burst forth in one general cry 'Oppossum! oppossum! oppossum!'[29]

This is construed as a call for the actor to sing 'Possum up a Gum Tree' and he promptly obliges, reverting immediately afterwards to some randomly selected Shakespeare: 'Now is de winter of our discontent, made de glorious summer by de sun of New York.'[30]

Other accounts by white contemporaries, reproduced in an invaluable documentary study of the African Theatre by George Thompson, give a similar picture of the performers as buffoons with delusory enthusiasms about their own capacities, engaged in preposterous attempts to mimic what white actors do. The standard narrative is one of debacle: the performance (and in one account the theatre itself) literally collapses in a heap of squirming bodies, locked into a scrum by their very attempts to fight their way out of it.[31] Such narratives are, of course, unreliable. The African Theatre's leading actor at the time of Mathews's visit was James Hewlett, whose own side of the story comes through quite substantially in Thompson's record. In an open letter to Mathews printed in the *National Advocate* (where an account of Mathews's *Trip to America* had appeared), Hewlett protested a betrayal of trust:

> You have, I perceive by the programme of your performance, ridiculed our African Theatre in Mercer Street, and burlesqued me with the rest of the negroe actors, as you are pleased to call us – mimicked our styles – imitated our dialects – laughed at our anomalies and lampooned, O shame, even our complexions. Was this well for a brother actor? – At your earnest and pressing solicitation, I performed some of my best parts; was perfect to a letter; and although it was a hazardous experiment, I even attempted your celebrated Mail Coach, which met with your unqualified approbation.[32]

The letter professes an endorsement of Mathews's inventive genius, but draws a clear distinction between the work of satirical delineation and the 'reflections on our colour' that lead to gross caricature. Hewlett had been ridiculed as a mere ape of classical actors whom he could not hope to emulate, so his payback was to demonstrate that he could better Mathews at his own game. He proceeded to compile his own *At Home*, closely based on a combination of Mathews's best-known sketches and featuring many of his characters. As a former ship steward, Hewlett was widely travelled and had visited theatres in France and Britain. He knew the styles of leading actors of the day well enough to quote them in his own satirical performances, just as Mathews did.

In a curious twist to the story, Ira Aldridge also believed he had been the actor lampooned as the African Roscius, and many subsequent accounts have assumed this to be so. From the evidence collected by Thompson the case for Hewlett is stronger, but what matters is the reactions of the actors themselves, and Aldridge's was remarkably similar to Hewlett's: to take over the reigns of the parody and drive it in a direction of his own. He took to incorporating 'Possum up a Gum Tree' as an interlude in his performances.[33]

Imitation was a *mise-en-abîme*, with no limit to the reflections and counter-reflections that could be practised. It might begin as a dedicated exercise in social observation and typological analysis, but it always retained the potential to take off into a sphere of its own, as an endless cycle of increasingly free-wheeling burlesque. The Mathews–Hewlett–Aldridge episode is one of the first indications that this was more likely to happen where impersonators were conscious of crossing the boundaries of race. The African-American was a new kind of challenge for Mathews. However satirical his impersonations of Yankee, French, Irish and Dutch men and women, their accuracy turned them into a form of recognition, a way of paying attention; but when it came to impersonating the 'Negro', the anchor in social observation seems to have come loose.

No doubt Mathews captured patterns of diction, intonation and gesture with the accuracy for which he was so celebrated, but the physical and psychological demands of working across racial difference may have skewed his technique towards the kinds of physical extravagance he professed to despise. Since the extravagances could be defended as an accurate reflection of the excesses of the other, he could take a freer licence and his audiences were clearly ready to endorse it. What was the order of difference between white and black races? How wide did the difference need to be in attempting the rendition of speech, posture and voice? Mathews's work became an enduring influence in minstrelsy, where grotesque caricature was passed off as accurate imitation, as if the distance between these two modes was no longer perceptible when it came to cross-racial delineation.

Mathews more than anyone could claim to have realised the eighteenth-century aspiration towards 'infinite variety' in comic acting. He widened the parameters of social observation so as to broaden the scope of stage characterisation in almost all genres, though his influence was strongest in farce, minstrel burlesque and other popular forms. Although his own career was over by the mid-1830s, his influence on popular performance continued to grow through the 1840s, when delineation became something of a craze. His finely observed Yankee characters prompted successful New York actors like James Hackett and George 'Yankee' Hill to follow his example so that, paradoxically, his visit was to have a catalytic effect on the development of the vernacular theatre that New York audiences were demanding. As specialist Yankee delineators, Hackett and Hill created a need for scripts that could provide effective vehicles for the roles they were developing, and the 1830s and 1840s saw a burgeoning of New York plays. The emphasis on social observation is evident from such titles as *The Spy in New York* (1843), *A Glance at New York* (1849), *New York as It Is* (1844) and *Life in New York* (1843).

Valentine copied Mathews more directly in the acts he created for the American Museum. He used the *At Home* format of the lecture desk as his central device, offering a comic lecture on phrenology, and various travel sketches in which he played all the passengers in a boat or coach. Winchell also based his act on travel narratives, concentrating on delineations of national types. His 'foreigners' represented the main immigrant groups that made up New York society and were continuing to flood into the Lower East Side: Irish, Scottish, Dutch, French, Chinese and German.

The discourses of natural history and evolution gave a new kind of significance to protean performance in the nineteenth century. Jonas Barish comments on the relationship between mimicry, the protean impulse and strategies of adaptation in Renaissance theatre, giving the Shakespeare characters of Hamlet and Edgar as examples:

> they reconquer their places in the world by giving their metamorphic instincts full scope, by experimenting with a variety of roles, finding the ones that fit, the ones that work best in the situations they face, and finding deep satisfaction in this exercise of their vitality.[34]

The implications here, though, were mainly social. As biologists committed themselves to the view that anatomy was destiny, impersonators who crossed human categories were calling into question the extent to which physical characteristics were really the determining factors in human life. What did human difference consist of? Impersonation was instant adaptation and, as such, made a mockery of the primordially slow process of variation in nature. Enactment was a way to test where nature set the boundaries between human types, and where these could be cheated through techniques of mimicry. A basic plot pretext for farces was that someone able to pass in the identity of another could use this skill to turn a situation to their advantage. *The Actor of All Work*, a farce written for Mathews in 1817, displayed 'the infinite variety of his transformations' as he worked his way through seven contrasting roles.[35] It was quickly matched by a female version, *The Actress of All Work*. These plays sparked a whole new genre known as protean farce, characterised by a plot in which multiple-identity switches showcased the capacity of the leading performers to cross the categories of gender, race, nationality, age and class.

The craze for protean farce caught on more than anywhere else in New York, where it reached its height in the 1830s and 1840s. The actor of all work was the thing to be, but he was quickly surpassed in popularity by his female counterpart. Going by Odell's records, *The Actress of All Work* became the more regularly performed of the two plays, and was especially favoured as a vehicle for showing off the precocious virtuosity of child actresses. Three female child stars – Jean Davenport, Mary Anne Gannon and Elizabeth Randolph – developed an escalating rivalry as proteans. Jean Davenport played six characters in *The Manager's Daughter* and Mary Gannon seven in *The Actress of All Work*; Elizabeth Randolph began to copy Gannon's repertoire, but was finally outdone in the 1840–1 season when Gannon took on nine roles in *Variety in One* and nine again in *A Wife for a Day*. She was 12 years old at the time. Mary Gannon began her stage career at the age of 6, playing female juvenile roles, but she soon diversified to play boys and then moved on to a range of adult roles, both male and female. When she trumped her rivals by playing the nine characters of *A Wife for a Day* at the Vauxhall Gardens, she shared top billing with Valentine, whose own galaxy of New York types may have appeared restricted by comparison.

The fashion for protean acting gave girls and women the opportunity to extend the range of roles they could play. The repository of female types grew exponentially under the influence of Mathews and other delineators whose female impersonations went well outside the scope of the stock female characters available to actresses. In addition to this, the protean convention licensed all performers to go outside the terms in which casting decisions would normally be made. Actresses could deliberately play as far wide of their own age and physical type as their skills would allow, and the opportunities for playing male roles were unrestricted. Favourite choices for young female proteans included Shylock, Richard III and Sir Peter

Teazle (the ageing baronet of *A School of Scandal*). The heightened distance between performer and role in protean acting also released women into burlesque, which became one of the most popular forms associated with the variety movement. Actresses began to freely display qualities of volatility, exhibitionism and knowing humour that made women dangerous as social adventurers capable of traversing the divisions of the class system.

Protean soloists continued to be popular in British and American theatre over the next two generations, and some female performers were quite successful in the genre. Emma Stanley, an English actress, made appearances in London and also at Niblo's Garden in New York in 1856, performing *The Seven Ages of Woman*. Besides displaying her capacity to play any age through from the infant to the crone, Stanley took on 'an extraordinary variety of dialects' and created character through instantaneous changes of voice and manner with minimal alterations to her costume. The finale, entitled the *polymelos*, was a thinly disguised version of the monopolylogue with the added embellishment of being performed in multiple languages – including Italian, Turkish, Swiss, French and Spanish – rather than only the foreign dialects assumed by other delineators.[36] Grace Egerton achieved major billing at the Egyptian Hall in London in two shows directly in the Mathews tradition. In *The Christmas Party* and *Latest Intelligence from at Home and Abroad*, she performed equal numbers of male and female roles including military men of various ranks, an African-American servant who sang 'two nigger melodies' and a Spanish dancer.[37] Also at the Egyptian Hall, Howard Liston, Alfred Burnett, Fleming Norton and Frank Lincoln were still making claims to the title of 'Successor of the elder Charles Mathews' through the 1870s and 1880s.[38] Where Mathews relied heavily on French delineations in building the genre, these performers shared a more transatlantic orientation, featuring Negro minstrels, Southern plantation-owners and an assortment of Yankees.

Protean impersonation was, among other things, a way of exploring difference by inhabiting it, by testing the ways in which human typologies formed themselves through differentiating characteristics of speech, movement, expression and gesture. By the 1850s, some delineators were consciously promoting their work as a form of ethnological research and some ethnological researchers were experimenting with impersonation as a means of communicating knowledge about human variety to general audiences. The skilled impersonator could sharpen the understanding of taxonomic difference to be gained from physiognomists by bringing out the distinctive qualities of the live subject whose dynamic account of him or herself might be infinitely more revealing than the stilted narratives of a would-be scientific observer.

London did not experience the massive influx of cultures and races that transformed the social fabric of New York across the mid-nineteenth century, and it was not a multicultural city in the same way, but Henry Mayhew came to see it as 'a distinct world', with its own forms of geographical and ethnological variety:

> Ethnologists have reduced the several varieties of mankind into five distinct types; but surely the judges who preside at the courts in Westminster are as morally distinct from the Jew 'fences' of Petticoat lane as the Caucasian from the Malayan race. Is not the 'pet parson', too, of some West End Puseyite Chapel as ethically and physically different from the London prize-fighter, and he again from the City Alderman, as is the Mongol from the Negro, or the Negro from the Red Indian. In the world of London, indeed, we find almost every species of the human family.[39]

Besides being a dedicated social analyst, Mayhew was one of the founding editors of *Punch* and had strong interests in dramatisation. His exhaustive firsthand researches into the lives of the London poor were published as an extended series of letters in the *Morning Chronicle*, beginning in October 1849 and then as a book, *London Labour and the London Poor* (1851). This was adapted for the stage in 1854 as *How We Live in London* but Mayhew's own solo performance, consisting of selected impersonations contextualised by an ethnological lecture, suited the material better. While there was an obvious lure for dramatists in the book's portraits of individual characters, captured through extended interviews, the Mathews approach, based as it was in a lecture format, enabled the complex taxonomic aspects of the research to be brought to the fore. Mayhew's entertainment was performed at St Martin's Hall in June 1857 and a provincial tour was planned, but an outraged reaction from his puritanical father seems to have scotched these plans.[40]

The London poor proved to be avid taxonomists in their own terrain, making clear distinctions between the many subgroups of hucksters, costermongers, street performers, woodworkers, needle-women, seamen, weavers and vagrants (to name but a few of his major categories). The impression gained from reading Mayhew's accounts is that the process of variation and category-splitting was at its most vigorous at the bottom of the social hierarchy. Such an impression runs counter to the interpretations of progressive evolutionists like Spencer, who saw variation and specialisation as a reflection of the increasing complexity of higher order groups. As social Darwinism took hold in the next two decades, though, its concerns were overwhelmingly with the problems associated with groups and here the investigative detail afforded by Mayhew provided a methodological example. Although Mayhew's own experiments with the stage presentation of his material were short-lived, his approach to social research is echoed in the work of leading dramatists of the naturalist movement – most notably Edward Harrigan (in New York) and Emile Zola (in Paris) – whose principal interests were in the experiences and conditions of the urban poor.

The delineation tradition fed into naturalistic drama as well as vaudeville and variety theatre. The work of Mathews himself might be situated in retrospect somewhere between these modes, but most of his followers veered towards the lighter, burlesque end of the spectrum. Few undertook any form of social research, but Edward Harrigan was a notable exception. Born and raised in the Lower East Side of New York, Harrigan was the son of a ship's caulker with Irish ancestry and his youth was spent exploring the urban jungle with its dense mix of inhabitants.[41] As he later recalled:

> I swam the docks and knew every inch of the city and watched it grow as I grew . . . . From boyhood I had exceptional advantages to become thoroughly familiar with the ragged edge of society. I knew every alley in the lower wards of the city, every street, every shipyard, every sailor's boarding house. So I had thoroughly familiarised myself with every existing type, not only from an inborn tendency to study human nature but by the actual commingling with these characters in their everyday life.[42]

The characters at the 'ragged edge' of society became the stock in trade of Harrigan's performances. From the time of his New York debut in 1870, he gained a reputation as his generation's leading delineator.

His early successes were in collaboration with Tony Hart, a runaway from a boy's reform school who, with his fine soprano voice, had a particular flair for female impersonation. Together they created a repertoire of comic sketches to fit the bills of the leading minstrel shows, starting with set-piece ethnic impersonations such as *The German Immigrants* (1872) and moving into more inventive scenarios in which characters from various immigrant groups were thrown together. Here their most successful vehicle was *The Mulligan Guard* (1873), which portrayed the adventures of a local militia led by an Irish grocer with an upwardly mobile wife. Mulligan's Guard was composed of Irish, Negro, German, Dutch, Italian and Yankee types, all pooling their particular national obsessions and incompetencies to precipitate comic disasters, with plenty of band music and dance thrown in. The enthusiastic popular and critical reception of the Mulligan sketches encouraged Harrigan to develop his characters further in comic plays with well-known local settings. The Lower East Side tenement, in particular, became the focus for these productions, which involved realistic stage reconstructions of recognisable streets and buildings. Determined to make his representations of both character and environment as accurate as possible, Harrigan took his research seriously.

> I've come to make a business of studying human nature. In the streetcars, on the elevator, in the restaurants, on the sidewalks, down in the Bowery, everywhere I take observations . . . . It has always been my aim to give as many of these types as possible and to make them as true to life as possible.[43]

The novelist and critic William Dean Howells called Harrigan the American Zola, and insisted that he was not taken seriously enough as a pioneer of naturalistic drama. In many ways Harrigan's interests and approach were exactly those of Zola, but he did not share Zola's explicit evolutionary rationale, or his evangelical earnestness. Struggle, competition and selective survival were the realities of life in the Lower East Side, as were the imperatives for adaptation in an environment that continually threw up new challenges and opportunities, and perhaps Harrigan, with his own urgent commercial priorities, felt no need for a theoretical account of these things. His view that 'experiments don't pay salaries' also distances him from the ethos of French naturalism.

Not all performers were as cavalier as Harrigan about the need for a theoretical and scientific framework for their innovations. There were some who advertised a scientific interest in human variety as an essential element in the popular appeal of their acts. One of these was Ernst Schultz, a visiting German artist, who performed at the

Egyptian Hall in the winter season of 1866 to 1867, offering a programme in four sections, each of which was devoted to a particular technique for analysing human typologies. He began with 'Humorous sketches of the varieties of mankind', in which he presented twelve characters based on the prototypes of the humours: melancholic, sanguinous, phlegmatic, choleric. Next was his particular speciality, 'Physiology of the beard'. Here he used a complex arrangement of candles, gas jets and mirrors to create light and shade in ways that changed the architecture of the face, so that its actual shape and features appeared to go through dramatic transformations. The third section was a 'Portrait album', consisting of a further twelve characters based on easily recognisable social types, including direct derivations from Matthews's repertoire. Schultz's finale, 'Types of race and nationality', was his most challenging experiment. The types included 'a Distinguished Arab, a Hungarian Peasant, a Chinese, an American Indian, a Negro and a Bosjeman Woman'.[44] The critics were impressed, commenting that 'Herr Schultz showed an almost preternatural talent for the destruction of his own identity'.[45]

It was one thing to give an impression of the general look and behaviour of various social types, but another to evoke the specific physiognomic characteristics of racial types from different parts of the globe. Schultz's theme was 'Masks and faces', and his conjuring presented a curious challenge to the anchoring assumptions of ethnological theory. If the features and complexion of an American Indian could be transformed in seconds into those of an African-American, and then into those of a Bosjeman woman, what did this say about the deep histories of racial typology upon which scientists were building assumptions about differential stages of evolutionary development?

Such questions were not explicitly raised in connection with Schultz's presentations, but they were implicit in the work of most performers who experimented with identity transformation across social categories. Schultz travelled widely with his show, making an extensive tour of the Americas following his London season and arriving in New York in the early 1870s. At the Théâtre Comique, he shared the bill with Edward Harrigan and Tony Hart (then in the early stages of their career), presenting himself as 'the man with 100 faces'.[46] Here he seems to have cut his multiracial segment. Since this was at the height of the minstrel craze, and Schultz was to make a number of subsequent appearances as a guest artist with various minstrel groups, it may have had something to do with a clash of approaches to interracial delineation. Indeed, he does not seem to have gone down well generally in the minstrel shows, where his billing recedes into supporting-act status. Perhaps his style was not robust enough for the raucous atmosphere of the minstrel variety programme. Schultz may have broken the unwritten ground rules of minstrel burlesque by taking racial difference a bit too seriously.

Valentine Vousden did not make this mistake. Vousden, an Irish vaudeville performer born in 1825, resuscitated his career in middle age by reinventing himself as the Polynational Character Actor in an act called 'The Unity of Nations'. This was effectively a one-man variety show, in which his impersonations of 'all the leading brands of humanity' drawn from the races of Africa, Asia, America and Europe were interspersed with singing and dancing and general comic patter.[47] Vousden took the protean tradition to its logical conclusion, creating a one-man ethnological congress in the early 1870s, a decade before even Barnum had managed to realise the concept.

Becoming Ethiopian

Charles Mathews's Ethiopian caricatures could be seen as the ultimate fulfilment of a mission to bring home all the human curiosities he encountered abroad in a repertoire graduating through distinct levels of foreignness, from the introductory range of regional types who were strangers to the metropolis, thence to the foreign accents collection from various parts of Europe, and on to the major challenge of racial difference in America. 'At Home', it seems that the delight of recognition escalated in relation to the degrees of strangeness Mathews succeeded in incorporating into himself until, in becoming Ethiopian, he demonstrated that even the major categories of human difference could be brought within the compass of the English stage vocabulary. In anthropological terms, then, he was using impersonation as a means of processing cultural strangeness through his own body, and thereby rendering it digestible to the intelligence of his fellow Englishmen. In this, was he not doing something that exactly paralleled the behaviour Darwin had seen in the Fuegians?

This encounter is described in *The Voyage of the Beagle*, where it is followed with some general reflections on powers of mimicry as an attribute of savages. The Fuegians demonstrated that besides performing 'hideous grimaces', they could do an astute impersonation of any European, repeating words and gestures 'with perfect correctness'. This talent may be explained, Darwin suggested, by the need for keener sense and more practised habits of perception among 'men in a savage state'.[48] Here he was expressing a commonly held view, though he put it more tactfully than was usual at the time. Mimicry was regarded as 'aping', an impulsive tendency to copy the behaviour and manners of savages and monkeys with no other strategies for relating to more sophisticated beings whose ways they could not understand.

In an illuminating commentary on Darwin's account of the Fuegian mimics, Michael Taussig draws in some additional information from Captain Fitzroy's version of the story, to point out that there was mimicking on both sides. According to Fitzroy, the Fuegians 'were highly pleased with the antics of a man belonging to the boat's crew, who danced well and was a good mimic'.[49] From here, Taussig turns to the question of why Darwin chose to notice only one side of what was effectively 'a competition in miming' with 'bewildering reciprocities'.[50]

> Who is mimicking whom, the sailor or the savage? We find the same problem and the same 'trick' of not seeing one's own indulgence in, and stimulation of, mimicry vis a vis the 'savage' when it comes to the way that adults in Western societies teach and relate to infants and children.[51]

In the case of Mathews and the delineators who followed in his wake, the denial took the form of a declaration that what they were doing was qualitatively different from the mere reflex behaviour of aping, and in order to explain this they needed to posit a hierarchical relationship between delineation and mimicry. 'Mere mimicry' was linked with the vulgarities of the grimace tradition; as a skill it was among the lowest in the scale of human activity, since it crossed the threshold between human and animal species. To *delineate* meant literally to capture in outline, and so carried connotations of definition. In this way it was linked with the discourses from natural history about the identification of specimens through defining characteristics. The Zoological Society of London published annual reports that included 'delineations' of the animals in its collections. The terms 'genus', 'species' and 'specimen' were also quite commonly used in a facetious spirit by popular entertainers.

The craze for Ethiopian delineation that gathered momentum from the early 1840s depended on a double convention. First, that 'darkies' were trying to copy the manners and fashions of white society, with the effect of demonstrating only that they were incapable of operating at the cultural level to which they childishly aspired. Second, that white Americans able to see these delusions for what they were could demonstrate their perceptiveness and afford great amusement for each other by capturing the symptoms of primitive mimicry in satirical sketches. Programmes and sheet music were often embellished with sketches of the minstrel troupes in two guises: first, in character, as buffoons with grotesque features in extravagant postures; second, as themselves, posing elegantly in formal dinner dress. Such dual images served to demonstrate that the minstrel persona was fully under the management of an identity schooled in the ways of civilisation. Some minstrel troupes emphasised their underlying dignity more strongly than others, but even for the most anarchic, the blackface mask served as a sharp signifier of distinction between the characteristics being demonstrated on stage and those the performer would be prepared to own as a white man.

The intended message was explicit: 'that a skilled man of intelligence is parodying a subhuman grotesque.'[52] These are the words of Ralph Ellison, whose 1958 essay on blackface minstrelsy was the first to consider the phenomenon from an African-American point of view. 'The figure in blackface looks suspiciously home grown, Western and Calvinist to me,' he says, and 'its adjustment to the contours of white symbolic needs is far more intriguing than its alleged origins.'[53] This is quite evidently the case, judging from the pervasiveness, endurance and sheer intensity of what *Punch* called 'Ethiopian mania' on both sides of the Atlantic. As Robert Toll emphasises, the blackface mask was 'a powerful theatrical device' that allowed for the playing out of fantasies.[54] In the debate that has grown up around minstrelsy since Ellison's essay was published, the ethnological scrutiny has been reversed, to focus on the anxieties of whiteness in mid-nineteenth-century America.[55] Recent studies of the minstrel craze have explored contextual factors, including the political tensions over slavery in the antebellum years, the pressures of mid-century immigration in working-class communities of New York, the formations of America's first proletarian youth culture, and the new social hierarchies of a nation in the process of asserting its independence.[56]

Such factors are interconnected, and the relevance of changing ideas about the evolution of human diversity should be considered among them. British and European Americans, whether recent immigrants or descendants of earlier settlers, were situated at an especially complex intersection of racial and cultural differences. Among themselves they represented a range of traditions that differed in language, religion, law and social practice but there were broader cultural frames they held in common, since they could look back to points in history from which their various traditions had diverged. When they compared themselves with indigenous American races, or with the races brought across into slavery from Africa, their sense of difference seems to have become confused and exaggerated. How were these distinct levels of diversity to be understood and negotiated?

Eric Lott writes of how minstrelsy brought out 'racialised elements of thought and feeling, tone and impulse, residing at the very edge of semantic availability'.[57] The forms of mimicry displayed in minstrel and other kinds of variety performance may be seen as a proto-language, an attempt to create forms of articulation around human subjects who are unfamiliar in their speech and behaviour. Minstrel programmes featured delineations of all immigrant groups, often mixing and mismatching them to create a hotpotch of burlesque internationalism. Bryant's Minstrels in the 1850s offered an African polka followed by an Italian opera, a sketch about an Irishman in Italy featuring an encounter with the Bourbon Arabs, and a farce set in the Chinese Embassy. Wood's Minstrels juxtaposed a Dutch drill with a Highland fling as prelude to a sequence of plantation scenes. They also performed an acrobatic sequence entitled 'Bedouin Arabs à la Ravel', which alternated on the programme with 'Chinese acrobats'. Christy's interspersed their plantation songs with Tyrolean yodellers, Hungarian warblers and Italian opera. Irish songs, dances and sketches were staple elements in the repertoire of most troupes.[58] Blackface was a distorting lens through which to caricature every form of national identity that captured the attention of the performers, but their roles as 'Ethiopian delineators' remained central. It was as if the Ethiopian mask served to amplify category differences, perhaps because it was itself a signifier of polar extremes in human difference.

If we take the case of the first encounter between the Fuegians and the crew of the Beagle as a prototypic example, mimicry may also be understood as a way to prepare the ground for communication where there is no shared social fabric and where attempts at direct dialogue would be premature. The resort to mimicry in first encounters is a phenomenon to which Michael Taussig devotes particular attention. On these occasions, he suggests, the distance between the races is 'a space permeated by the colonial tension of mimesis and alterity'.[59] If mimicry is, on both sides, a way of getting to know the other, this provides a way of explaining why cross-cultural and cross-racial impersonation was such a pervasive habit in mid-nineteenth-century America. Whites mimicking blacks were mirroring the behaviour of blacks imitating whites. However different the political loadings and underlying attitudes, the behavioural symptoms are certainly equivalent: the adoption of exaggerated versions of the other's costume and manners; heavily caricatured speech patterns; indulgence in facetious exhibitionism.

Blackface minstrelsy flourished in a hothouse atmosphere of contagious mimesis. Every exercise in impersonation was echoed in a counter-exercise, and mimics parodied each other in proliferating feedback loops that short-circuited within same-race communities. The African-American dancer Juba was one of those who recognised the syndrome and set out to trump any rivals by monopolising the circuits. In his advertisements, audiences are promised a finale with

> correct Imitation Dances of all the principal Ethiopian Dancers in the United States. After which he will give an imitation of himself – and then you will see the vast difference between those that have heretofore attempted dancing and this wonderful young man.[60]

To be imitated by a performer was to be recognised as a kind of performer oneself – someone whose behaviour constituted a source of amusement and spectator sport. A logical step for those who knew they were going to be mimicked was to perform in a way that would provoke and challenge imitation. In the case of a virtuoso performer like Juba, mimicry was an attempt at rivalry by those who sought to appropriate his success.

It was common for blackface minstrels to claim that their portrayals of 'plantation darkies' were accurate delineations based on firsthand study and observation, but most troupes created their repertoire by copying each other so that generic ingredients and structures rapidly fell into place. The more high-profile troupes regularly complained about their material being pirated, even as they promoted a repertoire consisting almost entirely of burlesque renditions of successful performances by their rivals.

Becoming Ethiopian was an experience whose special allure needs to be accounted for. Descriptions of Juba's impact on white audiences testify to levels of excitement they had never before experienced. The best known of such descriptions is Charles Dickens's account of a performance in a Five Points tavern:

> Instantly the fiddler grins and goes at it tooth and nail; there is new energy in the tambourine; new laughter in the dancers; new smiles in the landlady; new confidence in the landlord; new brightness in the very candles. Single shuffle, double shuffle, cut and cross cut; snapping his fingers, rolling his eyes, turning in his knees, presenting the backs of his legs in front, spinning about on his toes and heels like nothing but the man's fingers on the tambourine; dancing with two left legs, two right legs, two wooden legs, two wire legs, two spring legs – all sorts of legs and no legs – what is it him? And in what walk of life or dance of life does man ever get such stimulating applause as thunders about him, when, having danced his partner off her feet, and himself too, he finishes by leaping gloriously on the bar counter, and calling for something to drink, with the chuckle of a million counterfeit Jim Crows, in one inimitable sound.[61]

The spectator who was later to declare his repellence at the sight of the 'howling, whistling, clucking, stamping, jumping, tearing savage' in a misanthropic account of the Bushmen here allows himself to be caught in a whirl of sympathetic excitement as the shape-shifting Juba defies the laws of gravity and the natural order of the body.[62] It is easy to see how the impulse to try on the dance for oneself, with its accompanying exhilaration, became irresistible.

Becoming Ethiopian might involve emulating the extremes of skill demonstrated by Juba, but for blackface impersonators it also meant playing close to the human/animal divide upon which savages were supposed to be situated. Animal acts, whether in the form of animals behaving like humans or humans impersonating animals, were an essential component of variety programmes and had special prominence in minstrel shows. Signor Donetti's dogs, goats and monkeys appeared with several minstrel troupes in the early 1850s, and at Barnum's Museum they shared the bill with White's Serenaders. The monkeys, dressed as human gentry and their servants, rode the dogs as horses and performed an elaborate scene involving a carriage upset, after which the monkey drivers rescued their female passenger from a ditch, replaced a detached wheel and drove off again.[63] Minstrels often took on monkey roles, but also diversified to perform as giraffes and elephants in numerous parodies of menagerie shows. Bob Hart, Frank Brower and Jerry Bryant all played menagerists; Carncross and Dixey introduced Barnum with his elephant (1874); Wood's Minstrels advertised Von Ham-Bug's Menagerie (1863) and Haverley's Mastodon company burlesqued Fourpaugh's Menagerie (1880); Bryant's offered a horse opera (1857) and also featured Artemis Ward as a dancing giraffe.

Monkey-man acts with their inevitable missing link allusions were also stock in trade. *Jocko* was burlesqued by several minstrel troupes, notably Bryant's and Christy's. Almost as soon as Barnum introduced his 'What is It?' at the American Museum, Bryant's responded with one of their own, which remained in their repertoire for fifteen years. Bryant's 'What is It?' was in turn copied by Campbell's and Queen's. Barnum presented his 'What is It?' in the interval of Boucicault's *Octoroon* at the American Museum, but Christy's went one further in their *Moctoroon* (1860) by recasting the central character as a missing link. In Boucicault's play the heroine is an Octoroon girl, Zoe, who is the natural child of a white judge by a Quadroon slave. Several white men fall in love with Zoe without knowing about her compromised social status, and the drama descends into near tragedy as she is sold into slavery. *Moctoroon* replaces Zoe with Zoesy 'unhappily descendant of a gorilla', and invested with some newly fashionable Darwinian resonances.

As Darwinian interpretations of humanity gained currency, higher and lower levels of human status were increasingly read in terms of relative distance from animality. The Jim Crow and Zip Coon prototypes incorporated animal qualities in themselves, and were surrounded by animals in their narratives. 'My mammy was a wolf, my daddy was a tiger, and I'm what you call de old Virginia nigger', chants Jim Crow, whose social world is populated with animal species.[64] He has dialogues with the bullfrog and the mocking-bird, and battles of wits with the possum, the raccoon and the blue tail fly. There are tacit understandings with these peer groups. 'A jay bird sat on a hickory limb, he winked at me and I wink'd at him.'[65] Jim Crow's dancing, above all, is a form of inter-species communication:

I kneels to de buzzard and I bows to de crow;
And ebery time I weel about I jumps jis so.[66]

The songs often take the form of simple monologues, telling stories of flirting, fighting and feasting, as ingenuous versions of the 'three *fs*' still regarded by some sociobiologists as the primary motivating instincts of the human animal. Entirely controlled by appetite and impulse, the minstrels' darky generates a whirling chaos wherever he goes:

> Oh I met de pretty Miss Dinah,
> And I give her a buss,
> She slapt me in de face,
> And made a mouty fuss.
> And den I go to New Orleans,
> And feel so full of fight,
> Dey put me in de calaboose,
> And keep me dere all night.
>
> When I got out I hit a man,
> His name I now forgot;
> An dere noting left,
> 'Sept a little grease spot.
> I whipt my weight in wild cats,
> I eat an alligator;
> And tear up more ground
> Den kiver fifty load of tater.[67]

Much has been written about the class tensions underlying minstrel mania but images such as those in the song tell more immediately of species tensions.

In the 1860s, human evolution began to feature in minstrel shows as a hilarious topic. Soon after the appearance of Darwin's *The Origin of Species*, Christy's minstrels created a sketch about the controversy over human origins entitled '16,000 Years Ago'. Bob Hart, who made guest appearances with most of the leading minstrel companies in the 1870s, wrote and performed stump speeches on 'Mr. Darwin's Theory' and 'Vestages of Civilization' [*sic*]. A song by William Arlington entitled 'Darwinian Theory' spread into the repertoire of a number of minstrel troupes.[68] By the 1880s evolutionary theory had spawned a satirical language that was applied to the entertainments themselves: 'Away back in the silurian days of our country's history . . . there arose a species of entertainment called "negro minstrelsy".'[69]

Such conscious allusions to the scientific debate on human evolution are absent from the programmes of first-generation minstrels since the debate itself did not really take off in American circles until after *The Origin of Species* appeared.[70] By then blackface performers were already acting out an idea of their own species based on the polarities of savage infantilism and civilised adulthood. The pleasure of sliding between these poles was secured by the assumption that, as members of a superior race, they could control the shifts in behaviour through the delineator's art. Yet the pleasures of becoming Ethiopian were essentially hysterical. The screaming sketches, the flings and jigs and reels betrayed something other than simple *joie de vivre*: a compulsive need, perhaps, to try on the experience of those who were free of the constraints of civilisation, free to follow every impulse and let loose the most extreme energies. Seen in this light, minstrelsy was a form of regression.

Freud gave the term *regression* evolutionary connotations, especially when he applied it to collective rather than individual states in his later writings on society and civilisation. These texts provide some useful commentary on the craze for minstrelsy that swept America and then Britain at a time when the social order was being redefined in developmentalist terms. In an essay on group psychology published in 1921, Freud drew heavily on the ideas of the French social Darwinist Gustav Le Bon, to suggest that evolution was modelled in the psyche, with the ego situated between the primitive unconscious, repository of the instincts, and the super-ego as a control centre developed to serve the requirements of a highly evolved civilisation. Regression meant lapsing back into the primordial areas of psychic activity. The potency of group psychology is such, according to Freud, that it gives the individual 'a sentiment of invincible power which allows him to yield to instincts which, had he been alone, he would perforce have kept under restraint'.[71] The symptoms of 'a regression of mental activity to an earlier stage such as we are not surprised to find among savages or children' read like a prescription for blackface caricature:

> the weakness of intellectual ability, the lack of emotional restraint, the incapacity for moderation and delay, the inclination to exceed every limit in the expression of emotion and to work it off completely in the form of action.[72]

If those who have been schooled to occupy the upper echelons of the developmentalist hierarchy may thus be subject to overwhelming urges to regress to 'primordial states of mind which have been long ago overlaid', Freud wants to know why.[73]

He explores the question in 'Civilization and its Discontents', where his argument is driven by perplexity at the melancholy paradox 'that what we call our civilization is largely responsible for our misery, and that we should be much happier if we gave it up and returned to primitive conditions'.[74] No wonder the imagination of white America ran riot over the freedoms of a race they themselves had disqualified from the realms of higher civilisation. The presence of this race among them as cohabitants must surely have exacerbated a collective fantasy already primed by the psychological constraints of the Puritan tradition. Quakers, Shakers and Mormons were among the favourite targets of minstrel burlesque. The Chicago Troubadors featured a 'screaming sketch' entitled 'The Landing of the Pilgrim Fathers'.[75]

Gravity, reserve and uprightness were expressions of self-control crucial in denoting the status of the white man at the developmental peak of the racial hierarchy. From the mid-nineteenth century, a growing consciousness of behavioural codes is reflected in the popularity of etiquette manuals, some seventy of which, according to Rosemarie Bank, were published between 1830 and 1860, many of them running to several editions.[76] Since wildness was the primary defining feature of savage races, this meant taking special care with the control and containment of energy. Le Bon identifies 'energy' as one of the defining characteristics of superior racial groups, along with perseverance and will, but this triumvirate operates a harnessing process, so that energy is fed into productive labour. The blackface mask was a licence for white men to indulge instead in high-energy forms of expressive behaviour: to yell, cackle and whoop, to leap and spin, take pratfalls, sit at precarious angles, throw limbs around in chaotic disco-ordination, grimace, talk nonsense, sing falsetto and paint their faces. The Black Shakers and Shaking Quakers of minstrelsy put the upright, civilised body into a tailspin on its way to the rediscovery of that convulsive physicality which Freud claims it had been denied.[77] This was not the same thing as a Rabelasian inversion of bodily hierarchies; rather, the body was jigged and reeled into explosive effervescence and became a power-house of libidinal energy. This was a quintessentially performing body, making a spectacle of itself in its unremitting displays of pleasurable convulsion.

A review of the visiting Coloured Opera Troupe in *The Illustrated London News* in 1858 praised the 'extravaganza, in which the whole band furiously engages', to produce 'the excitement of the racecourse and of a house on fire'. But the writer was explicit on the terms of engagement: 'With white faces the whole affair would be intolerable. It is the ebony that gives the due and needful colour to the monstrosities, the breaches of decorum, the exaggerations of feeling.'[78] Ethnological shows gave spectators an opportunity to observe wildness contained in a framework of defined otherness, but blackface performances demonstrated that there was a need among the *soi-disant* civilised to embody wildness – to experience it in their own movements, expressions and vocalisations – not just to witness it. 'The feeling of happiness derived from the satisfaction of a wild instinctual impulse untamed by the ego,' Freud wrote, 'is incomparably more intense than that derived from sating an instinct that has been tamed.' The satisfaction of tamed impulse is mild and 'does not convulse our physical being'.[79] Putting on the body of the other meant expressing its sensations and attitudes, converting one's own physicality through the forbidden circuits of energy.

If the minstrel shows were the crucible of the variety movement, dance was the generative core of the minstrel show.[80] The following list of featured dances is gleaned from programmes in the Harvard Theatre Collection for performances between 1840 and 1870:

> Hong Kong bone dance, Congo green dance, Danse Metamorphose, Saint Anthony's dance, Bloomer dance, Corn-shucking dance, Ethiopian medley dance, Chinese dance, Polka de African, Polka à la militaire, Jim Crow polka, Jenny Lind polka, Excelsior jig, Rattlesnake jig, Somerset jig, Louisiana Plantation jig, Alligator reel, Sugar Cane reel, Zouave clog reel, Mazurka quadrille, Quadrille a la Clodoche, Pas de Danube, Pas de Coconut, La Tarentula, El Bolero de Cadiz, Ethiopian fling, Mississippi fling, Double clog hornpipe, Virginia breakdown, Grape Vine Twist.

The proliferation of names for dances may well have outstripped any genuine diversity in the choreography, but the names alone tell of the range of cultural references drawn into the Ethiopian whirl. Cavorting indiscriminately through the ballet, the polka and the fling to the clog-dance and the breakdown, minstrel groups crossed high culture codes of deportment with street exhibitionism. The burlesque adoption of the Shakers as a minstrel emblem points to a recognition that dance was the nemesis of Puritanism.

The permissiveness of blackface, though, carried its own forms of selectivity and suppression. African-Americans and women, as the two most popular targets for impersonation, were excluded from performing in the standard minstrel programmes, though there were African-Americans who infiltrated the genre by wearing blackface themselves. There could be no better expression of the principle that the categories of nature must be subordinated to the categories of performance. Some female troupes tried to break into the minstrel game, but the odds were against them. Drag acts were often the high point of minstrel shows, and real women could not hope to be as funny impersonating the ballerina Fanny Elssler, or singing Jenny Lind falsetto. They were less free to break the rules of physical decorum in the antics of 'screaming' farce. All-female troupes like the Buffalo Gals, who had moderate success in the mid-1840s, were not wild enough to achieve the epidemic popularity of the male troupes whose formula they had copied. The Lady Minstrels, who joined the Ethiopian Minstrels for a couple of seasons, were used as singers only, to enhance the musical impact of the opening section of the programme.[81] Some female groups tried to shift the basis of their appeal. Among these were the Arab Girls, who developed a gymnastics act in blackface. The Franklin Museum and the Palace of Beauty specialised in the presentation of scantily clad female 'minstrels' in mildly erotic poses, but their very passivity was the antithesis of what appealed to audiences in the male minstrel shows. Among the second generation of performers were Madame Rentz's Female Minstrels, actually a mixed company in which the men performed most of the comedy. They created a niche for themselves by deliberately cultivating a more upmarket style in which the quality of the music and the elegance of the female performers were the chief selling points.

The burlesque madness

A much more convincing female response to the Ethiopian mania was the craze for blonde burlesque sparked off by Lydia Thompson and her company when they arrived in New York in 1868. Burlesque had always been the keynote of minstrelsy, but Thompson's formula – male impersonation by statuesque beauties who presented themselves in a manner that verged on exhibitionism – was so successful that she managed to appropriate the label as her own. Thompson and her fellow blondes Pauline Markham and Ada Harland broke the monopoly of minstrel acts in a number of New York venues, tripling the box-office takings and provoking 'the wildest symptoms of delight' among the most jaded variety audiences. Their production of *Robinson Crusoe* (1869) put the minstrels firmly in their place: in the supporting cast, where a group of six blackface singers appeared in pageant, decisively outnumbered by

Amazon Warriors.[82] The Thompson Troupe also parodied minstrel songs and stump speeches, appropriating the breakdown dance competition as a finale. The *New York Times* credited them with 'beating Dan Bryant at his own trade', but they had a trade of their own whose practices were differently oriented.[83]

Minstrelsy was a developmental reversal, a plunge backwards into the state of polymorphous perversity in which mouth, eyes, hands and feet all did the dances of pleasure, but the instinctual terrain in which the Thompson Troupe specialised was adult and sexual. In the words of Robert C. Allen, leading scholar of American burlesque, they provoked 'mass male hysteria', encouraging the spread of stories about the chaos left in their wake on a recent European tour: suicides by admirers, men of the highest respectability drawn into abject pursuit of a stage Venus, extravagant gestures of courtship by members of the British and European aristocracy. Like Circe the ancient Greek sorceress who turned men into swine, these stage *femmes fatales* demonstrated a genius for stripping away the pretensions of those who thought they had risen far above animal nature. If the blackface mask was a passport back to the realms of instinctual pleasure, yellow hair licensed a more dangerous kind of regression, stirring the powerful energies of sexual obsession.

Press reportage did not pick this up immediately. There was no reason to anticipate anything especially hazardous from the visit of the British blondes. The stories of Thompson's conquests were no more extravagant than the promotional claims made for other forms of popular entertainment, and burlesques of various kinds dominated the New York season of 1868. Nor were female-dominated companies particularly unusual. The Thompson Troupe were contracted to appear at Wood's Museum, where they replaced Mademoiselle Morlacchi's ballet troupe, whose production of *The Cloth of Gold* was already being burlesqued elsewhere in New York by the Worrell Sisters. The success of the new arrivals at Wood's Museum was obviously something of a surprise to the *New York Times*, which reported briefly on the impressive box-office profits, and was politely enthusiastic in its review a few days later. The paper was already complaining of 'the meagreness of recent theatricals', writing about the failure of opera bouffe imported from France, and resorting to the perennial topic of 'high art and that which is not high', for the sake of finding something to discuss in a dull season.[84] But a few months later this topic was to return with a vengeance as reactions to Thompson's company intensified. Allen suggests that more heated critical attention was provoked by their move into prime middle-class territory at Niblo's Garden, but the anxieties that surfaced were many-faceted.

In an extended article on 'the Burlesque Madness', the *New York Times* echoed the style and imagery of *Punch*'s earlier responses to the invasion of London by Ethiopian minstrels:

> An epidemic, which the Board of Health is powerless to arrest, has seized upon New York and infects it in every part, counting its victims by the tens of thousands. It may be called the Mania for Burlesque. Slight touches of it have always been felt among us. Once there was an infected spot called Mitchell's Olympic, where it flourished in every season; after that the nest was swept away by advancing civilization, it came upon us intermittently . . . . At Niblo's Garden it has broken out with unparalleled intensity.[85]

The style here, though, has not the light touch that was Mr Punch's hallmark; there is a paranoid edge to some of the statements. How finally, after all, were the vestiges of lower forms swept away by the advancement of civilisation? In a report on the activities of the Smithsonian Institute published soon after Thompson first opened at Wood's Museum, the *New York Times* reported the view that 'the invasion and steady progress of a civilized population, while changing generally the face of nature, is obliterating many of the evidences of a former state of things'. Was there to be a reverse invasion? From the scientist's point of view, the lower orders of animal life were becoming extinct under 'the deadly influence of civilized man', but here in the theatre column, the story was looking very different. Savage life was staging a resurgence in the midst of domestic order, and in despite of higher cultural progress. 'It is feared that . . . the clotheless and convulsive symptoms may spread to every home and carry desolation to every hearth.'[86]

The Thompson Troupe's overt sexuality was powerfully female yet beyond the bounds of femininity as defined even by the conventions of stage eroticism. The female bodies displayed at the Franklin Museum and the Palace of Beauty were passive and compliant, posed for voyeuristic consumption in accordance with well-established aesthetic codes. It is small wonder that charismatic female impersonators often drew much stronger reactions, and provided more promising models for a new genre of female erotic performance based on male impersonation. Francis Leon – billed as 'the only Leon' to defy copy-cat impersonators – raised the minstrel drag act to a minor art form. Leon was a singer, dancer and choreographer whose stylish approach to stage image-making revealed new possibilities for female impersonation based on high glamour rather than grotesque caricature. Promoting himself as a fashion icon able to put any society lady in the shade, he created a range of stage personae that combined traditionally masculine qualities of boldness and physical display with traditionally feminine archness, vanity and curvilinear grace.

Leon, together with the transvestite equestrienne Ella Zoyara and the brilliant boy aerialist 'Lulu' (about whom more will be said later), were the leading male performers to provoke category confusion in staged sexuality. The blonde burlesquers exploited the opportunities they had created, escalating the crisis by transferring the sexualised feminine from that which was alluded to through techniques of imaging and performance, to that which was unmistakably present on stage. Sexual presence in the female burlesque was the more highly charged because it was undiluted by the kinds of virtuosity that cat
aylsed the performances of Zoyara or Leon. Thompson's company were not acrobats, they made no pretence at being skilled delineators, and were indifferent singers and dancers, yet burlesquers had techniques of their own that were revealed more starkly in the absence of other performance skills. William Dean Howells tried to identify their 'peculiar capabilities' and 'full-blown fascinations' in an essay for the *Atlantic Monthly*, attempting a detailed portrait of one (unnamed) leading player:

> This was a young person of powerful physical expression . . . and she triumphed and wantoned through the scenes with a fierce excess of animal vigour. She was all stocking, as one may say, being habited to represent a prince; she had a raucous voice, an insolent twist of the mouth, and a terrible trick of defying her enemies by standing erect, chin up, hand on hip, and right foot advanced, patting the floor. It was impossible, even from the orchestra seats, to look at her in this attitude and not shrink before her.[87]

If the stars of female burlesque were not actresses, there were aspects of role-play that they understood a great deal better than many women who were. They worked on the principle that all self-presentation was performative, and therefore manipulative and susceptible to facetious elaboration. All that was required to make it convincing was a certain physical rapport with the target audience. Howells found the tactics 'very unscrupulously clever'.[88]

Where minstrel burlesque tipped from the hilarious to the hysterical, female burlesque was characterised by a cooler but more thoroughgoing refusal of seriousness, in which every element in the performance became a pretext for drawing attention to the body. This was a technique involving shifts between ironic detachment and provocative directness. Ultimately, the formula was more destabilising than the performative hysterics of minstrelsy because it displaced the hysteria onto the audience, who might be 'infected' in earnest through the stirrings of sexual obsession. Here there was a paradoxical liaison between the lowest common denominator in human nature and the diversifying tendencies of role-play. On the one hand, burlesque revealed how easily social roles could be denatured because it involved the travesty of natural categories, whether of race, gender or species; on the other, it worked insidiously to confront society with the animal constants underlying even the most sophisticated demeanours of civilised man.

By the time the British blondes had completed their first season, the complacency of the *New York Times* on the high art/low art debate was well and truly dispelled. Erotic burlesque was triggering a crisis in public taste through its confusion of aesthetic hierarchies and cultural taxonomies. It was a form of drollery that involved more than simple descent into the grotesque, for the burlesque fed intimately on the substance of higher aesthetic forms, drawing them down the cultural scale while escalating the levels of excitation that might be attached to them. The prototypical stage production blended ingredients from the French ballet and opera bouffe, American minstrel shows and pantomime in a mock-up of Greek mythology. Scenes set on Olympus in the Thompson company's *Ixion* evoked the ornate formalities of court masque but also the obscene tableaux to be seen in the lowest dives of New York where, in George Foster's description, the 'same brawny female' equipped with a couple of gauze veils would appear every night as 'Venus rising from the sea' then 'Susannah in the bath'.[89] In Howells's account, the burlesque actress combined the insolent self-display of the prostitute with the courtly disdain of an unattainable lady. Her 'fierce excess of animal vigour' both allured and intimidated, and her gender ambiguity compounded the effect, merging 'the easy attitudes of young men' with the behavioural effrontery of the whore.

Richard Grant White, writing in 1869 on the 'outbreak of burlesque', dwelt on what he saw as its monstrosity. It was not, he said, wicked or disgusting or hateful, but 'monstrously incongruous and unnatural'.[90] The Thompson Troupe made their New York debut at Wood's Museum, where the ticket price also covered entry to the collection of natural curiosities and human freaks. From advertisements carried in the *New York Times* it is clear that the management were trading on the juxtaposition. Monstrosity, it seems, was entering the later nineteenth century in a new guise, no longer as the freaks of human or animal form, but as a bizarre convergence of overblown cultural forms, involving strange miscegenations of the high and the low, the masculine and the feminine.

These miscegenations were the more threatening in the context of widening interest in the social implications of evolutionary progress. Burlesque as low culture needs to be contextualised more specifically as the evolutionary low. Howells's opinions on it were expressed at a time when he was beginning to formulate an evolutionary view of cultural forms in which seriousness and realism were the defining qualities of highly evolved art. Henry Morley, picking up on the new emphasis on the brain-dominated course of human evolution, wrote obsessively of the burlesque threat to intelligence. It was 'all leg and no brains'. Its punning dialogue was a 'deficient use of human speech', appealing to 'the mind too feeble to lay hold habitually with its entire attention on the thoughts of which words are the signs'.[91] A writer in the London *Athenaeum* lamented the decline of burlesque as a genre that in the past had 'performed service in the cause of intellectual progress', and now served merely 'to amuse the feeble-minded'.[92] The insidious capacity of female burlesque to infiltrate middle-class culture and to fascinate men of the highest status had the potential to confuse the hierarchies of the natural order itself. According to Darwinian theory, lower forms of organic life gradually evolved into higher forms, but here lower and higher forms of culture were being confused with each other through sudden slippage. The female stars of burlesque were the precursors of the celebrated *demi-mondaines* who drew attention to the importance of sexual selection in determining the course of human evolution and, further than this, usurped the dominant role in sexual selection that civilised society had unequivocally awarded to the male of the species.

Burlesque was a monstrous outgrowth of the variety theatre culture. While the very principle of variety was diversification, burlesque brought about mergers and collapses of difference and, along with these, radical category confusions. In some ways it tapped into deeper cultural anxieties than the craze for blackface because of its foregrounding of sexuality, but the two 'manias' also shared common ground. Both provoked questions about what was natural in social categories and what was to be discovered about a common human nature underlying the social order. The surrender to wildness in minstrelsy and the unleashing of sexual energies in female burlesque demonstrated the anarchic potency of nature as a force at work in human behaviour. What was or was not out of the natural order could no longer be confidently determined by traditional decree: the way was open for experiment and discovery. Darwin's theory of natural selection introduced a view of nature as seething with incessant processes, and though he insisted that there was law at work in these, and wrote of natural selection as a law, he also insisted that the whole domain of activity was ultimately ungoverned.

The diversification of theatre forms across the mid-nineteenth century modelled the Darwinian paradigm in uncanny ways, stirring up some of the same troubling paradoxes about how nature operated. Were law and order coupled in nature, or was the law of nature truly expressed in wildness and anarchy? In the most important recent study of social Darwinism, Mike Hawkins emphasises the tensions surrounding this view of 'nature as janiform', as model and as threat.[93] Was civilisation an evolutionary process working in conjunction with natural law to produce ever more refined social beings, or (as Freud was later to conclude) an alien and therefore fragile imposition on the essentially unchanging raw material of human nature? During the 1860s and 1870s, scientists and social analysts were increasingly determined upon answering according to the first of these alternatives, while popular entertainments were providing evidence in support of the second. The stakes in the high art/low art debate were radically altered when lower forms of culture were seen as reversions to the primitive and when the primitive was seen not as some imperilled vestige of the past, but as an active force, capable of erupting anywhere and spreading its influence like a plague.

5

LOWLY ORIGINS

The fascination with wonderful difference that animates Darwin's writing in *The Voyage of the Beagle* gradually gave way to a more constrained and ambivalent outlook. Where his earlier focus on the variety of life forms gave a kind of exuberance to the spirit of his enquiries, his later preoccupation with the theme of human descent loaded his reasoning with a heavy burden of social responsibility. This was compounded by a change in his status from that of a maverick speculator at the time of the first release of *The Origin of Species* to that of a figurehead, the authority behind an expanding range of evolutionary approaches to psychology, sociology, ethics and human physiology. Correspondingly, the mood of second-generation Darwinism was darker and more intense than that which surrounded the earlier reception of his ideas.

'Man still bears in his bodily frame the indelible stamp of his lowly origin', Darwin states in his conclusion to *The Descent of Man* (1871).[1] Much of this book is concerned with an enquiry into how far and in what ways the marks of lowly origin still intruded into the lives of the most advanced members of the human species. In arguing the issues, Darwin was influenced by a number of writers who had extrapolated from his theory of natural selection to develop evolutionary approaches to social theory. He was thus receiving his own influence back from an expanded sphere of application, and in doing so found himself mediating between more and less optimistic readings of human tendency. From Herbert Spencer he had adopted the phrase 'survival of the fittest', with its upbeat connotations about the progressive effects of selection and struggle. Drawing support from Spencer's work on the moral sense, Darwin predicted:

> Looking to future generations, there is no cause to fear that the social instincts will grow weaker, and we may expect

that virtuous habits will grow stronger, becoming perhaps
fixed by inheritance. In this case the struggle between
higher and lower impulses will be less severe, and virtue
will be triumphant.[2]

Such confidence was tempered, however, by the recognition that
'progress is no invariable rule'. The English businessman Walter
Bagehot had emphasised this point, after an investigation into the
principles of adaptation as the basis for selection in humans. Progress
might appear to be the norm in human society, said Bagehot, but
the darker episodes of history taught otherwise and, paradoxically,
civilised nations could be most at risk of deterioration through their
determination to interfere with the process of natural selection. For
Darwin, the example of animal breeders – always an important reference point in his arguments – provided some salutary reflections on
this point. 'It is surprising how soon a want of care, or care wrongly
directed, leads to the degeneration of a domestic race; but excepting
in the case of man himself, hardly anyone is so ignorant as to allow
his worst animals to breed.'[3]

The work of Darwin's cousin Francis Galton was a strong influence
on this line of argument, since he had collected evidence of the reproduction rates among the higher and lower orders of society and drawn
some worrying predictions about the consequences of the tendencies
he identified. Thus natural selection and sexual selection became
interwoven in the argument of *The Descent*, but there were some tensions between them. Natural selection in the human was supposed to
have favoured brain development so that physiological and instinctual characteristics were subordinated to decision-making processes
based rationally on the demands of civilisation, while sexual selection
necessarily retained some basis in instinctual promptings:

> It deserves attention that with mankind the conditions were
> in many respects much more favourable for sexual selection
> during a very early period, when man had only just attained
> to the rank of manhood, than during later times. For he
> would then, as we may safely conclude, have been guided
> by his instinctive passions, and less by foresight or reason.[4]

Darwin remains idealistic about the benefits of having risen 'to
the very summit of the organic scale', but he likewise observes that
while civilised man has 'advanced in his intellectual powers' he has
'retrograded in his instincts'.[5] Savages choose their mates for their

physical attributes, whereas in more highly evolved races, 'men are largely attracted by the mental charms of the women, by their wealth, and especially by their social position; for men rarely marry into a much lower rank'.[6]

Sexual and intellectual tendencies pull in opposite directions and man bears in his bodily frame the indelible stamp of his lowly origins, yet the implications of this duality remain unexplored, despite strong emphasis on the significance of human sexual choice. Darwin quotes Schopenhauer: 'What it all turns on is nothing less than the composition of the next generation . . . It is not the weal or woe of any one individual, but that of the human race to come, which is here at stake.'[7]

Remarks about the dangers of allowing one's 'worst animals' to breed have one kind of relevance to what is at stake, but the dangers of sexual selection on the basis of economic and social factors have another, which Darwin neglects to explore. What might be the longer-term consequences of prioritising reason, wealth and social position over such qualities as strength, energy and physical form? The higher orders of society could be encouraging the rapid erosion of these latter qualities, and at the same time leaving themselves vulnerable to reversion, through the sudden resurgence of instincts that even European gentlemen still carried with them as part of the indelible stamp of their lowly origins. Female sexual choice – or, as Darwin terms it, 'the opposite form of selection' – is another potential source of trouble. He regards this as a more or less archaic phenomenon, since female choice is a characteristic of primitive humanity and the lower animals, but acknowledges that 'this form of selection may have occasionally acted in later times'.

The theatre, with its displays of performing bodies, was a high-risk environment in the eyes of those who feared the resurgence of base instincts, and the figure of the performer emerged as the focus for a range of anxieties about hierarchy and sexuality. Such anxieties lent themselves to burlesque exploitation, which in turn tended to exacerbate them. In the previous chapters I have considered the dialectic between performance and evolution as one in which entertainers created their own domain of burlesque commentary and interpretation, a domain free from the earnestness of scientific debate. Here, I am turning to another kind of perspective, one in which the performer him or herself comes under scrutiny as a destabilising influence in the uneasy balance of power between higher and lower modes of human being. This scrutiny was not new, in that the animal qualities of the actor had long been a matter for philosophical discussion, but the framework of social Darwinism gave a new urgency to the analysis.

The lure of the low

According to Darwin, man had 'ultimately become superior to woman' through the process of natural selection, which had caused the human male to develop higher order mental capacities more intensively. He noted the opinion of Carl Vogt (Genevan Professor of Natural History, and Honorary Fellow of the Anthropological Societies of Paris and London) that the difference between the sexes in mental capacity increased with the development of the race, 'so that the male European excels much more the female than the negro the negress'.[8] Along with this widening differential went the transfer to the male of the dominant role in sexual selection which, according to Sir John Lubbock (another influence on Darwin's views), may have been held by the female in earlier or more primitive societies where promiscuity still reigned and 'high honour was bestowed on women who were utterly licentious'.[9] Among the barbarous races, Darwin speculated, 'preference on the part of the woman, steadily acting in one direction, would ultimately affect the character of the tribe'.[10] The spectre of licentious women dragging the aristocrats and scions of society down to the lowest levels of human motivation was one Darwin himself did not raise, but his arguments provided the basis for such anxieties.

The brothel trade in the major industrial cities was becoming part of a complex underworld culture in which society men indulged their own alternative inclinations in ways prevented by the restrictions and rationalisations of marriage. In New York there was widespread concern about the tendency of the brothel to invade the theatre, with prostitutes using the cheaper tiers of the auditorium for soliciting. Theatre managers who sought to build a respectable clientele sometimes banned unaccompanied women in order to persuade women in families to attend. They promoted their theatres as agreeable places of family resort, especially suitable for ladies and children and, by implication, vigilantly guarded from the contaminations of the brothel trade. Even more important was the affirmation of respectability in what was presented on stage, since the temptation to cater to the lowest common denominator of male taste was always there.

If the brothel infiltrated the theatre, the theatre also entered the brothel, which developed its own forms of variety. Besides offering singing and dancing routines as excuses for physical display, brothel managers took to identifying their establishments with particular forms of role-play. Directories circulated for the New York brothels with listings for Mrs Hathaway's fair Quakeresses, Mrs Everett's beautiful senoritas and Miss Lizzie Wright's French belles.[11] Such role-play catered to clients who sought to indulge their fantasies, often in ways that blended the promise of physical gratification with elite domestic scenography. George Foster describes 'one of the most expensive and "aristocratic" homes of vice', a white carpeted parlour lit by a magnificent chandelier and decorated with colour-co-ordinated bouquets of flowers. The votaries in this 'modern temple to Aphrodite' are reflected in a vast Louis Quatorze mirror:

> Some are arrayed in the latest Parisian style, according to the cuts in Sartain's magazine – while others emulate . . . the Undine lately appearing in its pages, or the young lady combing her hair on the margin of the fountain of Vaucluse – her only garment having discovered the laws of gravity and slipped. On the sofa opposite the piano is a Miss in short frock and pantelettes who passes for fifteen.[12]

The temple of Aphrodite was in commercial terms the opposite extreme of the Walhalla where Foster saw 'Venus rising from the sea', revealed in her tin bath behind a filthy green rag of curtain, but the commitment to theatricality was central to both establishments, as was the sense that these were secret places, cordoned off from the legitimate social venues of the city. Those who worked in them could gain temporary prosperity, but this soon ran out as they grew older, or came to an abrupt end if they became sick. Prostitution offered no avenues of promotion and there was no route from the brothel back into society. For most women who had to resort to it, it was a terminal profession. Victorian social taxonomies relegated the prostitute to the lowest echelons; she might rise temporarily above criminals and vagrants in economic terms, but only by sinking even lower than they in the moral order. Her agency was limited to the fatal choice of selling her virtue, and the word 'ruin' expressed the finality and irreversibility of this. She had by definition relinquished any prerogative for choosing a mate, since her role was to make herself available to be picked and chosen by all those able to pay her price. Yet, in the later decades of the nineteenth century, the cultures of the brothel proved adaptable to the public arena in some ways that defied all rationalist assumptions about the controlling principles of a highly evolved civilisation.

Certain women began to gain notoriety through their ability to transform licentiousness into a theatrical currency so profitable and so potent in its influence on male spectators of all classes that they had become *de facto* duchesses, able to pick and choose between aristocratic suitors. From a Darwinian point of view, these stellar *demi-mondaines* were paradoxes in many ways. The rapidity and ostentatiousness with which they played their way to the top of the social scale (and often down again) made a mockery of the belief that social hierarchies were firmly rooted in a natural order which adhered to a law of steady and progressive change. They made their conquests by exuding animal sexuality but they were rationalists in the way they exercised choice over their suitors, being motivated by a quest for wealth and social cachet. Theatricality and role-play were the means of their success, even though in formal terms they may have been poor actresses. Indeed, in the case of such celebrities as Ada Isaacs Menken and Cora Pearl, the transparency of the pretence at acting served as a teasing veil over the physical exhibitionism that they and their slavish admirers well knew was the real purpose of the performance.

Menken and Pearl were contemporaries, but, since both were compulsive and highly unreliable autobiographers who gave variants on their birth dates and the circumstances of their upbringing, the parallels between them are easier to judge as matters of style than matters of fact. Whether or not either of them actually worked in a brothel in their youth, the cultures of the brothel were distinctly echoed in their sense of persona and their attitudes to male desire. The careers of both were fuelled by an interweave of precocious sexual experience and an instinctual flair for taking the stage. They led the way in creating a high-profile international market for the kinds of erotic role-play that had previously been confined to the brothel or to the private domain of the courtesan, and thus in creating new levels of celebrity and commercial value for the female stage icon. At the same time, they dismantled the historically precarious whore/actress divide by exercising their sexual power off stage, where it took devastating hold within the bastions of hereditary privilege, and then returning to the stage with a presence enhanced by the cachet of their widely publicised sexual conquests among the elite. They were a social taxonomist's nightmare, and a social Darwinist's fevered anxiety dream.

In the 1850s, Jenny Lind established the range of female stage personae acceptable to middle-class social values. Always demure and sweet-voiced, she appeared as a simple gypsy girl in a pastoral encampment, a shepherdess, the patriotic daughter of the regiment and, definitively, as La Somnambula swathed in clouds of white organza with her wide, innocent eyes vacant of expression. These roles were commemorated in sentimental porcelain figurines and other domestic accessories. By their very restrictions, they helped to define another set of personae celebrating all the female qualities they sought to exclude. At the height of Lind's career, Lola Montez was experimenting with this other set. On stage in her hallmark tarantella performances, Montez created 'the very poetry of avenging contempt . . . the head lifted and thrown back, the flashing eye, the fierce and protruded foot that crushed the insect'.[13] She was the dominatrix, the inflammatory Spanish gypsy, the daring horse-woman, expert with gun and whip. Off stage she played the courtesan, moving rapidly up the social scale to take on her most notorious role as mistress of Kind Ludwig I of Bavaria.

Montez became a role model for Ada Isaacs Menken, who emulated her Hispanic exoticism and her panache as a horsewoman. Like Montez, Menken found her way out of an unhappy early marriage and into a condition of economic and social independence by making herself into a successful theatrical commodity. This in turn enhanced her value to prospective partners so that she was able to exchange the role of deserted wife and mistress for that of the *femme fatale* who accepts and rejects entirely on her own terms. In her approach to sexual partnering she was taking on male forms of agency, but this was not the only way in which she experimented with masculine prerogatives. Her capacities as an actress were limited, but what talent she had lay in the direction of imperson-ation, especially male impersonation, which enabled her to incorporate athletically adventurous elements into her performances, besides providing a pretext for wearing short tunics to show off her much admired legs.

She was successful in a range of protean comedies, including one she claimed to have written herself entitled *Three Fast Women*. The plot concerned three women who sought to win back their dissolute husbands by dressing as men and following them into various dis-reputable haunts, themselves acting as swaggering youths, drunken sailors or wise-cracking rakes in order to blend in.[14] This was effec-tively a demonstration of Menken's strategy in life, which was to adopt the most demonstrative and expansive aspects of male behav-iour in order to heighten her impact as a desirable woman. The effect was at its most powerful in her performance in the title role of *Mazeppa*, a stage adaptation of Byron's poem. With her short black hair, vivid complexion and mesmeric eyes, Menken looked a little like Byron, and she clearly relished impersonating the adventurer whose high-voltage sexual attentions were so notoriously sought after. The role was normally played by a man for obvious reasons, not least of which was that the performer was required to engage in an act of bravado in the climactic scene. Captured by barbarous enemies, the hero is stripped, tied to the back of a wild horse, and sent off into the wilderness. Menken took the stripping and the riding more seriously than any of her male precursors in the part, daring to appear in cleverly minimal clothing that gave the impression of nudity and to take the wild ride in the most dangerous position, laid out back-to-back over the horse. The fusion of feminine exposure with masculine daring was apparently irresistible to audiences schooled to admire the most stringent forms of gender dualism.

Menken was nothing if not contradictory. While she collected gifts of heirloom jewellery from her admirers and spent her astronomical salary on an equipage in which to drive around London's Hyde Park with the best of the British aristocracy, she poured out a stream of abject self-pity in her poetry:

> 'My heritage!' It is to live within
> The marts of Pleasure and of Gain, yet be
> No willing worshipper at either shrine;
> To think, and speak, and act, not for my pleasure,
> But others'. The veriest slave of time and circumstances.
> Fortune's toy![15]

It was as if she needed to deny the agency she had achieved and revert to the conventional determinism of the eternal victim, though such fulsome self-dramatisations can also be read as expressions of the protean poseur in yet another guise.

Actresses like Mary Gannon exercised their protean virtuosity on the range of stage characters they could impersonate, but Menken transferred the protean impulse from character to persona, so that the game became one of constant self-invention and reinvention, conducted off stage as well as on it. This meant that there was no 'real' person to which the diversified impersonations would return. Ada Isaacs Menken was an adopted name accessorised with a largely invented life history. What she turned herself into was determined by the potential markets in which gains could be made, and in this sense her proteanism belonged quintessentially to the traditions of whoredom. At the same time, however, by creating new varieties of woman on stage and acting as a 'new free female species' off it, she also changed the terms on which the commerce between the sexes was traditionally conducted.[16] The dissenting voices were stern, but there was an edge of desperation in their tone that suggested they feared losing the struggle:

> It bodes an evil day for society in England, when it must be recorded that the theatre has been crammed to suffocation every evening during the past week by crowds of well-dressed people, a great number of whom had evidently gone with the hope of gratifying a prurient taste and gloating over a nudeness passing the bounds of propriety .... The exhibition is as low as it can be.[17]

Although Menken demonstrated repeatedly that she was prepared to run the gauntlet of the moralists, her melancholic writings are evidence that she was not immune to the punitive attitudes towards her as a woman who broke the rules. Cora Pearl left no such poetic expressions of misgiving. According to her biographer Baroness Von Hutton, Pearl feared nobody's condemnation because she had a genius for turning judgement inside out:

> realising her own defects, recognising the badness of her manners, her ignorance, the ugliness of her voice, what did she do? ... She exaggerated her coarseness, her loudness, her vulgarity. She created, in short, a new genre: the *genre d'écurie*; the 'genre Cora Pearl'.[18]

As an autobiographer, Pearl was as inventive as Menken and embroidered the difficulties of her early life so as to exaggerate the impression of a sharp upward trajectory.

Born in Plymouth, England, and originally named Emma Crouch, she was a late arrival in a family of sixteen children. By her own account, her father, at one time a promising composer, drank his way steadily to an early death while her mother battled to keep the children above poverty from what she earned as a concert singer. When the battle became too much, Emma was sent to London to live with a grandmother who alternately neglected her and subjected her to 'interminable lectures'. At the age of 14, she was accosted on her way home from church by a smartly dressed man who lured her to an apartment where she was drugged and raped. Further humiliated by the paltry recompense he offered, she tracked him down and found out that he was a diamond merchant. This episode, she says, instilled in her a lifelong resentment against men and launched her on a campaign of compensatory liaisons, in which it was she who created the humiliations and she who collected the diamonds.[19] She learned to pick and choose among available partners, playing one off against the other and in the process developing a persona that was an intoxicating blend of the princess and the tramp. As Cora Pearl, she moved to Paris with her first husband, then set out to work her way up the social scale by means of serial relationships, mythologising her own success by making the costs of these relationships – both emotional and financial – as public and as damaging to her lovers as possible.

Like Menken, she seems to have discovered that precocious sexual experience could be turned to advantage, though in Pearl's case, according to Sacheverell Sitwell's testimony, the suggestion of adolescent gaucherie was the secret of her appeal:

> A depraved and arrested childhood, which has still preserved its youthful health and high spirits, has been the means by which she has grown rich . . . Her pointed naïveté in all her dealings disconcerts and conquers men. She is twenty three years old, with nearly ten years experience behind her.[20]

Pearl's arrival on the scene in Paris caught the mood of the Second Empire as it reached its most capricious phase. This was the era of the *demi-monde,* the threshold society of pleasure-seekers escaping the hierarchical requirements of the social order for the theatres, hotels and bars that thrived as the underbelly of the city's economy. In such an environment those best adapted to survive were those whose skills lay in catering to the fantasies of others. Here Cora Pearl was a virtuoso who 'shed forth an aura or glamour of dissipation' or even 'an evil radiance' to which very few were immune.[21] She had not been in Paris long before the manager of the Bouffes Parisiens chose her to play Cupid in Offenbach's first full-scale operetta, *Orpheus in Hades* (1858).

The principal librettist for this work was Ludovic Halévy, a fierce social analyst who was satirising the decadence of his age even as he was providing a vehicle to cater to it. Halévy despised what he saw as a reckless dissipation of political power and control by the Napoleon family as they allowed themselves to be ruled by cupidity, squandering vast sums of money on their mistresses and neglecting the affairs of state while they pursued their other affairs. Cora Pearl, who a few years later was to become the mistress of Prince Napoleon (the Emperor's cousin), was the fatal choice for the Second Empire's Cupid, dressed from head to toe in jewels but wearing little else.

The stage Venus

In *La Belle Hélène* (1864), Halévy had turned the legend of Orpheus and Eurydice into a scathing political allegory in which Jupiter was a Napoleon figure driven by casual lusts and the rest of the Gods were sunk in pleasurable oblivion.[22] This left all power in the hands of the burlesque goddesses Venus and Cupid. His message was trenchant:

> Behold the state of Greece.
> It's one great bacchanalia,
> And Venus, Venus Astarte
> Drives the eternal round.
> Pleasure and sensuality are all.
> Virtue, duty, honour, morals,
> Are swept away in the current.[23]

'It has long been observed,' wrote Carl Vogt, 'that among peoples progressing in civilization, the men are in advance of the women; while among those which are retrograding, the contrary is the case.'[24] In the dramatic worlds created by Halévy and Offenbach, failure of masculine governance and determination left the feminine to hold sway, while on the actual stage the female performers ensured that the erotic held sway over the thematic concerns of the dramatist. The stage was in this sense a treacherous medium: it promoted the priority of physical presence over moral or intellectual claims on the audience's attention.

The novelist and theatre critic Emile Zola produced an evolutionary reading of this phenomenon, but he blamed the creators of satirical operetta for contributing to it, since, in his view, popular entertainment forms were the means by which widespread social degeneracy was taking hold:

> A kind of nervous erethism is unhinging our gilded youth. Aristocrats and scions live in lamebrained mirth. They applaud the cheap tunes ground out by Messieurs Offenbach and Hervé, they exalt wretched tightrope dancers cavorting on the legitimate stage. Their mistresses are street urchins who drag them down to their level of language and feeling.[25]

Zola was one of a growing number of commentators at this time who began to characterise the ruling classes as drained of energy and vigour, neurasthenic. Even their mirth and excitement, he suggested, were merely feverish, and in this condition they were ready victims for female sexual predators. In his fiction, Zola replaced the classical notion of character as destiny with a view of anatomy as destiny. 'Physiological man' was the focus, in a social world held in a state of critical tension between the impetus of progress and the atavistic forces in human nature. This was his theme in the ambitious cycle of Rougon-Macquart novels, subtitled 'the natural and social history of a family', the first of which was published in the same year as *The Descent*:

> I study the ambitions and the appetites of a family striving to forge its path through the modern world, making super-human efforts, prevented from getting anywhere by its own nature and by the external influences upon it, touching success only to fall away again, ending up by producing veritable moral monstrosities.[26]

One of these moral monstrosities was the actress/courtesan Nana, subject of the ninth novel in the cycle, *Nana*, published in 1879. Just as Geoffroy Saint Hilaire regarded physical monstrosity as reversion to an earlier organic type, Zola regarded moral monstrosity as the resurgence of primitive motivations. Nana was 'the fly that had come from the dungheap of the slums, carrying the ferment of social decay' but she was also a creature of the stage, who concealed her nature beneath the fatally delusive persona of the burlesque Venus.[27]

In *Nana*, Zola is polemically explicit in portraying his anti-heroine as 'a force of Nature' whose trail of destruction reveals that female sexuality is the very principle of degeneracy, working to reverse all the gains of evolutionary progress. He sets out to show that the social order is most vulnerable to destruction from an influence originating in the very lowest of its ranks. Nana is the child of a washerwoman and a drunkard, and her earliest experience of the social struggle is gained roaming the streets in the hopes of earning a five-franc piece. At the height of her career, this product of 'the dungheap of the slums' has become 'a woman of fashion, a beneficiary of male stupidity and lust, an aristocrat in the ranks of her calling'. When she drives out in her fine carriage, people identify her to each other 'with all the emotion of a nation saluting its sovereign'.[28] The brothel is in her blood, but the glittering trappings of wealth and position are in her head.

Entirely devoid of the intelligence and moral refinement that take hundreds of generations to evolve among the more elevated lineages of mankind, Nana divorces sex and money from all other values and sets them in exclusive relation to each other. At the same time, she demonstrates that men of the most elevated breeding will follow her in this, undoing the effects of centuries of refinement when they suddenly rediscover the primacy of animal instinct in themselves. As would-be lovers squander their energies and ruin their dignity in pursuit of her, their recklessness is most graphically expressed in their abject support for Nana's habit of literally throwing money away. 'Stories were told of crazy whims and fancies, of gold scattered to the four winds . . . of a handful of diamonds thrown on the fire during an evening's drunkenness in order to see whether they would burn like coal.'[29] Such stories echo those told of (and by) Cora Pearl, who recorded the extravagance of her admirers – and her own indifference to it – as a way of taking the measure of her sexual power. On one occasion she was sent a parcel of *marrons glacés*, individually wrapped in thousand-franc notes. 'The intention was commendable,' she commented, 'but the *marrons* were worthless.'[30] Her policy statement on such matters was more assertive than defensive:

> If coins were made to roll and diamonds to sparkle, no-one can reproach me with having diverted these fine things from their purpose: I sparkled with the one, and rolled with the other. It was all part of the system, and I sinned only in being too fond of the system, giving back into circulation that which was Caesar's, and to my creditors what was no longer mine. Honour and justice were satisfied. I never wronged anyone because I never belonged to anyone. My independence has been my fortune.[31]

The Nana effect reached its height during the Universal Exhibition of 1867. As the aristocracy and crowned heads of Europe were drawn to witness the great celebration of progress, they encountered its nemesis at the centre of the public stage. Hortense Schneider, Offenbach's favourite leading lady and another of the models for Nana, had one of her greatest triumphs at this time in *The Grand Duchess of Gerolstein*, a role which promoted her to the status of Duchess off stage as well as on it. Cartoons showed all the foreign dignitaries who had come to Paris to visit the Exhibition queuing up to pay court to her. Zola's anxieties about the primordial feminine converge with his anxieties about theatre, shown to be the milieu in which Nana's power is lifted from ordinary to extraordinary degrees of impact. It is the crucible in which she is transformed from a common whore into a public icon. The opening scene of the novel is set in the Théâtre des Variétés, designated to the fourth and lowest tier of Parisian theatres in the ranking established by Napoleon I in 1806. The upper three tiers were classified according to particular theatrical forms – classical comedy and tragedy in the first, opera in the second and comic opera in the third – but the fourth fell outside the taxonomy as institutions of indeterminate purpose, readily prostituted to the public tastes of the moment.[32] Zola suggests a radically symbiotic relationship between the theatre and the whore. In the first chapter of *Nana*, the manager of the Théâtre des Variétés is showing some gentlemen around the premises, and every time they make some remark about his theatre he corrects them: 'You mean my brothel.' This theatre is a brothel not just by virtue of its role as a place in which women are on display and assignations are made, but more fundamentally as the home of the operetta, which, in Zola's view, is the quintessence of depraved taste.

In his theatre criticism, Zola is savage about this form, declaring it 'a public enemy which, like a dangerous beast, should have its windpipe crushed'.[33] Those seduced by it are condemned for reneging on the struggle that has created progress, giving themselves wilfully to be blinded to changing environmental conditions at a time when the adaptive response of a scientific consciousness is imperative for the future of the race. Seeking an antidote for the social poison of libidinous theatre, Zola advocates the creation of fiction and drama on the strictly scientific principles of observation, research, experimental testing and analysis. In *Nana*, he uses the form of the novel to present a meticulously researched analysis of the social effects of the operetta and its courtesan star. His commitment to putting 'physiological man' under scrutiny begins with the investigation of environmental conditions. Zola's research for *Nana* included tours of the backstage areas in the Théâtre des Variétés, with his friend Halévy as guide, so that he could describe a performance in progress both from the auditorium and from behind the scenes.[34]

Zola's narrative accentuates the mismatch between the working areas behind the stage and the pseudo-environments on it. The medium of the theatre is seen to belie the formative influences of environment and embodiment, even as it concentrates their power.

Nana is posed as Venus on 'a cardboard Olympus, with clouds in the wings and Jupiter's throne on the right'.[35] Through its very denial of natural life, this tacky spectacle provocatively accentuates the physicality of the performers, and of Nana in particular. Nana's performance is technically incompetent and this too has the effect of accentuating her physical presence. Her embodiment is her sole asset on stage, and the more acutely it clashes with the mock-classical images in the charade that frames it, the more directly its power works on the audience:

> When she came to the end of the verse, her voice failed her completely, and she realised that she would never get through the whole song. So, without getting flustered, she thrust out one hip which was roundly outlined under a flimsy tunic, bent backwards, so that her breasts were shown to good advantage, and stretched out her arms. Applause burst forth on all sides. In the twinkling of an eye she had turned round and was going upstage, revealing the nape of her neck to the audience, a neck on which her reddish hair looked like an animal fleece. Then the applause became positively frantic.[36]

La bête humaine thus aroused in the audience manifests itself as a creeping hysteria. Their adulation is a response to the animal in Nana, whose very name, whispered like a mantra among them as they wait for her appearances, induces a state of infantilism. The whole show is designed to release them from the civilising disciplines of classical aesthetics, and the experience of conquering this audience leaves Nana herself 'sure of her future and wanting to shed her old skin'.[37]

In his fifth chapter, Zola follows the same performance through again, this time from behind the scenes where Nana, dishevelled and less than half-dressed, holds court before a marquis, a count and a prince. Description lingers on the trapped and overheated air, the glue on the back of the scenery, the chorus-girls' grubby clothing, the spilled paints and powders on the make-up table. Nana's cultivated male admirers, trained to relate to the world first and foremost through their eyes and ears, find themselves suddenly overwhelmed by the predominance of the sense of smell around her. The smell 'peculiar to the wings of a theatre' – an overpowering blend of sweaty clothing, acrid toilet water, soap and human breath – signals the dangerous presence of physiological woman.[38] Zola aims to make a scientific point about this backstage chemistry: it produces a toxicity whose effects spread far beyond the local, since they alter the balance between the cerebral and the sensory in the human brain, causing 'a great downward rush in the direction of fleshly madness'.[39]

As his biographer Frederick Brown points out, Zola was addressing anxieties that were becoming acute in his own social milieu: 'Just as evolutionary theory degraded mankind in general by linking it to bestial origins, so revolutionary doctrine raised the specter of a primitive horde subverting the middle class.' Brown cites the views of historian Adeline Daumard, who characterised the Parisian bourgeoisie as gripped by a 'siege mentality' and driven 'to disavow whatever elements of the primitive or the irrational survived in the civilization of their age'.[40] Although Zola set out to analyse these anxieties, he was also subject to them. He claimed to 'dislike classifications, as they always do violence to people and things', but the symbolic function of Nana exemplifies just such violence.[41] In his conceptualisation of the character, he made the classic ethnologist's error of assuming certain categorical incapabilities in those assigned to the lowest levels of the human order. Nana is a 'bird brain' whose chatty remarks about the smallness of her own skull reflect the research findings of craniometrists who set out to prove the evolutionary backwardness of woman.[42]

By presenting Nana as fundamentally stupid, Zola forecloses any serious consideration of her qualities or her impact as social performer. In his representation, the Nana-effect is simply a demonstration of anatomy as destiny, working to the exclusion of any sophisticated human agency. On stage, it is no more than an exhibition of mass cultural pathology for which the very absence of performance skills is one of the enabling conditions. But the talent of the stage Venus was precisely in her capacity to convert nudity into a commodity that travelled upmarket, through burlesque echoes of higher aesthetics. While she flagrantly breached these aesthetic codes, she also winked at them in a way that signalled close acquaintance. Sacheverell Sitwell records an eyewitness account of one of Cora Pearl's special 'at homes' for gentlemen:

> Cora Pearl was lying on a sofa, the focus of a hemicycle of diplomatists, senators and academicians, all seated with their chins leaning on gold knobbed walking sticks, their yellow gloves placed in the 'cylindres' at their sides, upon the floor. The Prince represented his 'jeunes amis', and they joined the hemicycle.

What they were contemplating, says Sitwell (writing in the 1930s), was an icon belonging strictly to the era:

> Heavy draperies, the velvet curtains of Garnier's Opera, descend from the cornice. This naked goddess, and it is necessary to think once more of the Olympia of Manet, has the curves and contours that present taste does not admire. She is sunning herself, like a lioness, and is silent and impels silence on those around her.[43]

This was brothel theatre outrageously elevated in the social order, and with its power dynamics reversed.

Zola takes a uniquely dismal view of the reversal. 'The day some woman conceives the brilliant idea of running around a stage naked on all fours and acting the part of a stray bitch,' he remarked after seeing a new operetta, 'that will be the day Paris cheers itself sick.'[44] Behind the image of Nana as Venus is the spectre of another Venus, who really was displayed naked and running around like an animal. This was Saartje Baartman, known as the Hottentot Venus. Baartman was first put on show in Piccadilly in London in 1810, and subsequently in Paris. The behaviour of her visitors shocked many observers, who recorded that she was allowed to be poked, that coins were thrown at her, and that she was dressed in minimal clothing designed to accentuate her highly developed buttocks, the main object of general curiosity. In London, there was a formal protest by the Secretary of the African Association, who stated that when he attended the exhibition:

> he there found a stage raised about three feet from the floor, with a cage, or enclosed place at the end of it; that the Hottentot was within the cage; that on being ordered by her keeper, she came out, and that her appearance was highly offensive to decency . . . . The Hottentot was produced like a wild beast, and ordered to move backwards and forwards and come out and go into her cage, more like a bear on a chain than a human being.[45]

In Paris she seems to have been persuaded to perform through flattery rather than bullying. 'Some sweets are given to her in order to induce her to leap and sing, and she is informed that she is the prettiest woman in society.'[46] Those who were most excited by this spectacle were the men of science, the kind Zola would have looked to for immunity to the sexual hysteria sweeping Paris during the decline of the Second Empire. Georges Cuvier and Geoffroy Saint-Hilaire examined her naked while she was alive, and Cuvier eagerly awaited the even more fascinating experience of dissecting her post-mortem.

Their reports display a prurient if not pathological curiosity about their subject's buttocks, breasts and genitalia, together with a line of commentary based on comparisons with the monkey and the orang-utan. In a recent study of the black Venus in France, T. Denean Sharpley-Whiting suggests that this obsession with Baartman's anatomy was a formative element in nineteenth-century French discourses about prostitution in general. Like Cuvier and Geoffroy, she says, Zola 'dissects and reads bodies in order to reveal propensities', and accordingly portrays the 'devouring sexuality' of Nana as racially and hereditarily determined.[47] Chronologically, only some three generations separate the literary creation of Nana from exhibition of the Hottentot Venus, but the association between them sets up deeper resonances of original human nature in Zola's fiction.

The beast actor

The cultural anxieties provoked by the stage Venus were gender-specific, but perhaps there was something atavistic about any kind of powerful stage presence. The call for evolutionary naturalism in acting, which Zola led in the early 1880s, may be seen as a new phase in a traditional debate about the balance between animal power and conscious craft in performance.

In his treatise on *Naturalism in the Theatre* (1881), Zola states that 'the great naturalist evolution . . . consists entirely in the gradual substitution of physiological man for metaphysical man'.[48] As his imagination gets to work on physiological man – and woman – he discovers *la bête humaine*, the bestial human situated at the animal edge of the species. Zola was as strident in his calls for *la bête humaine* to be taken off the stage as he was in his insistence that *l'homme physiologique* should be put on it, and here his portrayal of the Nana-effect points to a fundamental confusion in his evolutionary thesis about naturalism in the theatre. He wanted actors to break free of the codes and formulae taught to them at the Conservatoire and to portray full-blooded humanity, yet how was physiological man, whose anatomy was destiny and whose adventures were moderated by environmental determinants, to be kept from sliding down to the level of the beast, taking the whole representational apparatus of the theatre with him? Such anxieties underpin the rhetoric of Zola's essay on naturalism in the theatre, and although they do not surface explicitly in mistrustful views of the actor, they are evident in his quite explicit mistrust of audiences. The rallying cry of the crowd, he says, is always 'Lower! Lower!'[49]

The giant step forward – and upward – in the evolution of dramatic art must be made by 'a man of genius', a dramatist who can in every sense author the manifestation of physiological man on stage. 'And what an immense place this innovator would take in our dramatic literature! He would be at the summit.'[50] He would herd the bestial masses, whip in hand. This creator-evolutionist must make a new world in which the elements are drawn from life. An 'imperishable glory' awaits him in this work, but it is dangerous work. When he takes the clay of human nature in his hands, he may reveal the sedimentations in its deepest strata, but if he releases their energies, these will need to be kept under intellectual control so that they cannot run riot as they have done in response to the incitements of Queen Venus in the operetta.

If Zola's evangelical call for a naturalist revolution is fraught with contradictory insistences, the confusion is endemic to his subject. Five years previously, George Henry Lewes identified the problem in a collection of writings on actors and acting, about which, he said, the state of opinion was generally 'chaotic', with the most acute area of confusion being that of natural acting.[51] Zola's criticisms and appreciations of contemporary actors are oriented towards identification of where they have succeeded or failed in breaking free of codified forms of representation. Here, Lewes – whose primary focus is the actor – brings a very different perspective to the problem of naturalism in theatre. The actors he most admires – Edmund Kean, Frederic Lemaître, the French tragedians Talma and Rachel – are those whose energies carry the strongest animal and elemental power, but while he sees the actor as a channel for animal energies, Lewes also insists that s/he is a representational artist who must deal in 'symbols universally intelligible'.[52]

Where Zola regards codes of representation as alien excrescences to be shaken off, Lewes sees them as the very foundation of the actor's art. Both writers are deeply interested in evolutionary theory, but they draw different kinds of imperatives from their commitment to scientific modes of thought. To Lewes, the art of acting is an art of expression, which must have its origins in genuine feeling and experience, but must then be translated into communicable forms suited to the medium of theatre. The actor must pull back from the original feeling in order to select and craft its expression. The mere presence of genuine emotion during a performance, says Lewes, 'would be such a disturbance of the intellectual equilibrium as entirely to frustrate artistic expression'.[53] He sees the problem of bad acting as a complex one, since the art of the actor requires finely modulated judgement and technique. The actor needs, then, to draw on observation and experience in order to vitalise the code of expression which is his or her art, but there are no clear instructions to follow in this process:

> I have always emphatically insisted on the necessity of actors being true to nature in the expression of natural emotions, although technical conditions of the art forbid the expressions being exactly those of real life.[54]

'Naturalness in acting', says Lewes, 'is not the mere foisting of commonplace manner on the stage' and at the core of the actor's art is the double-bind problem of theatrical expression, which demands artifice in order to communicate truth.[55] This is 'the contradiction that perplexes judgement'.[56] Zola is confused not because he sees the perplexity, but because he does not. He posits a set of dichotomies – abstract man and physiological man, fixed rule and natural law, formulaic constraint and 'the great free air of reality' – in which one side violates the principles of naturalism, while the other carries them forward. For the actor who wants to escape the typical forms of bad theatre, it is simply a matter of making the right choice between the options. For Zola, observation and experience are in themselves enough to transform the art, and those who have this aim have only to follow Darwin 'who has upset all the old tenets, to open up a new path in which science is moving onward'.[57]

The goal is to see 'the abstract personage disappear to give place to the real man of blood and muscle'.[58] But the codes, the formulae and the conventions stand in the way. 'There is a physiognomic recipe for astonishment, one for terror, one for admiration, and so on, a whole collection of physiognomic recipes' that can be mastered by the most mediocre players, so perpetuating the reign of 'abstract man' on the stage.[59] Where did these recipes come from? The regimes of gesture and expression taught to actors were not, as Zola proclaims, based on 'abstract' views of human nature, but had their origins in studies informed by Linnaean taxonomy, comparative anatomy, physiognomy and zoology. As Joseph Roach cautions in his historical study of the scientific ideas underpinning the player's passion, 'the elaborate network of inhibitions called theatrical decorum . . . should not be understood as a capricious etiquette imposed by some bloodless notion of style'.[60]

Sketches of the facial expressions corresponding with the five 'universal passions' were included in Buffon's *Histoire Naturelle* (1749), where they were presented in relation to an enquiry into the causes of anatomical difference between species. David Garrick's 'Essay on Acting' (1744) was influenced by the work of George Christoph Lichtenberg, a professor of experimental physics, who wanted to establish a semiotics of affects on scientific principles.[61] One of the most influential eighteenth-century expositors of playing as a science was John Hill, whom Roach describes as 'physician, actor, playwright, pharmacist, botanist and prolific author on many scientific and medical topics'.[62] Hill's *General Natural History* (1748–52) was a major three-volume work that introduced Linnaean taxonomy to England; he was also a contributor to Diderot's *Encyclopaedia*, and translated an important French treatise on acting by Pierre Remond de Saint-Albine, a contribution that, according to Roach, 'brought theatrical theory in line with current science'.[63]

Zola, in his stylish and impassioned way, fails to recognise that the very conventions he is condemning first arose in just the spirit of scientific observation and experiment he advocates, but he does admit that what he is calling for is nothing new: every age has had its calls for reversion to the natural in aesthetics. He is ready enough to say that he is following in Diderot's wake, but insists that the naturalist imperative remains urgent and current, and therefore needs new champions. One wonders how carefully he had actually read Diderot's major treatise on theatre – *The Paradox of Acting* (1773) – since even the significance of its title seems to have escaped him. It is Lewes rather than Zola who restates Diderot's doctrine for the later nineteenth-century, echoing the terms of his paradox in a discussion of the contradictions inherent in the actor's art. Diderot consistently values technique in the actor over spontaneity: the paradox is a doubleness that must always underpin the actor's performance: 'He's listening to his own voice at the very moment he moves us, and his talent consists not, as you suppose, in feeling, but rather in rendering so meticulously the exterior signs of feeling, that you're taken in by it.'[64] The actor must maintain this 'double personality' – a term which became a catchphrase in nineteenth-century discussions of acting in France – as a dominant investment in the outward signs, which can only be effective if they are part of a system. Diderot does not deny that the actor can acquire or

169

simulate 'a kind of visceral mobility', but this, he says, 'is almost as dangerous as cultivating natural sensibility'.[65] The capacity to distance oneself from feeling is a mark of superiority: the actor, like the man of judgement in the social arena, is the one whose cool head allows him to stand apart from the crowd in a street disturbance. Through the actor's command over the chaos of human reactions, the stage becomes a medium for the promotion of cultural evolution: 'Your street scene is to the stage scene as a hoard of savages to an assembly of civilised men.'[66]

Between the mid-seventeenth and the later nineteenth century, the relationship between judgement and impulse was considered through changing frames of interpretation. Roach draws particular attention to this, and suggests that the works of Diderot and then of Darwin mark paradigm shifts in the meanings attached to nature and the natural. Diderot anticipated Darwin in many ways. His studies of anatomy and medicine made him a convinced transformationist before Geoffroy or Lamarck had given the term general academic currency. In his writings on physiology, Diderot puts forward a version of adaptation theory, as Roach notes, giving sensibility a central role in mediating between creatures and their environment.[67] Yet in his writings on acting, sensibility is characterised as something belonging to animal humanity, a retarding and destabilising influence:

> Sensibility, it seems to me . . . is a tendency that accompanies organic weakness, a consequence of mobility in the diaphragm, an overheated imagination, delicacy in the nerves; a tendency to empathise, to get the shivers, to wonder, to fear, to be moved, to cry, to faint, to shake, to flee, to shout, to lose reason, to exaggerate, to mistrust, to despise, to have no clear idea of truth or of the good and the beautiful, to be unjust, to be mad.

When the poet engenders 'the terrible beast' and the great actress Clairon makes it bellow, neither descends into bestial nature in order to create the effect.[68]

Later evolutionists broke down the generalised concept of 'sensibility' to identify developmental stages in the emotional tendencies of human beings. Herbert Spencer posits a scale of emotional development, the lower end of which (demonstrated in the behaviours of primitive races) is characterised by impulsiveness, reflex reaction, demonstrativeness and spontaneous, short-term excitability.

Gradually, the 'degrees and durations of social discipline' get to work on the 'fundamental trait of impulsiveness', promoting the evolution of more measured and complex responses, mediated by the organising activities of the intellect.[69] Diderot is thinking along the same lines, but without the concept of developmentalism to organise his account. Actors, he says, are specialists in mediated sensibility, who 'make an impression not when they are furious, but when they play fury well'.[70] In Spencer's framework of analysis, this means being able to conceive in the abstract of something called 'fury' through an exercise in classificatory thinking which involves identifying the defining properties of the state of fury, its outward signs and its motivating causes.

Lewes appreciates this art of abstraction, but while he stresses that 'fitful impulse' must always be subordinate to 'nice calculation' in a performance, he also writes of the 'animal power' of the actor. Indeed, in spite of his repeated theoretical statements about the actor as a technician of human expression, Lewes seems far more warmly engaged as a writer when he is describing the work of actors whose performances are charged with animal and elemental energies. He has a memory from his youth of seeing Edmund Kean as Othello:

> In the successive unfolding of these great scenes he repre-
> sented with incomparable effect the lion-like fury, the deep
> and haggard pathos, the forlorn sense of desolation, alter-
> nating with gusts of stormy cries for vengeance, the
> misgivings and sudden reassurances, the calm and deadly
> resolution of one not easily moved, but who, being moved
> was stirred to the very depths.[71]

The performance was technically flawed, he admits, but was 'irradiated with such flashes' that he would 'again risk broken ribs for the chance of a good place in the pit to see anything like it'.[72] One of Kean's greatest skills was in capturing the effect of 'subsiding emotion':

> The waves are not stilled when the storm has passed away.
> There remains the ground-swell troubling the deeps. In
> watching Kean's quivering muscles and altered tones you
> felt the subsidence of passion. The voice was calm but there
> was a tremor in it; the face might be quiet, but there were
> vanishing traces of the recent agitation.[73]

Kean is channelling elemental forces. The 'rush of mighty power' he brings to the stage evokes the ravening beast and the wild sea, and Lewes wants to be carried away by it, but he also wants to claim that nobody here has lost control. Kean is 'a consummate master of passionate expression'.[74]

Perhaps at some level Lewes was a little nervous about the actor's capacity to release the human beast. Here it is worth recalling Fanny Kemble's comments on acting and wildness. Writing in the early 1860s at a time when the debate on passion and control was raging everywhere, Kemble demonstrates an almost startling independence of vision. In general, contributors to the debate divided themselves approximately into those who felt immediate passion should be excluded from performance altogether and those (like Lewes and the great actor Talma) who felt it was an essential element in great acting, provided it was truly 'mastered'. Anxieties about the resurgence of primitive and animal tendencies are clearly at the heart of the debate on both sides. Kemble shows no such anxiety and is actually prepared to argue that there is too much mastery going on. She warns against 'the various adverse influences of a state of civilization and society which fosters a genuine dislike of exhibitions of emotion', and contends that 'our stage is and must be supplied, if supplied at all, by persons less sophisticated and less civilized'.[75]

Many nineteenth-century critics had creeping misgivings that indeed actors were, fundamentally, persons less sophisticated and less civilised. From Lewes' account, one gets the strong impression that the most compelling actors were themselves half-beast, and their lure was the lure of the low, always threatening to break free of the technical mastery with which it was overlaid. Among the luminaries of classical acting there were more than a few who had started their careers as acrobats and street performers, making a physical spectacle of themselves. Every generation had its 'beast actors' famed for their virtuoso displays of animal energy: David Garrick, Talma, Rachel (described by Lewes as 'the panther of the stage'), Edmund Kean, Frederick Lemaître, Edwin Forest, Henry Irving. In an innovative study of theatricality in the lives of the Victorians, Nina Auerbach remarks that 'the cult of the beast stimulated the cult of the actor' in ways that were linked with cultural anxieties about 'men who are inseparable from the animals they are supposed to have risen above'.[76]

The American actor Edwin Forrest established a style of physical acting in the 1840s that made him a cult figure among the New York Bowery B'hoys. He was described by detractors as 'a muscular tragedian of body without brains' and 'a vast animal bewildered by a grain of genius'.[77] Forrest studied anatomy with leading physicians and drew on this knowledge as the very basis of his art, adopting a muscles-first approach to training for his roles. He did rounds in the gymnasium with a punch-bag as a way of limbering up for *Macbeth* and *Spartacus*, in which he demonstrated to other cast members that 'powerful acting' meant literally knocking out his six assailants in a stage fight.[78] When he was not limbering up in the gymnasium, Forrest liked to visit asylums and talk to physicians who specialised in the study of the mad. Frederic Lemaître, another performer with 'great energy of animal passion', plumbed dangerous depths in his role as the scoundrel Robert Macaire. According to Lewes, there was something 'offensive to good taste' in Lemaître's acting, 'a note of vulgarity, partly owing to his daring animal spirits'.[79]

The most controversial and thrilling of the later nineteenth-century beast actors was Henry Irving, who himself played a heated role in the paradox debate. Irving, says Auerbach, 'with his aptitude for converting himself from the diabolical to the divine', carried about him the most unnerving suggestion of hybridity. He was the model for Bram Stoker's *Dracula*, the first of the great *fin-de-siècle* beast men of literature. As Irving's manager, Stoker had more than enough opportunity to observe the metamorphoses of the beast actor, and he left some resonant descriptions of them, like this one of the climactic scene in the melodrama *Eugene Aram* (1879): 'As Irving played it, the hunted man at bay was transformed from his gentleness to a ravening tiger; he looked the spirit of murder incarnate as he answered threat by threat.'[80]

Of all the actors who tried to bring together the art and science of expression, Irving was perhaps the most volatile experimentalist, verging towards horror rather than classical terror, and with a repertoire of physical behaviours that were always suggestive of a barely submerged savagery. The philosopher Mary Midgley's comments on the bestial/human divide seem especially relevant to the impact made by Irving. 'Human and humane are words of praise,' she says. 'Being inhuman is something terrible. It is easy from here to connect the notion of vice with other species. The use of words like bestial, beastly, shows how readily we do this.'[81] In illustrations from Irving's production of *Faust*, the scene in the witches' kitchen is a descent into the mixed nightmares of Freud and Darwin, with the witches portrayed as monkeys crouching and chattering on the floor of the cave. The fearsome potion bubbling away in their midst carries the ever active promise of bestial transformation.[82]

If Irving made his admirers nervous, this was because he threatened to dissolve the hierarchical relationships between instinct and intellect, primitive and modern. In Irving's technique, impulse and calculation were intricately cross-wired. His sense of human typology was itself like a predatory tracking instinct, helping him to sniff out the features and habits that would enable capture:

> He had studied individuality so thoroughly, and was so familiar with not only his apparent characteristics but with those secret manifestations which are in their very secrecy subtle indicators of individuality grafted on type, that he had recreated him – just as Cuvier or Owen could from a single bone reconstruct giant reptiles of the Palaeozoic age.[83]

Reconstituting ancient life forms was one thing, but reanimating them was another. From an evolutionist's point of view Irving was playing with fire, but in doing so he may have come closer than any other actor to a strictly Darwinian grasp of the problematics of expressive acting.

Darwin's own study of *The Expression of the Emotions in Man and Animals* upsets traditional distinctions between the intellect and the emotions. He focuses especially on the intricate combinations of small muscles involved in the typical expression of common emotional states, and points to the complex interplay of voluntary and involuntary muscular activity, together with associated breathing patterns, blood flow and the flow of what he calls 'nerve force' (which is what we might call adrenalin). The state of rage, for example, is characterised by a strongly marked frown, glaring eyes, clenched teeth, clenched fists and rapid speech, all of which could be voluntarily simulated. However, the mobility and animation with which these attitudes are invested produces a number of other manifestations that are entirely involuntary. These may include hairs bristling, pupils contracting, a rush of blood to the face, quivering nostrils and paralysed lips that 'refuse to obey the will'. There are further elements that hover between the voluntary and the involuntary, such as rapid breathing, trembling of the muscles and the effect of strangulation in the voice due to tension in the throat muscles.[84] Darwin acknowledges that people vary in their capacity for gaining voluntary control over the small sets of muscles involved in facial expression, and those who have high degrees of such control are especially useful to him in his observations. He describes them as good actors and notes that their facility is often hereditary, as in the case of the lady with the power 'to bring the grief muscles freely into play' who belonged 'to a family famous for having produced an extraordinary number of good actors and actresses'.[85] He evidently views the acting profession as specialists in the voluntarisation of spontaneous and reflex patterns of expression.

Darwin notes that many researchers who have specialised in the study of expression point to the role of thought in giving rise to emotions, sometimes quite unintentionally. He himself cites a number of instances of this, so illustrating that thought itself moves in and out of conscious control. There is thus no clear-cut relationship of control between the mental and emotional aspects of human response. Following this premise, the paradox of acting becomes more to do with the way the actor can trace a Moebius strip from deliberately thinking about something that may give rise to anger, so provoking the involuntary expressive symptoms of anger, then voluntarily selecting from among these in such a way as to produce a visually and aurally effective impression upon an audience. But this is not a smooth ride. The implication of Darwin's analysis is that no one who wishes even to simulate expressive states can stay safely in the zone of voluntary control. There must be points of abdication, leaps into the dark, moments of potentially reckless surrender to the animal energies of passion. The jerky style and aggravated texture of Irving's performances may bear witness to this.

The passions in which Irving specialised were those that crossed the borderline into ferocity. His definitive performance was in the melodrama *The Bells*, playing the role of a murderer haunted by uncanny reminders of his crime. Irving was celebrated for his capacity to carry the escalating intensity of the drama as his character, Mathias, moved in stages from subliminal fear through overt anguish and animal terror (his wolf-like howl was a high moment in the performance), into a tranced state of horror. As an actor, he took himself into the kinds of extreme expressive states that Darwin learned about through consulting physicians who specialised in the treatment of the insane. One of these was Henry Maudsley, himself a committed social evolutionist, who recorded that what he witnessed in the asylum prompted him to pose the question:

whence come 'the savage snarl, the destructive disposition, the obscene language, the wild howl, the offensive habits, displayed by some of the insane? Why should a human being, deprived of his reason, ever become so brutal in character, as some do, unless he has the brute nature within him?'[86]

Maudsley was also of the opinion that in the process of enactment, the emotion itself was 'intensified and made definite by the bodily action'. Darwin sets this point together with evidence provided by a hypnotist that states of passion may be induced by putting someone into the bodily attitudes suggesting them.[87] His own deduction is that:

> He who gives way to violent gestures will increase his rage; he who does not control the signs of fear will experience fear in a greater degree . . . . These results follow partly from the intimate relation which exists between almost all the emotions and their outward manifestations; and partly from the direct influence of exertion on the heart, and consequently on the brain.[88]

Where commentators on acting from Diderot to Lewes form their views on the assumption that emotion can be separated from expression, and that the latter can be manipulated at will, Darwin treats emotion and its expression as virtually the same thing. He also reverses the priority in their co-dependency, so that instead of seeing emotion as the substance and expression the shadow, he sees expression as the very matter of emotion.

So where does this leave the actor? Certainly not in the position Lewes wants to give him as 'perfect master of effects'.[89] The hereditary transmission of reactive patterns, Darwin insists, precludes any such level of control in any human being:

> I have often felt much difficulty about the proper application of the terms, will, consciousness, and intention. Actions, which were first voluntary, soon became habitual, and at last hereditary, and may then be performed even in opposition to the will.[90]

In many ways, the actor is him or herself the paradox that epitomises the emerging contradictions in social Darwinism. On the one hand, the actor is a throwback, playing with the primordial matter of human nature and continually threatening to raise the beast. On the other, he or she is purporting to be uniquely qualified in a form of voluntarism that may enable some control over this beast. The actor's art is to keep its resurgence under selective management, and to ensure the beast's return to confinement after it has been paraded for public view. Darwin hints that the second of these roles may be a logical impossibility, but since will and control remain areas where he acknowledges 'much difficulty' in coming to any conclusion, the hint remains just that.

Joseph Roach sees Darwin's *Expressions* as the trigger for a paradigm shift in the theory of acting, from a model in which the passions are regarded taxonomically as states that can be represented through fixed formulae of expression, to one in which the focus is on variation, mutation and interplay.[91] He points to André Antoine and William Archer as exponents of a new Darwinian interpretation of acting that is zoocentric, 'nourished from the depths of animal nature'.[92] There is an important and useful observation here, and one that is based on a subtlety of distinction that Zola, with his blanket attack on the formula, was not able to articulate. However, the complexities warrant further exploration. There is a tendency among late twentieth-century critics writing in a climate heavily dominated by the Darwin industry to portray Darwin as some kind of break-through point in human understanding. Roach focuses on a change in the vocabulary of performance criticism resulting from Darwin's influence, and emphasises how this opens out the terms in which passion and expression may be understood, so that acting can be seen as a dynamic living art, concerned not with the capture of states of feeling, but rather with the flows and transitions of human reaction. However, Darwin is concerned to identify complexities in the nature of these flows and transitions: he raises questions about what prompts them, what governs them, the paths they follow and the feedback loops they create between impulse on the one hand and conscious thought on the other. He does not reach a break-through point with these questions, but rather speculates in ways that are biased towards a materialistic and deterministic philosophy. The actor was in many ways the greatest challenge to this kind of determinism.

A spectator mentioned Irving's wolf-like howl as an unforgettable moment in *The Bells*. 'It makes my hair stand on end just to think of it', he recorded.[93] Here the very thought of a simulated expression of animal passion serves to create an instinctual physiological reaction. The reaction may be seen as a reflex hardwired into this man's anatomy as part of an ancient survival instinct, but there is also a sense in which Irving is the author of it. Actors lived and worked with the contradictions that loomed as crisis points in Darwin's system of interpretation. For William Archer, setting out to formulate a Darwinian theory of acting, the feedback loop between reflex and intention was not a critical issue at all, but something to be taken for granted: 'No one denies, I think, that the primary emotions of an imagined character do in fact tend to communicate themselves to the nerve centres of the actor, and to affect his organs of expression.'[94]

The reverse is also a commonplace fact to the profession, as evidenced by 'the practice, attributed to several great artists, of mechanically mobilising the nerve centres by means of that reaction from external manifestations of passion which Hartmann describes as "auto-suggestion"'.[95] Archer is drawing on Darwin's account here, but does not seem to recognise that the relationship between reflex and intention is much more problematic to Darwin than to himself. André Antoine, the actor-director who took up Zola's call for a naturalist revolution in the theatre, describes his mission in a statement that interweaves chance and human agency as if they are a seamless continuum:

> Here then the field of battle, the occupiers of the place to be won, the troupes ready for possible assault; but who would coordinate so many scattered elements? Who would give the signal? Quite simply, chance.[96]

When writing about actors, though, Antoine, like Zola, prefers to situate human agency with the author. He goes further, in fact, portraying actors as voided of any determining role:

> They are, in reality, mannequins, marionettes more or less perfect, depending on their talent, whom the author clothes and manipulates according to his whim . . . the actor's ideal must be to become a keyboard, a marvellously tuned instrument on which the author can play at will.[97]

He describes his own performance as Oswald in Ibsen's *Ghosts* as an act of self-abdication such that 'after the second act I remembered nothing, neither the audience nor the effect of the production, and, shaking and weakened, I was some time getting hold of myself again after the final curtain had fallen'.[98] The paradox here is in the presentation of the actor as someone who makes a voluntary renunciation of the will, and undertakes an intentional process of self-surrender.

The fears of the Diderot camp – that any such surrender would ruin the artistic dimensions of the performance – proved unfounded. Antoine's portrayal of Oswald was one of his greatest critical and popular triumphs. But the phenomenon of this kind of acting also calls the bluff on Darwinian speculations about the transgenerational dominance of reflex and nerve force over individual and conscious intention. Antoine is unable to regain a hold on himself 'for some time' after the performance, but the effect of the surrender is not permanent.

Antoine founded the Zola-inspired Théâtre Libre in Paris in 1887, employing mainly amateur actors who were free from the mannerisms instilled by formal training, and using the contents of his mother's house to furnish the stage. His repertoire in the first three years included dramatisations of stories by Zola and plays by Oscar Métenier, Leo Tolstoy and Henrik Ibsen, and was later to include new works by August Strindberg and Gerhart Hauptmann. These dramas had certain things in common: they portrayed tragedies emerging in the lives of middle- and lower-class people, and they had confined, small-scale settings that were redolent with the material details of everyday domestic and working lives. The passions they dealt in were not the high-flown archetypal states of anger, love, grief and terror, but those connected with the struggle for human survival in a hostile environment. These were the 'low' passions of greed, violence, lust, jealousy, fear and animal dominance, and they were played out between ordinary individuals. The dramatists associated with Antoine had in common an interest in questions of heredity and environment and an analytical concern with the pathologies and weaknesses of the human species as they were played out among families. With the domestic environment as the primary focus of their explorations, Antoine and his collaborators turned the stage into a room from which the fourth wall had been removed, to allow the audience to see into it, a space that shared the same optical and aural scale as the auditorium. The contents of a small sitting-room in a nearby street could be transferred to it without any problems of perspective, so that human voice and gesture could also be kept within their natural registers. From the actor's point of view, this meant that the details of emotional expression became as important as the broad outlines that could signal the grand passions.

In Darwin's analysis the involuntary manifestations of expression were often in its subtler aspects, such as sweating, blushing or blanching, twitching of small facial muscles, constriction of the throat, bristling of hairs. While these create only minor visual signals (such as would be missed in the optic of traditional staging), they are associated with more intense internal sensations than those larger movements of the face and limbs that are under voluntary control. A clenched fist and bared teeth are less immediately connected with affect than a blanched complexion and dry throat, but the cumulative impression of several small involuntary reactions is to convey to an observer that the body is charged with the energies of intense affect.

In the optic of naturalist staging, where the audience were positioned to register the human scale of the actor's body, an impression of 'nerve force' at work could have a powerful impact, as some actors proved. The observer's hair might stand on end as a sympathetic reflex reaction crept up on them. A Darwinian interpretation would suggest that both actor and spectator were experiencing a moment of throwback: physiological man was being tapped on the shoulder by the human beast. Yet Antoine's removal of the fourth wall at the Théâtre Libre did not leave the audience's perception unmediated. In the dramas he staged, forms of distancing were in operation, so that the glimpses offered of lower humanity were framed with intellectual concern. Ibsen and Tolstoy (especially in his *Power of Darkness*) devised theatrical techniques for conveying the deep histories behind critical events in the present and for suggesting the atavistic elements in human personality. Their plays were about characters whose lives were in the grip of hereditary criminality, alcoholism, promiscuity and mental illness, but those who acted them out were not supposed to be in the grip of these things other than for the duration of the performance. The Théâtre Libre's analytic concern with the motivating forces in human nature purported to be distinct from more prurient curiosities about what actually went on in those forbidden scenes of human interaction where violent and sexual impulses rose to the fore. This was the new paradox. Antoine's stage room allowed the primitive sedimentations of human nature to be released but also to be encased, or at least that was the intention.

The beast was not supposed to slip its confines and run riot in the civilised world, but Zola was right to be acutely mistrustful of its capacity to find escape routes, especially through the murky area of audience taste. Here, the lure of the low had its own powerful drag. What was to stop an audience becoming more interested in the gory details of the execution described in Oscar Métenier's *En Famille* than in the sociological insights to be gained from the narrative, especially as he was so well placed to cater to audience fascination with the more sensational aspects of Parisian low life? As former secretary to the Paris Police Commissioner, Métenier had inside knowledge of the kinds of characters and situations he featured in his plays, and had been known to draw his cast members from old acquaintances with long entries in the criminal records book. He once took Antoine to a private viewing of an execution, reputedly shocking him with the ambiguity of his own interests in violent death. In his five years with the police, Métenier became intimately acquainted with the roughest areas of Paris, getting to know the living conditions, mannerisms and speech rhythms of those who inhabited them. He also learned to identify with the battlers of the Paris underworld, seeing them as victims of heredity and environment and refusing to endorse the middle-class values according to which they were condemned. In this world, acts of violence were also acts of strength, crimes were feral survival strategies and prostitution a necessary resort for women whose hereditary lot had cast them adrift from the support systems of the bourgeois world. Métenier knew that prostitution usually began as a family affair, often starting in childhood – 'half the prostitutes in Paris had a brother or sometimes their father as their first lover' – and continuing as a vital means of financial support for small children and ageing parents.[99]

Métenier pioneered a new genre of documentary drama known as the *pièce rosse*. *Rosse* meant ruffian or thug, and *rosser* was to beat up. These plays were about life in the raw among the underclasses, and were usually structured to lead to a violent climax, so veering towards another new genre in which violence became an end in itself and any pretence of analytical detachment was dropped. In 1897, a decade after the inauguration of the Théâtre Libre, the naturalist movement spawned a bastard second progeny, the Théâtre du Grand Guignol, of which Métenier was one of the founders. The Grand Guignol adhered to the techniques and tenets of naturalism in many ways. To begin with, the new theatre employed the same dramatists: seven of the works in its first season were by writers who had contributed to Antoine's select repertoire.[100] It operated from a small, intimate theatre with a stage that replicated the proportions of a domestic room. Details of everyday living were evoked through minute attention to props and sound effects. Ideas for action and situation were drawn from newspaper reports of actual events in the criminal underworld. The portrayal of emotion was based on scientific studies of human expression, particularly those conducted in asylums for the insane, and characterisation was influenced by new psychological theories. Stock characters included the doctor, the policeman, the prostitute, the scorned mistress (with vitriol at the ready) and a gallery of assorted lunatics.[101] The name of the new theatre alluded to the 'guignol' puppet show and implied that the actors were giant puppets, an image that directly echoed Antoine's view of actors as marionettes, but here the departure point also became evident.

Antoine's marionettes were for the author to clothe and manipulate according to his whim. They were the instruments upon which he played. If the guignol actors were giving themselves up to possession and manipulation it was not to the genius of the author, but to the indelible mark of their lowly origins. Here fantasy and science were well and truly embroiled, as Peter Hutchings demonstrates in a new study of 'the criminal spectre' in late nineteenth-century discourses.[102] The darker mood of *fin-de-siècle* atavism is epitomised in a statement by Frederick Courtney Selous, an avid Darwinian who discovered profoundly troubling things about his own nature and impulses while fighting the Matabele in Rhodesia:

> in the smooth and easy course of civilised existence it is possible for a man to live a long life without ever becoming aware that somewhere deep down below the polished surface of conventionality there exists in him an ineradicable leaven of innate ferocity, which, although it may never show itself except under the most exceptional circumstances, must and ever will be there – the cruel instinct which, given sufficient provocation, prompts the meekest nature to kill its enemy – the instinct which forms the connecting link between the nature of man and that of beast.[103]

This extraordinary meditation situates the savage, the monster and the missing link within, where they had always belonged.

So, too, did the Théâtre du Grand Guignol, which in every sense brought the beast home: into the domestic arena and 'the heart of an apparently rational social order'.[104] Here Freud met Darwin in a return of the repressed that drew its power from the deepest repositories of the human psyche, as all emotions were subsumed in the single overriding affect of terror, and all impulses slid towards the baseline drives of lust and murder. The idea of a return of the repressed, in evolutionary as well as psychoanalytic terms, was brought out in one of the key texts of the Grand Guignol movement, André de Lorde's 'The Theatre of Horror' (1909), whose evocative Preface celebrated terror 'elevated to the status of a natural law'. The cry went up, 'Who is going to give us back our fear, our lost fear, the fear that stuns, the great fear of our ancestors?'[105] This primordial terror was a kind of genius in itself.

Zola chose *La bête humaine* as the title for what is perhaps the grimmest of all the twenty novels in the Rougon-Macquart cycle. The story begins with a hideous episode of domestic violence, and the plot develops through the inextricable linkage of violence and sexuality. At least three of its characters are presented as potential killers, but the real serial killer is heredity itself, tainting one generation after the other with the overwhelming compulsion to murder. Such compulsions were the driving force of the Grand Guignol, where the beast was no longer what it had been in the fairgrounds, an objectified figure to be gawped at. It became a transformative energy that could generate horrifying images in sudden, unpredictable turns of events. Instead of bringing down the curtain between the audience and the ultimate scene of horror, the Grand Guignol drew the spectators in, implicating them as witnessing presences. Victor Emeljanow stresses the significance of this. 'Violence must be seen and shared, thereby stripping away the veneer of middle-class theatregoing conformity.'[106] To watch was to want to watch, and patrons of the Grand Guignol could no more claim innocence of the drives underlying the spectacle than could the clients of the theatricalised brothel.

The performances demonstrated that 'human reason is precarious, the brain is the most vulnerable of our organs'.[107] This meant that the distinctions between the civilised and the savage, the mad and the rational, the moral and the criminal were all vulnerable too, and the Grand Guignol specialised in showing their dissolution. The homicidal surgeon and the lunatic psychiatrist were the favourite catalysts for the horror finale, and the house dramatists – most notably André de Lorde – specialised in showing how the beast in the head had a propensity to show itself among the most revered intelligences. In *The System of Dr Goudron and Professor Plume*, one of de Lorde's best-known plays, a rebel lunatic poses as the director of the asylum, his ambiguous behaviour being equally convincing as that of an expert with psychotic tendencies or a psychotic with some expert knowledge.[108] The scenario was based on an actual situation which occurred when, a few years earlier, the distinguished psychologist Gilles de la Tourette began to display symptoms of hysteria during a special lecture he had agreed to give for the theatre audience:

After all that exertion through a whole lifetime of relentless labour, the great scholar began to present before the
public the first symptoms of the mania in which his great
intelligence was soon to be immersed. A few days later, he
was committed.[109]

The finale in which the lunatics run rampant became one of the stock
in trade elements of the Grand Guignol. Here was the ethnological
savage show in a new guise, with its whoops and yells and blood-
thirsty mimes performed by authentic Europeans keen to demonstrate that the bedrock of human nature was a seething mass of
violent energies always ready to erupt through the fragile uppermost
strata of civilisation.

6

NATURAL VIGOUR

The blonde Venus, the beast actor and the Grand Guignol lunatic played upon the fraught nerves of a society that was becoming obsessively concerned with its own symptoms. From one point of view they may be seen as embodiments of these symptoms, projections of a fevered cultural imaginary. Yet the performers who created the roles on stage skewed the deadly serious figures of the whore, the lunatic and the animal human towards the burlesque, exposing their status as phantasms. Here, though, burlesque itself was tinged with hysteria and melancholy. The anxious hypotheses of social Darwinism did not lend themselves to the kind of hilarious treatment that suited the broad themes of evolution taken up in the circuses and variety theatres of the mid-nineteenth century. While the Barnum principle of humbug remained strong in the freak shows through to the end of the century, the recklessly exuberant sense of diversity conveyed in the variety theatres across the middle decades of the nineteenth century was fading in the harsh light of a new kind of analytic scrutiny focused on the figure of the performer. Dancers and acrobats could be seen as a social threat, and the circus itself a dangerous counter-zone to that of civilised society.

The dialectical relationship between the two cultures of science and show business became muddier, more complex, as they confused each other's principles and priorities. The sharpest insights about the evolutionary implications of role-play were offered by those who combined analytic and performative approaches to it, and whose allegiances were not necessarily to the rational mindset of civilised humanity. A sense of crisis was looming, and the figure of the performer on stage was somewhere at the heart of it.

Energy trouble

Towards the end of the nineteenth century, the growing emphasis on degeneration became bound up with radical misgivings about the strength and directions of the life force, which was coming to be understood in terms of the first and second laws of thermodynamics. The first law, formulated by Hermann von Helmholtz in 1847, was that 'the sum of all the forces capable of work in the totality of nature remains eternal and unchanged throughout all variations'.[1] Helmholtz was no metaphysical vitalist, and his law was based on an assumption that 'no other forces than common physical chemical ones are active within the organism'.[2] William Thomson radically qualified Helmholtz's picture through the formulation of a second law, which acknowledged the necessary co-presence of wastage and loss, identifying the principle that later became known as entropy. Thomson was also to be one of the most relentless critics of the theory of natural selection, undermining Darwin's estimations of the age of the Earth with a much reduced estimate based on calculations that took into account the phenomenon of heat loss in the Earth's core. But it was in interpretations of human evolution that the 'second law' had its most troubling implications.

The double vision presented in thermodynamics was paralleled in early ethnology, with its concern to account for both the advancement of civilised peoples and the condition of races considered savage or primitive. In the view of some interpreters, such races were in a regressive rather than a static condition, having declined from the condition of man at the point of creation in the Garden of Eden. The eighteenth-century naturalist Buffon commented that the Indians of the New World lacked vitality, and their organs of generation were 'feeble and small'. Hunger and thirst, he said, were the sole motivating forces in the savage, who without them would 'remain either standing there stupidly or recumbent for days at a time'. Perhaps Buffon was already envisaging something akin to Thomson's second law operating with regard to primitive humanity, a condition defined as one of general failure in 'natural vigour'.[3]

Two years before Darwin had published *The Origin of Species*, Benedict Morel produced the first general treatise on 'the physical, moral and intellectual degeneration of the human species'. Here, he suggested that the process of natural variation might produce strains that were 'a morbid deviation from an original type' containing 'transmissible elements' so that whoever inherited them became 'more and more incapable of fulfilling his functions in the world'.[4]

Morel, a precursor of Lombroso in his approach to diagnosis, proposed that the signs of degeneracy included stunted growth, asymmetrical features, malformed ears and squinting eyes. It was as if the vital force was losing pressure and regulation, and the resulting deviations of form made effective function impossible.

The confident assumption that energy trouble was a disorder of the primitive, remote from the experiences of civilised peoples, began to lose ground with this growing concern about degeneration within European races. Arthur Gobineau, Morel's contemporary, put forward a theory of racial vitalism, with the premise that the Aryan or white races possessed the most vital energy, and that their aristocracies were the ultimate repository of the life force. However, the very strength of these peoples led to their dispersal through the globe, and consequently to intermarriage and the loss of racial purity. In 1856, Gobineau declared that the causes of enervation were gathering, and that the degeneration of the finest European bloodlines would soon be complete.[5] In the 1870s, the notion of degeneration turned from a troubling hypothesis to a raging cultural hypochondria following the claim by an American physician named George Miller Beard that a disease whose primary symptom was 'want of nervous force' had reached epidemic proportions. Neurasthenia was a degenerative condition to which the finest sensibilities were prone, and its sufferers soon included Herbert Spencer and Charles Darwin.

The prime cause of the debilitating condition, according to Beard, was civilisation itself, since the demands of progress were 'carried to a degree from which nervous diseases must be the inevitable results'.[6] The implications of this took some time to process, but the ironies were not lost on astute social observers. While Spencer was complaining that he could not work more than two hours a day without inducing a state of nervous collapse, and Darwin excused himself from after-dinner conversation on the grounds that he 'was an old woman' who must retire early, members of the lower orders were engaged day after day in hard manual labour without succumbing to nervous exhaustion. While eugenicists agonised about the propagation rates of degenerates and mental defectives, Henry James's *Washington Square* told the story of a brilliant New York medical man whose only daughter moves into terminal spinsterhood. The mad and the violent were exploding with excess energy, but refined members of society had to wear galvanic belts and take water cures to compensate for loss of precious nerve force. How did such anomalies sit with Darwin's own theories of adaptation and natural selection? One lurking misgiving was that perhaps the high and the low in the social hierarchy did not correspond with levels of fitness in natural selection. In this atmosphere of neurotic speculation, the 'electric force of a strong personality' on stage was a disturbing phenomenon.[7] Powerful energies such as those exuded by Irving had a sinister quality.

The human energy crisis was imaginatively bound up with a spreading crisis of definition that threatened to dissolve existing rationales about what constituted higher and lower tendencies, human as distinct from animal behaviour. The narrator in Stevenson's *Dr. Jekyll and Mr. Hyde* (1886) confesses: 'it was . . . in my own person that I learned to recognize the thorough and primitive duality of man.'[8] Bram Stoker's Count Dracula (1897) is a stalking category crisis: man and beast, aristocrat and criminal, a lord of the living dead, whose activities leave him filled with vigour even as he spreads the poison of terminal decay. His castle, 'that awful den of hellish infamy', is a hotbed of spontaneous generation where 'every speck of dust that whirls in the wind' may be 'a devouring monster in embryo'.[9] Darwin himself entertained the hypothesis of spontaneous generation in his earlier writings, so this malevolent version of it, however steeped in supernatural fantasy, was not so far from the speculations of science. Stoker drew on the work of Lombroso in rendering Dracula as a criminal type, 'an atavistic being who reproduces in his person the ferocious instincts of primitive humanity and the inferior animals'.[10] In a culture seduced by the generative powers of Dracula's theatre of horror, how could anyone be sure whether the energies in the biological world were indeed working towards the formation of what Darwin called 'good and true species'?

Here the speculations of the artist and the scientist tended to diverge. Darwin may have been unable to state definitively what constituted a species, but this does not mean that he resigned from the work of definition. The weaknesses he observed in crosses and hybrids served to demonstrate that natural vigour might generate a thousand branch lines but would only retain its full strength in the main channels of speciation. Yet the idea that the strongest energies were the darkest, most shape-shifting and most primeval was compelling. Stephen Arata sees in Dracula a narrative of 'reverse colonisation' in which 'the "civilised" world is on the point of being colonized by "primitive" forces'. This is a guilt narrative, says Arata, where 'in the marauding invasive Other, British culture sees its own imperial practices mirrored back in monstrous forms'.[11]

By the end of the nineteenth century, images of invasion and counter-invasion were haunting all the major category divisions upon which the upper echelons of European and American society had built their sense of cultural identity. Gender difference became a critical issue. Bram Dijkstra sees the level of anxiety attached to this as veering into the realms of the psychotic:

> The anthropologists, biologists, and sociologists who, in the later nineteenth century, developed 'the science of man' are often so extreme on the subject of the relationship between the sexes that reading their remarks is like entering into an insane asylum in which the inmates have written all the rules.[12]

Elaine Showalter has also investigated examples of the spreading cultural hysteria created by late nineteenth-century fears of sexual anarchy resulting from the loss of clear demarcation lines between the sexes and between sexualities.[13] There was intense and contradictory speculation about the true 'nature' of woman. Bram Stoker saw gender polarity itself as an outcome of higher evolution, so that

> the attraction of each individual to the other sex depends upon its place on the scale between the highest and lowest grade of sex. The most masculine man draws the most feminine woman . . . and so down the scale till close to the borderline in the great mass of persons.[14]

Whether woman was to man as lower was to higher, or as one pole of higher being to the other, there were crucial questions about what kinds of vital power resided in the female form as the defining other of masculinity.

The natural history of the ballet girl

Behind the *fin-de-siècle* crisis in gender relations explored by Dijkstra and Showalter was a long history of cultural anxiety about feminine energy. The female dancer, who became an increasingly important element of the stage repertoire from the early 1840s, was a magnet for such anxieties and fascinations. Albert Smith offered an ironic perspective on the cult of the female dancer in his short satirical book *The Natural History of the Ballet Girl* (1847). The satire focused on the essential contradiction between the image of the ballet girl on stage – a weightless vision in gauze – and her natural life off stage as a member of the human species. 'Once upon a time', Smith begins, and proceeds to recount the fantasy of the ballet girl as a magical species who transcends physical life, having been initiated as a child into the realms of the fairies where she once danced by moonlight on the primrose banks, skipped from bough to bough among the trees, and travelled wherever the breezes carried her.[15] In other words, she caters to a fantasy that is still trying to escape the world view offered by natural science. As a counterpoint, Smith provides a physical life history of this species, 'considered as of the industrious classes'.[16] No magical being but a small, pale child, who works long hours, eats poorly on her shilling a day salary, and walks home alone late at night, she is the product of her workplace and 'looks as if she had been generated from the atmosphere of the play-house, as spontaneously as were the galvanic mites of Mr. Crosse, apparently from nothing'.[17] Smith manages to convey, more deftly and in some ways more incisively than Zola, that the cult of the ballet girl is in denial of physiological humanity. The etherealised feminine forms of the ballet, appearing as fairies, wilis, naiads, sunbeams, zephyrs, sprites and sylphs, were the starkest antithesis of the human body whose secrets were revealed on the anatomy table and whose life course was determined by heredity and environment. There was no natural vigour in the sylph. Being substanceless she was moved by the very breezes, wafting rather than stepping her way across the stage.

The pale child in Smith's account dreams of being 'a second Taglioni'.[18] Marie Taglioni epitomised ethereal femininity, creating its definitive expression in her portrayal of the sylph in *La Sylphide*, a ballet choreographed for her by her father Filippo Taglioni at the Paris Opera in 1832. Théophile Gautier, the leading Parisian dance critic, described her as 'an idealised form, a poetic personification, an opalescent mist seen against the green obscurity of an enchanted forest'.[19] Since Victorian stereotypes associated femininity with passivity and weakness, the portrayal of purely feminine energy on stage was an aesthetic challenge of a special kind; Taglioni achieved the perfect illusion of movement without the faintest sense of muscular activity behind it. A series of lithographs depicted her floating above the ground, her pointed foot tantalisingly promising momentary contact. Jules Janin, the second major Parisian dance critic of the era, wrote of a Taglioni revolution. The traditional *danseur noble* and his partner, says Janin, look like grotesque caricatures in contrast: he goes red in the face and displays swelling veins as he executes a few basic jumps, while she pirouettes with 'a large foot usually squashed and flattened by exercise, before they proceed to the *pas de deux*. "Tic tac toc"; the floor cries out. Their hips groan; their hearts leap in their breasts and bounce like their jowls; it is a punishment.'[20]

Taglioni appeared to transcend the material condition of humanity, yet she achieved apotheosis through arduous training, systematic physical discipline and stylistic precision. Once the impression was created it took on a life of its own in the writings of the more eloquent ballet critics, and Gautier in particular. Having assembled the vocabulary in which to capture his impression of Taglioni's performances, Gautier transferred the descriptive formula to other dancers, such as Emma Livry. 'Catching a glimpse of her through the transparency of her veilings,' he wrote, 'one was reminded of a happy shade, an Elysian apparition at play in a bluish gleam; she was possessed of imponderable lightness, and her silent figure darted through space without one hearing the quivering of the air.'[21] The illusion was tragically dispelled when Livry's costume caught in the flame of a stage light and she suffered fatal burns.

Mortality was a condition that sat gossamer-light on the shoulders of the *taglionesque* dancer. *Giselle* (1841), of which Gautier was one of the co-writers, features a heroine who goes out of her mind, then leaves her body – expiring in the midst of a dance of despair – to become the quintessence of feminine grace. Reading Gautier and Janin, one gets the impression that the romantic ballet was an orgy of sublimation, and in *Giselle* the ideal was already showing signs of a split. Felicia McCarren writes of the ways in which *Giselle* reflects pathologies coming under attention from the new science of psychiatry, finding 'a doubleness at the core of the dance that is responsible for the genre's fascination'.[22] In Act I of the ballet, the heroine is a village girl whose love of dancing expresses an infectious *joie de vivre*, but in the second act she has been transformed into one of the Wilis, a race of unearthly spirit girls who exact revenge on mortal men by luring them into a dance of death. Natalia Makarova, re-creating the role in the 1970s, studied photographs of Taglioni, who inspired the ballet, and of Carlotta Grisi, who first performed it, to find a way of inhabiting the work. The breakthrough came, she says, when she confronted its fundamental duality:

> I suddenly understood why the plot itself had never excited me: the poor village girl, the count pretending to be a peasant and deceiving her, insanity, death – the whole ordinary little melodrama, interpreted and reinterpreted a thousand

times, completely uninteresting. Beyond the primitive plot I suddenly had a clear vision – not just of a romantic drama, but of a drama of the dualism of body and spirit, of their fatal incompatibility.[23]

This archetypal dualism had acquired a particular inflection in the cultural climate in which Gautier was writing. Giselle's escape from the reproductive cycle through a quantum leap into insubstantiality was like a sublimation of the evolutionary process itself, which in the 1840s was already being imagined as one of progressive rarefication. The female dancer in the nineteenth century provoked an intensely ambivalent heterosexual response. On the one hand, she was supposed to epitomise physically desirable femininity, and incited a great deal of overtly sexual interest by appearing scantily clad to allow public appraisal of the moving contours of her body. On the other, when her idealisation was pushed beyond a certain point she became asexual, an image without a body. Growing popular awareness of anatomy and of the animality of the human body complicated audience reactions to its public display, so that there was a tendency for desire to kick back into cold-blooded observation, and thence sometimes into outright disgust. As Zola's portrayal of Nana demonstrates, desire and disgust almost inevitably went together for the spectator who brought a physiological perspective to his appraisal of the female body. Where this body was also energised and motivated, as it was on stage, reactions were all the more intense.

Gautier, though less overtly concerned with taking a scientific view than Zola, also showed acute symptoms of repugnance for the material realities of the female anatomy. If Taglioni evaded these by conjuring the illusion of an almost supra-physical condition, her rival Fanny Elssler was the dancer who brought tensions between eroticism and fastidiousness to the fore. Widely agreed to be second best to Taglioni, Elssler was a dancer 'of the earth', whose vivacity on stage compensated for her never quite transcendent technique. If Taglioni was the prototype for the supernatural Giselle of the ballet's second act, Elssler was the prototype for the charming village maiden of the first. When she first came to Gautier's notice she was put under exhaustive scrutiny:

Mlle Elssler has rounded and well shaped arms which do not reveal the bone of the elbow and have nothing of the miserable shape of her companions' arms, whose frightful thinness makes them look like lobster claws dabbed with wet-white. Her bosom is full, a rare thing in the world of entrechats where the twin hills and the snowy mountains of which students and minor poets sing appear totally unknown. Nor can one see moving on her back those two bony triangles which are like the roots of torn off wings.[24]

This is not the late twentieth-century fastidiousness about excess flesh, but a more radical disgust with the actual architecture of the body. The dancer was to be all flesh, moulded into perfect curves and cylinders whose shape would never reveal the grotesque evidence of supporting bones or muscles. Elssler may not have been able to take flight like Taglioni, but at least she was not (as were some of her peers) scarred by the unsightly stumps of the wings she did not have. One might ask what kind of test she had passed under Gautier's relentless eye, but his growing admiration for her over the next few years indicates her capacity to maintain her position on the extraordinarily slippery middle ground between the ideal and the abject in the masculine imagination, so that her dancing retained some warmth and erotic appeal without creating a backlash of withering distaste.

If the dancer was acknowledged as a physical body, moved by her own energies rather than wafting on currents of air, questions arose about the nature of those energies and the extent to which they were sexual. As McCarren points out, 'dance touches the mysteries of femininity: the sexual freedom implied by freedom of movement, in public, by women, in an erotically charged context'.[25] Lynn Garafola emphasises how, at the time when the vogue for romantic ballet in Paris was at its zenith, behind the scenes at the opera 'became a privileged venue of sexual assignation, openly countenanced and abetted'.[26] As a child, Elssler was sent to a children's ballet school in Vienna where the pupils were paraded for inspection by one of the city's most notorious aristocrats, whose tastes ran in the direction of under-age girls. Elssler herself took on the courtesan role as a young adult, becoming the mistress of an ageing statesman with a long career of promiscuity behind him. On stage she always retained the allure of a potential mistress. One of the New Yorkers conquered during her American tour in 1841 enthused:

Her eyes charm the Pit and Boxes by a mightier spell than the boa constrictor's. He who yields to her influence must, for that moment, become a voluptuary. Her influence is sensual, her ensemble the incarnation of seductive attraction.[27]

Elssler's reputation for exhilarating renditions of the Spanish *Cachuca* and *Tarantella* helped to establish acceptable forms for the display of feminine energy. Both dances involved fast spins and jumps, deep backbends and pounding rhythmic footwork. Barnum, who saw her perform in New Orleans while he was touring with the dancer John Diamond, was so impressed that he instantly arranged for Diamond to offer a minstrel parody, 'the Black Bayadère'. Barnum was even more impressed by the profits gained through the efforts of her clever manager Henry Wikoff, whose publicity campaign generated a widespread outbreak of 'Elsslermania'.[28]

Taglioni and Elssler established enduring prototypes for the ideal feminine, but from the outset these were destabilised by underlying tensions between the animal and the ethereal. Elssler was the more controversial figure because she crossed over from the terrain of the sylph to that of the sexual woman, so allowing the colours of the flesh to leak back into the airy spectre. Yet, as Sally Banes suggests, there were dangers of another kind of seduction inherent in Taglioni's roles. 'La Sylphide,' she says, 'acts as a cautionary tale, admonishing men on pain of death to marry inside their own community and not to be lured outside their own folk into a world portrayed as Other and inhuman.'[29] What Banes calls 'the marriage plot' in the romantic ballet might be seen as a crisis of sexual selection, in which the drama is triggered by an error of choice across order, class or species.

Views of the physical and the cerebral as competing for evolutionary dominance in the human species led to an elite distaste for displays of strength and muscularity in either sex. Stoker's 'highest grade' and 'most feminine' woman should ideally be entirely devoid of natural vigour, and if this was not humanly possible the stage offered some trans-human realisations that fulfilled the criteria. The sylph and the wili were the antithesis of the higher masculine, but also of the animal human. While some social Darwinists (including Darwin himself) claimed that, as the less evolved of the two sexes, women were closer to the condition of animality than men, the sylph provided a model of the higher feminine as further away from this condition than any of the prevailing images of Victorian masculinity. Yet the sylph, as a symptom of denial, had her own form of doubleness, which emerged in performance, if not in the sanitised lithographs that showed her wafting above ground. Banes emphasises the perverse sexuality of the wilis in *Giselle*, and their capacity for suggesting a kind of radical slippage between species. 'At the end of their dance, moving across the stage in arabesque penchée, they look like animals crawling or insects skimming the lake's surface.'[30]

When Barnum paid tribute to Elssler by naming his favourite orang-utan 'Mademoiselle Fanny, the connecting link between man and brute', he was parodically drawing attention to a pure antithesis in the evolved order of nature.[31] Fanny the Orang – who acquired a considerable popular following of her own – wore pink tulle and danced, so reminding everyone of how, undisguised by art, the plain physicalite of motion was a low thing indeed. Taglioni was also juxtaposed with the ape dancer early in her career, when she danced in a ballet *Jocko* with Joseph Mazilier, but here there were mixed messages of parallelism and polarity. Her grace and lightness contrasted with Jocko's solid muscularity, yet they shared the capacity to defy gravity.

The sylph reached her zenith in the 1830s and 1840s. As *The Era* complained in 1870, 'we have not the dancers now that we had then. Lucile Grahn, Cerito, Fanny Elssler, Carlotta Grisi, Duvernay, and, greatest of all, the ethereal Taglioni, have carried their graceful art with them from the stage.'[32] Nostalgia for the sylph who wafted rather than moved surfaced strongly at this time, when neurasthenia was setting in as the prevailing cultural hypochondria. Magazines were advertising 'Pulvermacher's Glavanic Chain-Bands, Belts, and Pocket Batteries', guaranteed to impart 'renewed energy and vitality to constitutions enfeebled by various influences', and carrying endorsements from members of the Royal Society, the Royal College of Physicians and the Royal College of Surgeons.[33] As neurasthenia became epidemic it filtered through to the labouring classes, but at this stage it was considered to be a disease to which those with the most refined sensibilities were the most prone. The culture of neurasthenia created a fear of physical effort. Extremes of human movement were enjoyable as spectacle but only on condition that no effort was apparent.

In the 1860s and 1870s, fascination with the airborne body transferred from the image of the wafting sylph to that of the tumbling acrobat, who turned movement into something approaching miracle. Flying rather than floating was the sought-after illusion, achieved most easily by women and children who conveyed a sense that they defied gravity through insubstantiality rather than muscular power. Two of the leading acrobatic stars began their careers as young boys and took on female identities in their teenage years. Louisiana-born Omar Kingsley captured the imagination of critics from the time when he started performing as an equestrian at the age of 6. 'There

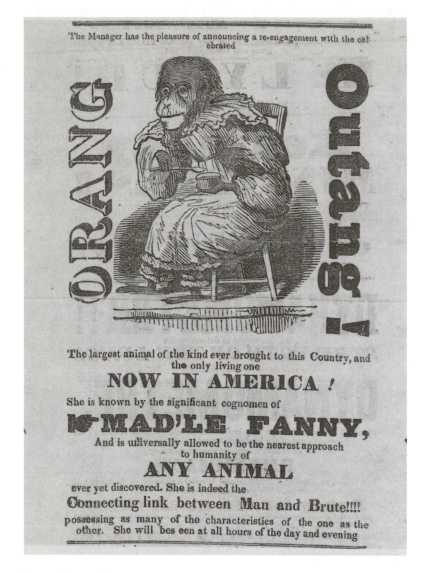

Figure 6.1 Mademoiselle Fanny the Orang Outang at the American Museum, 1845

Source: Courtesy of the Harvard Theatre Collection

was actually something about that boy,' recalled one journalist, 'that made him quite unlike any mortal I ever saw on a horse. He was a marvel.'[34] Also described as 'a sprite, a fairy, an embodiment of grace', Kinglsey decided to cultivate audience tendencies to feminise him.[35] As Ella Zoyara, Kingsley's impact was most memorably evoked by Thomas Baile Aldrich:

> She was a most daring and startling gymnaste, with a beauty and grace of movement that gave her audacious performance almost a sense of prudery. Watching her wondrous dexterity and pliant strength . . . it seemed the most natural thing in the world that she should do those unpardonable things. She had a way of melting from one posture to another, like the dissolving figures thrown from a stereopticon. She was a lithe, radiant shape out of Grecian mythology.[36]

This passage captures brilliantly the flickering gender perceptions that were so disturbing for audiences whose sexual tastes were educated according to sharply dichotomised views of male and female physicality, and of homo- and heterosexuality. Zoyara was a leading attraction at Niblo's Garden in New York in the 1860s, and continued to sustain 'her' identity for several years after publicly admitting she was a man in 1861.

The fatal dancer

Zoyara's sexual ambiguity gave her an aura of danger. There are accounts of heterosexual men being more powerfully smitten by her performances than by those of any woman, then being devastated when they learned the truth. Equally mesmerising was Lulu, protégée of the great aerialist Farini, whose career followed a similar pattern. Originally billed as Farini's son El Nino, this performer had his debut in London in 1866. He performed a high-wire act involving jumps and catches of unprecedented daring. Four years later in Paris, El Nino resurfaced as Mademoiselle Lulu, gaining an ecstatic reception for a performance of astonishing technical virtuosity.[37] The highlights were a triple somersault and a twenty-five-foot leap between mid-air platforms. Lulu won equal acclaim on a return trip to London. *The Era* published a preview notice calling her the eighth wonder of the world and proclaiming that 'the term "extraordinary" was never more properly applied to any entertainment'. She had succeeded Taglioni as queen of the air, and with a bolder, if equally effortless approach to flight. 'If Mdll. Lulu is an angel, her wings are hidden; but flying is, without doubt, her peculiar *forte*.'[38] At her first London performance, attention was focused on the apparently miraculous 'Lulu leap':

> excitement was visible in every countenance as Lulu prepared for the seemingly impossible bound of twenty five feet upwards. Standing before the enclosure of the ring, with eyes fixed upon the narrow bridge above her, she waited for the signal to go, and every eye throughout the building was directed towards her in the vain endeavour to discover the mystery of her flight. It is not too much to say that the bound is made 'in the twinkling of an eye'.[39]

Lulu reinvented the sylph for a new era, but she was also a precursor of Peter Pan from the gravity-free Never-Never Land, caught in a state of magical androgyny. Masculinity was allowed to leak back into the stage persona by degrees, so that during a tour of the United States in 1873 there were open speculations about her gender from all sides, but these do not seem to have detracted at all from her popularity or from the idolatry inspired by her image in performance. She spawned imitators by the dozen, and the leap – made even more spectacular through improved equipment – started to attract attention as a technological innovation. Electricity was the secret, but this new power called electricity had a mysterious relationship to the human presence. According to the *New York Times*, Lulu's performance was 'so intensely emotional as to impart an electric shock to the beholders'.[40] There is more than a hint here that Lulu's power was sexual.

As Shane Peacock observes, there may be a direct association between Lulu and the character of that name created by Frank Wedekind, who had a lifelong fascination with acrobats.[41] This is moving forward another generation into the early 1890s, but the connection is worth exploring for what it can tell us about changing perceptions of the performing body and its energies. Wedekind spent two years in Paris from the beginning of 1892, immersing himself in the night world of Montmartre which drew together acrobats, dancers, whores, writers and artists from all over Europe and North Africa. For writers in this milieu, major intellectual speculation about society and culture became bound up with immediate issues about what to eat and where to sleep, where to go and whom to meet up with, what pleasures were on offer and how they were to be paid for. Wedekind, who was born shortly after his German parents had moved back to Europe from a period of living in America, and was brought up in Switzerland, had himself no clear sense of national or social belonging. His Paris diaries show that he submerged himself in the social melting-pot of the Parisian *demi-monde* as if it were his natural element, alternating between feverish bouts of work alone in his room and excursions into the night-life of the city.

These excursions, as described in the diaries, usually involve the pursuit of women via the performance venues in which dancers and acrobats seek clientele of all kinds. Those he associates with are, like himself, hanging loose from the formal structures of the legitimate social world. He follows Jeanne la Folle, a cabaret dancer whose tensed presence and daring technique made her a cult figure until she began to sink into the terminal stages of morphine addiction. He is also strongly attracted to an Arabian woman, a trapeze artist turned belly-dancer, who has spent her adult life touring Europe and Russia, speaking only fragments of the several languages in which she has to negotiate her living. Circus performers in particular fascinate him, and he frequents those cafés where the strong men, equestrians, clowns, animal-tamers and trapeze artists collect when they are visiting Paris. His interest in their explorations of the limits of the body is bound up with his ongoing account of his own experiments to test the boundaries of sexuality.

The figure of Lulu is like a kaleidoscope into which he collects some facet of every woman with whom he becomes involved. One of her most disturbing associations is with the image of a small child whom Wedekind saw performing in a music-hall show while he was visiting London:

> The greatest applause is earned by a dancing-girl of about four years of age dressed in a brief white princess frock, with bare legs, short socks and little shoes in gilded morocco leather. She sticks a monocle in her eye and sings the Monte Carlo song, showing her scanty white lace knickers up to the waist at each beat of the drum. As she withdraws into the wings, a veritable battle cry goes up, a howl such as you might hear in a Kaffir kraal, a brawling, screeching and whistling as in a menagerie when the meat appears in front of the animal cages.[42]

This is no blonde Venus, but the impact of the little girl's presence seems equal to that created by any of the stage women who are behind Zola's portrayal of Nana.

Wedekind's milieu was one in which sexual energies were becoming explosive, taking dangerous and perverse turns. It was also during his visit to London that he gained a vision of the more sinister extremes to which these impulses could run. Only five years previously, Jack the Ripper had terrorised the feral districts of the city's East End. When Wedekind returned to Paris, the image of the Ripper continued to roam the edges of his own imaginative world, influencing a series of dramas about the power of human sexuality. The diaries portray a world of unstable and often violent dynamics, a world in which assaults occur routinely, people disappear without trace and abandoned children wander like lost souls. Everyone practises their own form of prostitution, and anyone may at any time find their impulses running in the darker channels of human nature.

Lulu is the catalyst for all kinds of obsessions and compulsions. Like the women who most fascinated Wedekind in Paris, she is a creature of the circus and the theatre and, like them, she has come permanently adrift from her origins. Every man with whom she becomes involved creates a new name for her, but her birth name is unknown and her parentage a deeper mystery. It is said variously that she is 'a born actress', that she 'came into the world as a dancer', that she was born in a Pierrot costume, and that she must have been spontaneously generated from somewhere behind the scenes in a theatre. There is a curious echo here of the image Albert Smith chooses in his account of the genesis of the ballet girl, but Lulu has no natural history. She is a repository of some powerful form of energy that goes to work in the sphere of the natural, yet is not quite of it. She is the quintessential category-crosser: adult and child, boy and girl, guttersnipe and aristocrat, murderer and murderee. Most significantly, she is the animal human, who triggers a symbolic crisis about whether man or beast will win in the eternal struggle for dominance taking place within every individual.

Jennifer Ham suggests that the spectacle of exotic animal-taming at this time reflected the Darwinian ideologies of colonisation, demonstrating 'the simultaneous narrowing and widening "distance within" the civilising process'.[43] Wedekind moves outside Darwinian frameworks of interpretation in his portrayal of the struggle between animal and tamer, so that instead of presenting it as an allegory of the progressive triumph of civilisation over barbarity, he focuses instead on the immediacy of the clash of forces, stressing its unpredictability. *Earth Spirit*, the first of the Lulu plays, has a prologue by an animal-tamer who invites the audience into his circus tent to watch man and beast 'fight it out' in a narrow cage.[44] As the forces engage, they also begin to merge and exchange their different forms of power.

Lulu is carried on stage by the circus strongman to be introduced as the snake that coils around its chosen victims, drawing out of them the primordial instincts that answer to hers. She is the meeting point of sexuality and evil:

> She was created for every abuse,
> To allure and to poison and seduce,
> To murder without leaving any trace.[45]

The idea of 'lust-murder' captured the imaginations of a number of writers and artists in the furore surrounding the Ripper murders of 1888, but the term had actually been coined two years previously by the German psychologist Krafft-Ebing, in a study of sexual pathology heavily influenced by Lombroso's theories of the throwback. Lulu, though, is not a throwback resembling any of the images Lombroso compiled, nor, by virtue of her gender, does she conform to the profile of the lust-murderer drawn by Krafft-Ebing, whose work Wedekind was reading while he was in Paris. She is rather the carrier of lust-murder as a social gene, engaging each new sexual partner over the body of the old one, so that the killer impulse transfers immediately to its next scenario. Eventually, her course is terminated when she encounters the quintessential lust-murderer Jack the Ripper at the end of the second play, *Pandora's Box*.

Lulu is a brilliantly effective expression of Wedekind's antitaxonomic view of the world. He rolls together the qualities of rejected humanity and mixes them with everything that is desirable in her, so that instead of producing an image of the despised other needing to be eliminated through the process of natural selection, he shows the mixture itself to be essential. Through his portrayal of Lulu, he raises radical questions about what natural energy consists of and how it gets converted to destructive ends. One of the impulses behind Wedekind's work is a sharp dislike of the naturalist movement, which was becoming dominant in both France and Germany at the time when he started writing. He refused to be claimed by it, and has his animal-tamer pour scorn on its pallid 'domestic beasts', contrasting them with his own menagerie of red-blooded animals.

Zola and his followers wrote from a Darwinian point of view, seeking to warn of the dangers to civilisation from spreading forces of depravity, but Wedekind targeted civilisation itself as the perverting influence. While Lulu is no creature of civilisation, she creates havoc by embodying its icons, changing her costume and her environment as she establishes each new base for her influence. She is not the simple cause of the fatal encounters shown in the drama, but rather a catalytic agent, whose strange vitality reacts dangerously with the compulsions of those formed in the social mould. In Wedekind's dramatic world, civilisation is not a state or an order but rather a dynamic, whose operations produce patholog-ical side-effects, one of which is a death struggle between man as master and man as beast. She is referred to as a 'second Taglioni', but this is a Taglioni fused with the performing genius of 'a splendid animal' of the circus. She is also a kind of missing link between the figure of Taglioni and the stage Venus as embodied in Nana. Like Nana, her true domain is the backstage dressing-room, where she negotiates with prospective lovers while incessantly changing her clothes.

The backstage scenes in *Earth Spirit* seem to be a deliberate echo of those in *Nana*, but the chemistry is shown to work on different principles. One of Lulu's admirers is Prince Escerny, a colonial explorer. 'Would not this woman's children be more aristocratic in soul and body,' he wonders, 'than children whose mother had no more vitality in her than I have left in myself.'[46] The theatre is Lulu's crucible, the site at which her vitality is generated and regenerated. It is a vitality that could, as Escerny recognises, be transmitted as a healthful and strengthening influence, but not through him or his like.

The performer who in Wedekind's time made the strongest impression in the role of Lulu was Tilly Newes, whose memoirs were entitled *Lulu – the Role of my Life*. The double meaning in that phrase – that Lulu was both the best role of her life as an actress, and the role her life turned into – may or may not be intentional, but it is appropriate. Newes became Wedekind's wife and was photographed with him as Lulu, wearing a short ballet skirt and boots. Wedekind himself played the role of Schon, the man who first found Lulu on the streets at the age of 12 and adopted her, then later became her lover. According to Newes, he also coveted the role of Jack the Ripper and played it in one production.[47] For both of them, then, the roles leaked from the stage into life. As Brecht said of Wedekind, 'his greatest work was his own personality'. If Wedekind was drawn to Tilly Newes for some mesmeric quality of vitality in her, Brecht bears witness to how Wedekind himself exercised just this fascination on others, both in performance and in his day-to-day persona:

> He filled every corner with his personality. There he stood, ugly, brutal, dangerous, with close-cropped red hair, his hands in his trouser pockets, and one felt that the devil himself couldn't shift him. He came before the curtain as ringmaster in a red tail coat, carrying a whip and revolver, and no one could forget that hard dry metallic voice, that brazen faun's head with 'eyes like a gloomy owl' set in immobile features. A few weeks ago at the Bonbonnière he sang his songs to guitar accompaniment in a brittle voice, slightly monotonous and quite untrained. No singer gave me such a shock, such a thrill. It was the man's intense aliveness, the energy which allowed him to defy sniggering ridicule and proclaim his brazen hymn to humanity, that also gave him this personal magic.[48]

The Lulu plays are, among other things, about experiments with the power of persona, experiments of a kind in which Wedekind himself was perpetually engaged. His charisma was that of the dandy, whose willing embrace of decadence created a highly charged presence in which the neurasthenic weakness of the aesthete and the feral potency of the libertine were combined. The dandy refused all investments other than those of persona, and this enabled a wide-ranging recklessness. What Wedekind's biographer Sol Gittleman calls his 'argument with civilization' was conducted from outside the systems of value and belief upon which social Darwinism was founded.[49]

His characters are the mouthpieces through which the argument is conducted, and in *Pandora's Box* he introduces some self-parody into the character of Alwa, a young entrepreneur:

> To bring about a rebirth of a genuine vigorous art we should go as much as possible among men who have never read a book in their lives, whose actions are dictated by the simplest animal instincts. In my play *Earth Spirit* I did my utmost to work on these principles.[50]

Wedekind's rejection of those processes of self-fashioning associated with cultural and biological superiority is sharpened by an identification with the circus world, where instinct is valued over self-control, physical strength over mental refinement, a culture of raw competition over one of moral management. As Alwa proclaims, respectable society has produced 'nothing but half men for the past twenty years. Men who can't beget children and women who can't bear any. It's what's known as the modern problem.'[51] Lulu is at this time married to a circus strongman who intends to train her to become 'the most magnificent trapeze artist in the world'.[52]

The circus, however, is not presented as any idealised solution. Even Lulu and her strongman fail its challenge, and by the second act she has been prostituted to a libertine aristocrat who wants to sell her to a brothel in Cairo. Wedekind was too much of an anarchist to be to the business of offering model examples of evolutionary fitness. In choosing the circus rather than the laboratory as the site for his inquiry into human nature, he rejects the four-square clinical architecture of the scientific domain in favour of a space that is circular, impure and volatile. Circuses are where accidents happen, where triumphs and failures are never predictable, where control is achieved through the actions of the moment, not through the 'moral ethical tribunal' of the social order.[53] Here the laws of performance decree that a struggle is resolved only until the next time it is played out, usually on the following evening. The ring is a zone of whirling energies, a testing ground in which events are cyclical, just as Lulu's life cycle is a series of bouts with whoever finds their way into her arena. Each of these bouts has its own performative values, its own feats of virtuosity and displays of charisma.

Wedekind's Paris diaries record that he spent hours at a time reading Nietzsche, whose influence is evident in his fascination with inverting the values of Darwinian moral management. 'All those things which we now call culture, education, civilization must some day appear before the judge, Dionysos whom no man can deceive', wrote Nietzsche in 1872.[54] Dionysus for Nietzsche was the genius of dance and the nemesis of modern civilisation because his laws were the laws of impulse and savage desire. What was at issue in the Dionysian judgement was health, the great area of failure for refined Europeans. Nietzsche expressed contempt for 'the school of Darwin' because of its failure to identify the real dynamics of the modern power struggle which, in his own analysis, was not a struggle for life but a struggle for power. The wrong side had gained the upper hand in this struggle, he asserted, because 'the weak possess more mind' and this was how they dominated the strong.[55] In the category of mind, he included all those qualities identified by Spencer as the later and therefore more highly evolved capacities of mankind:

foresight, patience, conscience and self-control. 'He who possesses strength divests himself of mind', said Nietzsche, but the reverse was also true, which was why 'a general decay of vitality' had now brought civilisation to the point where it was doomed.[56] This was the moment for the resurgence of Dionysus, who would orchestrate 'the symbolism of the entire body, not just of the mouth, the face, the word, but the full gesture of dance with its rhythmic movement of every limb'.[57]

In Nietzsche's writings, this scenario is developed in the context of an increasingly complex and idiosyncratic philosophy, but the figure of the fatal dancer appeared in the work of a number of writers and artists in the late nineteenth century. Salomé, the prototype for this figure, became a major icon of *fin-de-siècle* culture, especially in Paris, where Gustave Moreau painted her, Mallarmé wrote about her and that doyen of the decadents Joris Karl Huysmans tried to translate her dance into the overblown language of *A Rebours* (1884):

> Her breasts rise and fall, the nipples hardening to the touch of her whirling necklaces; the strings of diamonds glitter against her moist flesh; her bracelets, her belts, her rings all spit out fiery sparks; and across her triumphal robe, sewn with pearls, patterned with silver, spangled with gold, the jeweled cuirass, of which every chain is a precious stone, seems to be ablaze with little snakes of fire.[58]

And so it goes on through several more lines of luxuriant description. The florid vision is offered in conscious reaction against what Huysmans sees as a gesture of avoidance common to the biblical versions of the Salomé legend. None of them, he complains, have 'enlarged on the maddening charm and potent depravity of the dancer,' which may be accessible only to such as himself, 'to brains shaken and sharpened and rendered almost clairvoyant by neurosis.'[59]

A Rebours (the title is usually translated as *Against Nature*, but actually means 'against the grain') is an anti-naturalist treatise written partly as a breakaway gesture from the young Realism movement inspired by Zola. In it, Huysmans creates an alter-ego, a decaying aristocrat called Des Esseintes whose parents died early of nervous exhaustion and who is obviously going to be the last of his line. Having tasted every imaginable experience, this world-weary aesthete abandons society, retreats into his elaborately decorated mansion and sinks wilfully into a state of lethargy: 'If in the name of pity the futile business of procreation was ever to be abolished, the time had surely come to do it.'[60] He concludes that the best way to deal with 'the cruel and abominable law of the struggle for life' is not to be born in the first place and, failing that, to drift far from everyday life into the land of dreams.[61] Here he dwells on Moreau's image of the 'weird and superhuman Salomé', the incarnation of undying lust in a dying world, the goddess of hysteria and also 'the monstrous Beast, indifferent, irresponsible, insensible'.[62]

Lulu carries more than a touch of this Salomé, but Wedekind's version of the fatal dancer bears the nature of the wild and present circus beast rather than the chimeric Beast of the apocalypse. Wedekind is not renouncing the struggle for survival like Huysmans, and for him as for Nietzsche, the dancer carries the promise of a renewal of vital sexual energies; if the promise is not fulfilled, it is because the grip of a moribund civilisation is too strong. Huysmans has no wish to rescue the sinking ship of a degenerate culture, but is rather seeking means to help it go down faster, with stronger dramatic effect. No natural body could carry the metaphoric weight with which Salomé is loaded by Huysmans and Moreau. Who could perform the dance they imagine?

Oscar Wilde, one of the most committed admirers of *A Rebours*, decided to create a dramatic version of her story in which the dance would indeed have to be performed. Wilde's Salomé, like Wedekind's Lulu, was conceived in Paris in the early 1890s with inspiration from the dancers at the Moulin Rouge, and one in particular, a Romanian acrobat who danced on her hands. The story is told by Stuart Merrill, his companion at the time:

> There was fat Oscar all wrapped up in this spectacle and trying to send this dancer his card inviting her to supper. 'I want to see this woman,' he said. 'I particularly want to see her to make her an offer to play or still more to dance the part of Salomé in a play that I am going to write. I want her to dance on her hands like in the Flaubert story.'[63]

In Flaubert's 'Herodias', Salomé's dance becomes increasingly contortionary as it progresses, creating strange angles and inhuman relationships between the head and limbs; in her finale she throws herself on her hands, heels in the air, and circles the royal dais 'like a huge scarab'.[64] Wilde's own contribution to the realisation of the dance was a one-line stage direction: 'Salomé dances the dance of the seven veils.' As Felicia McCarren stresses, it is 'a black hole at the centre of the play'.[65] He was tempted by the image of a naked

Salomé, adorned only with jewels, who would have been directly evocative of Cora Pearl as Cupid, but later envisaged the character in a glittering green costume that would give her the look of 'a curious and poisonous lizard'.[66]

He claimed that the role was not written with any particular performer in mind, but was delighted when Sarah Bernhardt expressed an interest in playing it. This was not to be, as rehearsals were halted at an early stage by a ban on its performance from the Lord Chamberlain's office, but the identification of Bernhardt with Salomé caught the imagination of many people, not least because of its obvious perversity. Bernhardt was in her late forties at this time, and Salomé is supposed to be a teenage girl; it is her father-in-law who is seduced by the dance, and the generational difference between them is crucial to the dynamics of the whole story. In addition, Bernhardt was no dancer, so speculation as to how (and even whether) she would perform the dance was intense.

Yet Bernhardt had a reputation for delivering on just such impossible demands. 'It would require some ingenuity to give an idea of the intensity, the ecstasy, the insanity . . . provoked by Mademoiselle Bernhardt', wrote Henry James.[67] She was, in many ways, the Salomé of her age, a stage presence of unrivalled charisma and an actor who brought a sense of cataclysm to her most celebrated roles. This is how Lytton Strachey responded to her performance as *Phèdre*:

> To watch . . . all the dark forces of destiny crowd down on that great spirit, when the heavens and the earth reject her, and Hell opens, and the terrific urn of Minos thunders and crashes to the ground – that indeed is to come close to immortality, to plunge shuddering through infinite abysses, and to look, if only for a moment, upon eternal light.[68]

Bernhardt's glory, said Jules Lemaître, was that of the great conquerors in the first age of empires: 'an immense, concrete, drunken, devastating glory.'[69] If she did not dance, perhaps she did not need to. When she came down the spiral staircase of her hotel, remarked one observer, it was as if she remained perfectly still and the stairs turned around her.[70] Maurice Baring, an English theatre critic who followed her career from the early 1880s, compared her impact on audiences to an electric shock, and said that it was 'impossible to exaggerate or to overestimate her energy'.[71]

Wilde's own justification for his vision of Bernhardt as Salomé indicates that what he wanted to see in the role was not so much the dangerous sexuality of youth as the sense of an uncanny presence conjured from the abyss of deep time. 'What has age to do with acting?' he protested. 'The only person in the world who could act Salomé is Sarah Bernhardt, that serpent of old Nile, older than the Pyramids.'[72] Like Lulu, Bernhardt had a reptilian quality that was brought out through her affinity with all kinds of wild animals. While staying in London in 1879, she made a special trip to Liverpool to consult with Edward Cross (formerly manager of the Exeter Change menagerie), returning with a cheetah, a wolfhound and six chameleons, which then shared her house with her collection of dogs, parrots and a monkey called Darwin.

Bernhardt on stage was often compared to a panther or a cheetah, but in her youth she could also, like Marie Taglioni, create an illusion of insubstantiality. This was most effectively described by Ellen Terry:

> How wonderful she looked in those days! She was as transparent as an azalea, only more so; like a cloud, only not so thick. Smoke from a burning paper describes her more nearly. She was hollow eyed, thin, almost consumptive looking. Her body was not the prison of her soul, but its shadow.[73]

There are resonances of Taglioni in Flaubert's description of Salomé ('lighter than a butterfly, like an inquisitive Psyche') and in the way she is described in the opening pages of Wilde's text.[74] 'She is like a dove that has strayed,' croons a forlorn admirer, 'like a narcissus trembling in the wind. . . . She is like a silver flower.'[75] However, his Salomé is no sylph. With the appearance of Jokanaan (John the Baptist), the lens swivels and she is labled wanton and harlot, 'daughter of adultery'; she behaves accordingly, becoming obsessed with the young saint's mouth and escalating her advances in response to his disgust. It is she who is going to do the sexual selecting, and when a besotted suitor of her own shoots himself at her feet she is as indifferent as any of the great courtesans to the blood on the floor. In the climactic scene, Herod has his first moment of misgiving as he realises that those feet like 'little white flowers that dance on trees' are actually going to dance in blood.[76]

Salomé's energies, like Bernhardt's, are powerfully certain, and therefore dangerous to the febrile, neurasthenic sensibilities of a decadent world. Their effect is not reinvigorating but cataclysmic as they tear through the worn threads of declining vitality against which they vibrate. If, as Huysmans claims, those most drawn to them are decadents like himself, rendered clairvoyant by neurosis, perhaps this is because there is a suicidal impulse in the attraction. Witnessing the dance of the seven veils is like succumbing to an overdose of some hallucinatory narcotic: a destruction to long for and one which must, ultimately, rebound on its instrument. Clearly the fascination of the Salomé story to Wilde and other decadents at the *fin de siècle* indicates that, whatever personal fantasies it appealed to, they were reading it as an analogue of the crisis in modernity. Since this was an energy crisis, the dance was a fitting way to symbolise its epicentre.

The more particular symbolic significance of the dance in Wilde's text, though, is far from clear. For all his ostentatious recklessness, Wilde bore in mind that 'the calm Gods of the Parthenon looked down impassively on the passion of the Dionysiac Theatre'.[77] He makes Herod as strong a presence as Salomé, and presents him as a paradoxical figure: a hysteric, whose intelligence is torn between symbolism and rationalism. If his seduction by the dance shows the triumph of impulse over moral management, this is not portrayed as any cause for celebration or reversal of values, but rather as a crucial but inevitable step in his deteriorioration. He demands the dance against all entreaties, including Salomé's own, and as he reaches desperation and makes her the fatal offer of whatever she may ask him, his urgings literally reach fever pitch. After tearing off the garland of flowers that he claims is burning his forehead, and raving about the blood red of the roses in it, he instantaneously sobers up, reminding himself that one 'must not find symbols in everything'.[78]

Wilde himself was deeply contradictory. He did not so much hold views as adopt positions, changing them to suit different personae, so that those expressed in one work could be quite out of keeping with those expressed in another. When playing the moral philosopher, as in his Oxford writings, he took his Darwinism seriously, espousing Herbert Spencer's ideas about evolutionary cultural progression and concerning himself with questions about the material basis of consciousness. When playing the dandy, he posed as a facetious anti-naturalist, whose opinion of natural selection was that 'nature has good intentions, but unfortunately . . . cannot carry them out'.[79] As the aesthete Vivian in 'The Decay of Lying' (1889), he poured contempt on the school of Zola, advocating instead the creative art of lying as a means of rescue for 'poor, probable, uninteresting human life – tired of repeating herself for the benefit of Mr. Herbert Spencer'.[80] Salomé's dance might be seen as part of the rescue package – a concentrated dose of exotic fantasy – but, like all else in human culture, its deep history was in simple biology:

> The splendour and grace of swift limbs, the grave beauty of girlish foreheads, the physical ecstasy of sensuous life – do we love these things less because the germ of man is to be found in the formless protoplasm of the deep seas, or in the hideous sluggishness of the Lower Amoebae.[81]

The dance of the seven veils had its own more particular resonances with the culture of natural history, as Elaine Showalter points out. Francis Bacon's metaphors of nature as a woman who must be unveiled and forced to reveal her secrets became institutionalised as, for example, in the hall of the Paris medical faculty where there was a statue of a young woman representing nature unveiling before science.[82] But this is hardly an evocation of what Wilde calls 'the physical extasy of sensuous life'. Sculpture and Dance are two very different mediums of expression, and in this case they offer polarised renditions of the power dynamics at issue in the act of unveiling. Where the half-revealed body immobilised in the statue offers herself as the passive object of scrutiny, the dancer in the role of Salomé seduces the observer through her movements and creates a force-field in which she is able to exercise command over a powerful ruler. Unveiled, she is at the height of her own powers and assumes the prerogatives of an autocrat whose decision overrides all other considerations. If her display is ultimately a phenomenon to be understood in evolutionary terms, it shows the operations of nature in a more disturbing and complex perspective than Bacon and his followers ever brought to them.

Wilde was aware of the apparently contrary directions of symbolism and biologism in his thinking, and his approach to the Salomé legend brought them into conjunction in the most challenging way. 'Is the voice of one crying in the wilderness merely the result of the molecular action of locusts and wild honey?' he speculates in his Oxford notebook.[83] If it is, and if Salomé's dance is a development from the gyrations of formless protoplasm, the fatalism of both has more to do with science than with superstition. The dance and the voice are the instruments of destinies meted out by natural selection, but who are the dying and who the survivors in the struggle of which they are part? The voice of John the Baptist is both the herald of a new dawn and the harbinger of imminent doom (his own included); Salomé's dance is a triumphant display of her powers, but it also puts her on course to meet her death. (Here it is worth remembering that Wilde originally wanted to draw on a version of the legend which ended with her own beheading, and that his first choice of title was *The Double Beheading*.)[84] She is thus no Nietzschean symbol of the survival powers of raw energy. Molecular action is itself a dance of destiny, in which the degenerative and the regenerative currents in nature may cross and whirl together, though in *Salomé* degeneration emerges clearly as the dominant tendency in the whole situation. None of the three central characters are survivors, and a point is made of the fact that Herod has been unable to produce an heir.

Wilde's belief that he was himself one of the rejects of natural selection underlies much of his work, emerging in its full strength in the fatalism of *De Profundis*. It is also evident in earlier works where the author as dandy seems to be suggesting that the gesture of relinquishing the struggle for survival has a kind of glamour that makes it irresistible. In *Salomé*, all three main characters are running to their ruin, and aspects of their author are reflected in their fatal tendencies: Salomé's fixation on young male beauty; John the Baptist's suicidal intoxication with the sound of his own prophetic voice; Herod's elevation of sensual indulgence over moral intelligence. Their luxuriant and overblown language marks them as decadents from their first appearance, an impression Wilde wanted to reinforce by using yellow – which stood for decadence and decay in the Symbolists' colour code – as the dominant tone in the costumes and set design.[85]

This was the kind of effect that caused Max Nordau to scoff with contempt about 'an atmosphere of yellow broth'.[86] In *Degeneration* (1892), Nordau launched a virulent attack on the Symbolist movement, whose condition of mental decay, he insisted, was not an organic evolution such as Morel or Gobineau had imagined, but rather a ludicrous imposture, a fashion set among members of the spoiled upper classes who suffered from egomania and whose behaviour was characterised by a relentless theatricality. Their obsession with the *fin de siècle* was an affectation capable of doing real damage simply because of the credulity with which their indulgent melancholia was received:

> Only the brain of a child or a savage could form the clumsy idea that the century is a kind of living being, born like a beast or a man, passing through all the stages of existence,

gradually ageing and declining . . . after being afflicted in its last decade with all the infirmities of mournful senility.[87]

While he acknowledges 'the vast fatigue' with which those who have lived through the birth of steam power and electricity have to contend, Nordau calls for a new wave of determination to grasp the future, to think of the new century coming. Humanity is still young, he declares, 'and a moment of over-exertion is not fatal to youth'. The species has not reached the term of its evolution or exhausted its vital powers.[88]

The Fairy Electricity

Nordau was convinced that the mental epidemic of decadence had its genesis and its most severe outbreak in Paris; yet it was also in Paris that the symbolism of the century's turn was to be most enthusiastically expressed, in the Universal Exposition of 1900. Here the mood of progressive (and aggressive) optimism that had never lost its impetus, even during the most intensive phase of anxiety about degeneration, came to the fore. The Eiffel Tower, built in 1889, expressed in the words of Edouard Lockroy (Minister of Commerce, Publication and Arts) 'the image of progress such as we conceive it today: an unending spiral where humanity gravitates in its eternal ascension'.[89] The illuminated Tower was the centrepiece of the Exposition of 1900. The Chicago exhibition had drawn on techniques of theatrical performance and scenography to celebrate the triumph of the will to progress, but the Paris Exposition, with electricity as its primary symbol, raised spectacle itself to a level that suggested a whole new evolutionary phase for the human species.

Here electricity was no longer (as Beard saw it) a remedial application for lost human vigour, nor (as Nordau saw it) a driving power alien to human vitality, but was united with the human form in ways that promised a vast and ever-expanding new source of energy to draw on. The Hachette Guide portrayed it as nothing less than a new life force:

> Without electricity the Exhibition is merely an inert mass devoid of the slightest breath of life . . . . A single touch of the finger on a switch and the magic fluid pours forth: everything is immediately illuminated, everything moves.[90]

This narrative shaped the visitor's whole experience of the exhibition. Entry through the Porte Binet was a passage through the deep history of life forms. The dome-shaped extravaganza was widely criticised by some but fervently defended by others as a work that captured the spirit of its time. René Binet was an avid student of palaeontology who, in his regular visits to the Musée d'histoire naturel had 'observed the laws of transformism and noted how, with the lower beings, the natural kingdoms converge and intermingle'.[91] His fascination with evolutionary biology was impressively projected in sculptural decorations based on the vertebrae of the dinosaur, the cells of the beehive, shell and coral forms. At night, these competed for visual focus with the dense scattering of electric bulbs that covered the dome, creating a foretaste of the explosion of colour, light and sound to be met with in the exhibition grounds.

Electricity produced its own strange hybrids, born of the cross between science and fantasy, illusion and technological design. The new hybridity was personified in the presiding deity of the Exposition, the Fairy Electricity, in whom high modernity was united with the magic worlds of childhood:

> She is progress, the poetry of rich and poor; she generates light; she is the great Signal . . . . It is Electricity that enables the espaliers of fire to climb the monumental arch . . . . The Seine is violet, pigeon's-throat pink, ox-blood. Electricity is drawn up, compacted, transformed, stored in bottles, drawn out in cables, wound around drums, then they unleash her into the water, through the fountain jets, they set her free across the roof tops, they pour her out amongst the trees.[92]

'She' was a symbolic presence diffused throughout the exhibition and multiplied in a range of images, but at the same time everyone was conscious that there was really only one Fairy Electricity, and that was the very human Loie Fuller, the performer who may be credited with at last bringing Salomé's dance out of the heated closet of the imagination and on to the stage.

On the avenue leading in from the Porte Binet, Fuller had her own theatre with a sweeping art nouveau façade, mounted by a statue of herself with her hallmark swathes of gossamer fabric billowing around her like a swirl of ectoplasm. Inside the theatre Fuller danced the Fire Dance, her interpretation of Salomé's dance of the seven veils, to Wagner's 'Ride of the Walkyries'. This performance had been developed over six years, during which the lighting and costume technology had become increasingly sophisticated. The

Figure 6.2 Loie Fuller in the Fire Dance from *Salomé* by Jules Cheret

Source: Courtesy of the Theatre Museum, London, and the Victoria and Albert Museum

London critic J. E. Crawford Flitch recorded a description of it in its ultimate version:

> The dancer's dress was a voluminous smoke-coloured skirt, to which strips of the same material were loosely attached. She danced in the center of a darkened stage before an opening in the floor through which a powerful electric light shot up flame-coloured rays. At first only a pale indecisive bluish flame appeared in the midst of the surrounding darkness; little by little it took shape, quickened into life, trembled, grew, mounted upwards, until it embraced all the stage in its wings of fire, developed into a mighty whirlwind in the midst of which emerged a woman's head, smiling, enigmatical while the shifting phosphorescence played over the body that the lambent flames had held in their embrace.

This vision of Salomé's head floating serene above the chrysalis of her own immolation struck Flitch as 'superhuman'.[93] Fuller's genius was to take the emphasis in the dance away from the body and its fetishisation. Instead, she made an impact on the senses of the observer by escaping the limits of natural form, to create a kaleidoscope of virtual forms extending several metres beyond its boundaries.

This effect was achieved through a combination of technical innovations, all devised by Fuller herself, for some of which she held patents. Her early experiments involved manipulating the illumination of costumes made from fine silks and gauzes. By her own account, she first hit upon the idea when, as a young dancer, she was given a Hindu skirt as a gift. The garment, which incorporated dozens of yards of silk, was so fine that it could be threaded through a wedding ring. When she danced in it, she found that it would respond to her movements with fantastic aftermaths of form. The silk behaved like smoke or vapour rather than tangible matter, and when combined with lighting changes produced a display of pyrotechnic metamorphoses. To develop the technique further, Fuller experimented with ways of bias cutting and seaming the fabric in variously angled panels so that not dozens but literally hundreds of yards of it could be draped around the body. By extending her arm-span with lightweight 'wands' of bamboo or aluminium held in each hand, she was able to control this vast mass and create forms on a gigantic scale. These were then lit from diverse angles and in sliding colour tones. As Fitch explains in his description of the Fire Dance, some of the most spectacular illusions were created through the use of sub-floor lighting which, projected into an entirely blackened stage space, made the dancer seem to float in mid-air.

In Fuller's performances, the fantasies that had surrounded Taglioni were reinvoked and given fuller, freer realisation than even Taglioni herself could have imagined. 'She is the butterfly, she is the fire, she is light, heaven, the stars,' wrote one admirer, 'frail under floating material, flowery with pale gold, with chalcedony and beryl, Salomé passed in her power.'[94] Here the romantic illusion of biological transcendence through dematerialisation is strengthened and enriched, so that it merges with the potent dream-scape of the Symbolists. Mallarmé recognised a kindred spirit in this conjurer of giant petals and butterflies, this figure that merged with fleeting clouds in the 'oxyhydrant phantasmagoria of dusk'.[95] Indeed, from one point of view Fuller could be taken for a doyenne of the decadence movement, since her work displayed all the signs Nordau had identified with the condition of degeneracy. Everything she did was in the cause of 'exciting the nerves and dazzling the senses'; her preference for uncertain lights and colours, her addiction to 'half-transparent wash, problematical vapour, shimmer and sheen' would in his view have been a sure indication that she was suffering from the same disease as those painters who portrayed the phenomena of nature 'trembling, restless, devoid of firm outline'.[96]

Fuller, though, was far too healthy and unpretentious to be a decadent. She was frequently described as 'a straightforward, unaffected American girl', and seems to have been happy to maintain an off-stage image that was entirely devoid of glamour.[97] She was also no anti-naturalist. If she agreed with the Symbolists about colour (stating that it was 'a fact' that yellow caused enervation and mauve was soporific), this was because she had made her own empirical tests. She also went out of her way to study the natural forms she evoked in performance, seeking out exceptional private collections such as that of Monsieur Groult, a businessman who had 18,000 butterflies from all parts of the globe. Groult, who rarely admitted anyone to the collection, became one of Fuller's most committed admirers and described her as 'a painter of nature'.[98] If Nordau liked to see natural forms solid and stable, Fuller was scientifically as well as artistically interested in their mobility. The word *evolution* was frequently used by and about her as a way of describing the dynamics of her art. Her creations unfurled, grew, spread, diversified and went through transformations, while her techniques reached complexity and sophistication in progressive stages, from simple beginnings. Her interest in human reactions, too, focused on transitional and unsettling states, and she defended it in terms Zola or Antoine might have endorsed:

> I have motion. That means that all elements of nature may be expressed. Let us take a *'tranche de vie'* that expresses surprise, deception, contentment, uncertainty, resignation, hope, distress, joy, fatigue, feebleness and finally death. Are not all these sensations, each one in turn, humanity's lot?[99]

She was above all fascinated by power and energy. She carried out a particular study of radium, making notes for a lecture on phosphorescence and the production of rays.[100] Many of her dances explored forms – the lily, the serpent, the butterfly – but others attempted to stage elemental forces.

Loie Fuller was impossible to categorise. Her early career was as a variety artist, working in pantomimes and burlesques. She played 'the Prairie Waif' in Bill Cody's *Wild West Show* and appeared at the *Folies Bergère* with La Belle Fatma and Karl Kaps, the Kangaroo Boxer from Monte Carlo.[101] As she developed her own independent style, she took a more serious interest in other artists, creating an important collaboration with the Japanese performer Sada Yacco, who was also interested in the fusion of ancient and modern aesthetics. Ronda Garelick argues that what Fuller staged at the 1900 Exposition was an inversion of the images of women offered in the ethnological 'villages' set up in the Trocadero. She danced inside a glass booth, as if to parody the presentations of specimens; she created patterns of light, which played across her body like tattoo designs. Playing 'both the butterfly and the taxidermist', she returned the colonising gaze trained on the specimen.[102]

Fuller was the very personification of 1900. A journalist writing in 1899 remarked that 'any account of Paris in these, the dying days of the nineteenth century, would be incomplete without mention of her'.[103] But if as a glittering presence on the stage of the Folies Bergère she expressed the mood of the *fin de siècle*, she was, in her other guise as scientist and inventor, a woman of the future, charged with the energies of an age about to dawn. Her capacity to inhabit the image repertoire of decadence enabled this to be brought into conjunction with a new kind of excitement about the electrified body, a body freed from the nervous crises of old biological humanity.

At the turn of the century in a millennium that was entering its final segment, the idea of a critical evolutionary transition point was compelling indeed and Fuller as the Fairy Electricity, with her Valkyrie music, was one of its definitive expressions. Such an idea was not compatible with the gradualism central to Darwin's theory of natural selection in the animal world, but it was not hard to reconcile with theories of cultural evolution such as Spencer's or Bagehot's. The theory of natural selection, with its vision of change randomly generated and infinitely slow to take recognisable form, was difficult to interpret in performance, but evolutionary theory fused with an archaic vision of cyclic change – and all the accompanying symbolism of death, regeneration and metamorphosis – was inherently dramatic. 'Transformism', the term used in the 1820s by anatomists making the first attempt to express a concept of evolutionary change in the organism, took on new meaning in Loie Fuller's personifications, which also implied that science and human agency might drive all forms towards higher levels of being. Of course, the euphoria of the new century was as much fed by illusion as the indulgent melancholia of the old, but in focusing both of them at once, Fuller's performances were a genuine catalyst for new thought and for a change of mood.

Fuller's visual and conceptual experiments may be seen as fundamental contributions to an extraordinary revitalisation of dance in the early twentieth century. In the work of Isadora Duncan and that of the dancers and choreographers who joined Diaghilev's Ballets Russes, there was a movement away from the rigidities of classical style towards the representation of movement in natural forms of all kinds. Fuller's work demonstrated that evolution was essentially a matter of energy and formation, and reminded audiences that these were mysteries which science had only begun to explore. Her performances at the 1900 Exposition may, in retrospect, be seen as precursory to Diaghilev's production of *The Rite of Spring* (1913). 'This is a biological ballet,' wrote Jacques Rivière. 'This is spring seen from the inside; spring in all its striving, its spasm, its partition.' Seeing the work as a primordial drama of cell division, Rivière nevertheless experienced an intense personal reaction to it. 'I felt on my heart the weight of physical matter, a mineral inertia! For the first time, I saw in the doctrine of evolution a kind of heartbreaking possibility.'[104] The lens of Darwinism that had narrowed to an obsessive focus on human physicality in the 1880s and 1890s began in the new century to open out again onto diversity, but with a powerful hangover of anxiety.

Intimations of heart-breaking possibility belonged to the nervous climate of a new era, in which the decadent fascination with closure gave way to radical uncertainties about what the future might hold. Striving, spasm and partition were words that expressed the unstable political dynamics of a world in which the major power blocks were in crisis. Evolution was once again seen as forward movement, though no longer of a kind to support the colonial idea of steady linear progression based on the gradual accumulation of superior characteristics. The notion of evolutionary superiority headed instead towards hysterical extremism, inspiring violent forms of social engineering, while species anxieties became oriented towards the human–machine interface, rather than the human–animal divide. But fascist visions of progress were offset by avant-garde cultures that foregrounded the experiences of splitting and convulsion.

In the twentieth century, evolutionary theory came to mean Darwinian theory. It no longer encompassed a range of competing analyses and interpretations, and was accorded monolithic status as one of the great paradigm shifts of modern intellectual history. This change in perspective was partly a consequence of 'the new synthesis', an interpretive approach that combined the theory of natural selection with Mendelian genetics and fostered the development of more specialised forms of scientific expertise. New kinds of disagreement arose, but the great themes of evolution – species definition, variation, struggle, progress and degeneration – became matters for verbal controversy rather than direct enactment.

Darwin died in 1882 and Barnum in 1891. By the time of their deaths, both had become celebrated patriarchs. Barnum's image had changed from that of the Prince of Humbugs to that of an Emperor and Sage, spreading new world enlightenment to all the people. His head, framed as a round or oval portrait, appeared on all his posters and publications like that of a monarch. If he was not on the dollar bill, this hardly mattered. Barnum was his own currency. Yet what he had made of himself was never entirely what he wanted to be. His envy of seriousness and science always haunted the art of humbug by which his elevated status was acquired. One of his most important gestures to posterity was the endowment of the Barnum Museum of Natural History at Tufts College in Massachusetts. In some part of himself, Barnum would have liked to be Darwin. Darwin, meanwhile, had been buried in Westminster Abbey, and no legacies were needed to persuade universities and science museums to adopt his name. As I write in 2001, it is Darwin who is celebrated as the Sage and Emperor of the new Enlightenment, with his image honoured on the homepage of tens of thousands of websites and his face on the £10 note.[105] He is the subject of countless television programmes; huge commercial investments are made in what is known as the Darwin industry in publishing; hyperbolic claims are made about his importance and his impact. Darwin has become Barnum, with more than a little humbug in the promotional mix – but who is to call it? As the Darwin wars rage, the voices of experts and pedagogues have taken over and drowned out the kinds of undisciplined, miscellaneous, parodically deflationary engagements that were generated in the popular domain during the age of Darwin.

NOTES

INTRODUCTION

1 *Punch*, vol. 17, July–December 1849, p. 242.
2 Thomas Henry Huxley, 'On the Relations of Man to the Lower Animals', in *Man's Place in Nature and Other Essays*, London, Dent, 1911, p. 52.
3 Richard Altick, *The Shows of London*, Cambridge, MA, Harvard University Press, 1978.
4 Peter J. Bowler, *The Non-Darwinian Revolution: Reinterpreting a Historical Myth*, Baltimore, MD, Johns Hopkins University Press, 1988, p. 3.
5 Michael Ruse, *The Darwinian Revolution*, IL, Chicago, University of Chicago Press, 1999, p. 86.
6 Alvar Ellergård, *Darwin and the General Reader*, Chicago, IL, University of Chicago Press, 1990, p. 20.
7 James G. Paradis, 'Satire and Science in Victorian Culture', in Bernard Lightman (ed.), *Victorian Science in Context*, Chicago, IL, University of Chicago Press, 1997, p. 146.
8 Ibid., p. 170.
9 Joseph R. Roach, *The Player's Passion: Studies in the Science of Acting*, London and Toronto, Associated University Presses, 1985, p. 12.
10 Bram Dijkstra, *Idols of Perversity: Fantasies of Feminine Evil in Fin de Siècle Culture*, New York, Oxford University Press, 1986, p. 161.
11 Robert C. Allen, *Horrible Prettiness: Burlesque and American Culture*, Chapel Hill, University of North Carolina Press, 1991, p. 32.
12 Peter Stallybrass and Allon White, *The Politics and Poetics of Transgression*, Ithaca, NY, Cornell University Press, 1995, p. 5.
13 Sigmund Freud, Lecture 18, *Introductory Lectures on Psychoanalysis*, The Pelican Freud Library, vol. I, trans. James Strachey, Harmondsworth, Pelican, 1984, p. 326.
14 Daniel Dennett works hard to convey this impression in his influential book *Darwin's Dangerous Idea: Evolution and the Meanings of Life*, London, Penguin, 1995.

1   OUT OF NATURAL HISTORY

1 Gottfried Leibnitz, 'An Odd Thought Concerning a New Sort of Exhibition' (1675), in Philip P. Wiener (ed.), *Leibnitz Selections*, New York, Charles Scribner & Sons, 1951, pp. 586–94.

2 Francis Bacon, *The Advancement of Learning*, ed. G. W. Kitchen, London, J. M. Dent, 1861, p. 70.
3 The history of collecting and exhibition has been the subject of a range of scholarly studies over the past thirty years or so. With the exception of Richard Altick's remarkable work *The Shows of London* (Cambridge, MA, Harvard University Press, 1978), the specifically performative and dramatic aspects of collection are not the main focus of these studies, though some emphasise theatricality in metaphoric terms and make it an important theme. This chapter is indebted to the scholarship in a number of these works, in particular: Harriet Ritvo, *The Platypus and the Mermaid and Other Figments of the Classifying Imagination*, Cambridge, MA, Harvard University Press, 1997; Susan Stewart, *On Longing: Narratives of the Miniature, the Gigantic, the Souvenir, the Collection*, Durham, NC, Duke University Press, 1993; Paula Findlen, *Possessing Nature: Museums, Collecting and Scientific Culture in Early Modern Italy*, Berkeley, University of California Press, 1994; Katie Whitaker, 'The Culture of Curiosity' in N. Jardine, J. A. Secord and E. C. Spary (eds), *Cultures of Natural History*, Cambridge, Cambridge University Press, 1996; Eileen Hooper-Greenhill, *Museums and the Shaping of Knowledge*, London, Routledge, 1992; Tony Bennett, *The Birth of the Museum*, London, Routledge, 1995.
4 John North, 'A Lecture on Monstrosities, Part One', *The Lancet*, 7 March 1840, pp. 857–8.
5 John North, 'A Lecture on Monstrosities, Part Two', *The Lancet*, 14 March 1840, p. 918.
6 Lorraine Daston and Katherine Park, *Wonders and the Order of Nature, 1150–1750*, New York, Zone Books, 1998, p. 20.
7 Cited in Henry Morley, *Memoirs of Bartholomew Fair*, London, Chatto & Windus, 1880, p. 147.
8 Ibid., p. 133.
9 Ibid., pp. 250–1.
10 Ibid., p. 303.
11 Ritvo, op. cit., p. 3. Another well-researched account of the dilemmas expressed by Shaw and others is offered by Ann Moyal in *Platypus*, Sydney, Allen & Unwin, 2001.
12 Albert E. Gunther, *A Century of Zoology at the British Museum through the Lives of Two Keepers, 1815–1914*, London, Dawson & Sons, 1975, p. 52. Linnaeus in his 'Observations' stated that 'like always gives birth to like', and that hybrids and other paradoxa (monsters) are natural impossibilities. However, he accepted the authenticity of mermaids (Carolus Linnaeus, *Systema Naturae*, trans. M. S. J. Engel-Lederboer, Amsterdam, Nieuwkoop & B. de Graaf, 1964, p. 19).
13 Ritvo, op. cit., pp. 3–4.
14 Morley, op. cit., p. 252.
15 North, 'A Lecture on Monstrosities, Part One', p. 858.
16 Morley, op. cit., p. 388.
17 *Punch*, 4 September 1847, p. 90.
18 *The Illustrated London News*, 3 April 1847, p. 242. This issue of *The Illustrated London News* celebrates April Fool's Day, so the issue of imposture is highly topical.
19 Matthew Buchinger and Miss Biffin were especially popular as 'armless wonders'. Ricky Jay offers an account of their careers in *Learned Pigs and Fireproof Women*, New York, Warner Books, 1986, ch. 4.

20 Samuel Taylor Coleridge, *Biographia Literaria*, George Watson (ed.), London, Everyman, 1967, p. 169.

21 Daston and Park put the view that in medieval cultures of wonder, credulity was not an issue in the way it became for modern audiences. Medieval travel books and bestiaries, they suggest, 'demanded emotional and intellectual consent rather than a dogmatic commitment to belief' (op. cit., p. 60).

22 John Evelyn, diary entry for 13 September 1660, in Philip Francis (ed.), *John Evelyn's Diary*, London, Folio, 1963, p. 121.

23 Phineas Taylor Barnum, *Struggles and Triumphs, or Forty Years' Recollections*, New York, Warren, Johnson & Co, 1872, pp. 11 and 293.

24 William Clift's annotations to his drawing of the mermaid, cited in Ritvo, op. cit., p. 179. The story of early investigations into the mermaid's authenticity is also traced in detail by Jan Bondeson in *The Feejee Mermaid and Other Essays in Natural and Unnatural History*, Ithaca, NY, Cornell University Press, 1999, pp. 36–63.

25 These details are recorded in A. H. Saxon's meticulously researched biography *P. T. Barnum, the Legend and the Man*, New York, Columbia University Press, 1989.

26 Phineas Taylor Barnum, *The Humbugs of the World*, London, John Camden Hotten, 1866, p. 31.

27 Barnum, *Struggles and Triumphs*, p. 129.

28 Ibid, p. 128.

29 The Charlestown Mercury, 21 January 1843, cited in Neil Harris, *Humbug: the Art of P. T. Barnum*, Boston, MA, Little Brown & Co, 1973, p. 311.

30 Edwin H. Chapin, cited in Saxon, op. cit., p. 122.

31 Daston and Park, op. cit., p. 62.

32 Correspondence from C. R. Bree, *The Lancet*, 21 March 1840, p. 959.

33 Robert Fox, 'Report on Two Cases of Monstrosity', *The Lancet*, 21 December 1839, p. 471.

34 Definitions are from *The Shorter Oxford English Dictionary on Historical Principles*, Oxford, Clarendon, 1973. Hooper-Greenhill notes that the term *theatre* 'generally referred to a "compilation" or "compendium"' (op. cit., p. 98).

35 Findlen, op. cit., p. 192.

36 Ibid., pp. 27 and 17.

37 Arthur MacGregor, 'The Tradescants: Gardeners and Botanists', in Arthur MacGregor (ed.), *Tradescant's Rarities*, Oxford, Clarendon Press, 1983, p. 15.

38 Inventory of the rarities in the Anatomy School in 1709, reprinted in R. T. Gunther, *Early Science in Oxford Volume III: The Biological Sciences and the Biological Collections*, Oxford, Oxford University Press, 1925, pp. 264–75.

39 *Museaum Thoresbyanum*, cited in Whitaker, op. cit., p. 78.

40 Thomas Sprat, *The History of the Royal Society of London for the Improving of Natural Knowledge*, London, J. Martyn, 1667, p. 362.

41 Robert Hooke, cited in William T. Stearn, *The Natural History Museum at South Kensington: A History of the British Museum (Natural History), 1753–1980*, London, Heinemann, 1981, p. 8.

42 P. J. P. Whitehead, 'Museums in the History of Zoology', *Museums Journal*, vol. 70, no. 2, 1970.

43 Michel Foucault, *The Order of Things*, London, Routledge, 1991, p. 161.

44 Albert E. Gunther, op. cit., p. 59.
45 Ibid., p. 248.
46 Ibid., p. 351.
47 Gunther was promoted from the position of specialist (ichthyology) to that of Head Keeper in the Zoological Department in 1875. In this capacity, his agenda was to oversee the exhaustive cataloguing of each department, seeking out additional assistants and assistant keepers with expertise in 'systematic work'. He records that in 1880 the total number of zoological specimens in the collection was 1,300,000, and that it had risen to 2,245,000 by 1895 (Albert E. Gunther, *History of the Collections Contained in the Natural History Departments of the British Museum, 1856–1895*, London, Longmans, 1912, p. 47).
48 S. Zuckerman, Introduction to *The Zoological Society of London, 1826–1976 and Beyond*: *Proceedings of the 150th Anniversary Symposium of the Zoological Society of London*, London, Academic Press, 1976, p. 10.
49 Cited in Altick, op. cit., p. 300.
50 Article on Polito's Menagerie in *Nottingham Journal*, 28 September 1805, cited in E. H. Bostock, *Menageries, Circuses and Theatres*, New York, Blom, 1972, p. 8.
51 Bostock, p. 7.
52 For a fuller account of Chunee's stage career, see Altick, op. cit., pp. 13–16 and Bondeson, op. cit., pp. 70–2.
53 William Wordsworth, *The Prelude* (1805), bk 7, lines 702–5, eds J. Wordsworth, M. H. Abrams and S. Gill, New York, Norton, 1979, p. 264.
54 Transcriptions from handbills, recorded in Morley, op. cit., pp. 336, 303, 246, 263, 248 and 251.
55 Altick, op. cit., p. 339.
56 This claim was made in advertisements for 'The Royal Institute of Anatomy and Science' in Oxford Street, *The Athenaeum*, 14 May 1859.
57 Advertisement for 'Dr Kahn's Museum and Gallery of Science', *The Athenaeum*, 19 December 1857, p.1591.
58 Peter Stallybrass and Allon White, *The Politics and Poetics of Transgression*, New York, Cornell University Press, 1986, p. 31.
59 Barnum, *Struggles and Triumphs*, pp. 120–1.
60 Ibid., p. 114.
61 Hooper-Greenhill, op. cit., p. 78.
62 A detailed discussion of this situation is offered in Bruce A. McConachie, 'Museum Theatre and the Problem of Respectability', in Ron Eagle and Tice L. Miller (eds), *The American Stage: Social and Economic Issues from the Colonial Period to the Present*, Cambridge, Cambridge University Press, 1993, pp. 65–80.
63 Barnum, *Struggles and Triumphs*, p. 104.
64 Henry James, *A Small Boy and Others*, London, Macmillan, 1913, p. 163.
65 Barnum, *Struggles and Triumphs*, p. 698.
66 Charles Willson Peale, 'To the Citizens of the United States of America', 1 February 1790, reproduced in Edgar P. Richardson, Brooke Hindle and Lillian B. Miller (eds), *Charles Willson Peale and his World*, New York, Harry N. Abrams, 1983, p. 144.
67 American Philosophical Society, 'Certificate of Membership to Charles Willson Peale, Philadelphia, 21 July 1786', reproduced in Lillian B. Miller

(ed.), *The Selected Papers of Charles Willson Peale and his Family*, New Haven, CT, Yale University Press, 1983, p. 449.

68 Charles Willson Peale, advertisement for 'The Famous Grisly Bear' (1804), reproduced in Richardson, Hindle and Miller, op. cit., p. 134; Peale, advertisement for 'Ourang Outang or The Wild Man of the Woods', reproduced in David R. Brigham, *Public Culture in the Early Republic: Peale's Museum and its Audience*, Washington, DC, Smithsonian Institute Press, 1995, p. 131.

69 Peale, First Advertisement for the Museum, *Pennsylvania Packet*, 7 July 1786, reproduced in Miller, op. cit., p. 448.

70 Peale, letter to Ebenezer Hazard, 26 July 1787, cited in Miller, op. cit., p. 486.

71 'Inventory for the Peale Museum', Philadelphia, cited in Charles Coleman Sellers, *Charles Willson Peale*, New York, Charles Scribner & Sons, 1969, p. 346.

72 Barnum, *Struggles and Triumphs*, p. 410.

73 John Richard Betts, 'P. T. Barnum and the Popularisation of Natural History', *Journal of the History of Ideas*, no. 20, 1959, p. 361.

74 See Adrian Desmond, 'Science on the Stump' and 'Huxley and his Workers', in *Huxley*, London, Penguin, 1997, pp. 636–43.

75 Charles Dickens, *Hard Times*, ed. Kate Flint, London, Penguin, 1995, p. 12.

76 Preface to *Barnum and Bailey's Handbook of Natural History*, 1888, HTC.

77 Advertisement for 'The American Museum of Living Curiosities', *Barnum's Advance Courier*, June 1889, p. 11, HTC.

78 *The Wonder Book of Freaks and Animals in the Barnum and Bailey Greatest Show on Earth*, London, Walter Hill & Co, 1898, p. 3, TML.

79 Barnum and Bailey, programme for *The Greatest Show on Earth at Olympia*, 1898, p. 3, TML.

80 One of these is reproduced in Philip B. Kunhardt Jr., Philip B. Kunhardt III and Peter W. Kunhardt, *P. T. Barnum, America's Greatest Showman: An Illustrated Biography*, New York, Alfred A. Knopf, 1995, p. 253.

81 Robert W. Rydell, *All the World's a Fair: Visions of Empire at the American International Expositions, 1876–1916*, Chicago, IL, University of Chicago Press, 1984, p. 2.

2   MISSING LINKS AND LILLIPUTIANS

1 Preface to *The Gardens and Parks of the Zoological Society of London Delineated*, London, Thomas Tegg, 1830, vol. 13.

2 Adelard of Bath, cited in Lorraine Daston and Katherine Park, *Wonders and the Order of Nature, 1150–1750*, New York, Zone Books, 1998, p. 109.

3 For a more detailed discussion of debates in anatomy see Adrian Desmond, *The Politics of Evolution: Morphology, Medicine and Reform in Radical London*, Chicago, IL, Chicago University Press, 1989.

4 Harriet Ritvo, *The Platypus and the Mermaid and Other Figments of the Classifying Imagination*, Cambridge, MA, Harvard University Press, 1997, p. 11.

5 Ibid., p. 6.

6 Phineas Taylor Barnum, *Struggles and Triumphs, or Forty Years' Recollections*, New York, Warren, Johnson & Co, 1872, p. 238.

7 Ibid., p. 349.
8 *Journal of the Ethnological Society of London*, cited in Douglas A. Lorimer, *Colour, Class and the Victorians: English Attitudes to the Negro in the Mid-Nineteenth Century*, Leicester, Leicester University Press, 1978, pp. 134–5.
9 James Cowles Prichard, *The Natural History of Man*, London, Schulze, 1843, p. vii.
10 For a detailed discussion of Prichard's influence in pre-Darwinian ethnology, see George W. Stocking Jr., *Victorian Anthropology*, New York, The Free Press, 1987, ch. 2.
11 Jules Joseph Gabriel de Lurieu, *Jocko ou le singe du Brésil*, Paris, Chez Quoy, 1825, ANL.
12 These summaries are based on listings in George Odell, *Annals of the New York Stage*, New York, Columbia Press, 1931, vols 3–5.
13 Report on the temporary cancellation of *Pongo* in the *New York Times*, 19 June 1856, cited in John Purdy Blair Jr., *Productions at Niblo's Garden, 1849–1862*, Ph.D. thesis for the University of Georgia, Ann Arbor, University Microfilms International, 1984, p. 183, NYHS.
14 *The Times*, 27 April 1847, p. 4.
15 For details of Leech/Nano's experience as 'What is It?' and of his other performances, see James R. Cook Jr., 'Of Men, Missing Links, and Nondescripts: The Strange Career of P. T. Barnum's "What is it?" Exhibition', in Rosemary Garland Thomson (ed.), *Freakery: Cultural Spectacles of the Extraordinary Body*, New York, New York University Press, 1996, pp. 140–3.
16 *The Times*, 29 August 1846, p. 2.
17 Advertisement for 'The Wild Man of the Prairies or "What is It?"', *The Times*, 29 August 1846.
18 For a detailed account of this incident see Richard Altick, *The Shows of London*, Cambridge, MA, Harvard University Press, 1978, pp. 265–6.
19 Advertisement for '"What is It?" at the American Museum', 17 March 1860, HTC.
20 Advertisement for '"What is It?" at the American Museum', 11 April 1860, HTC.
21 Advertisement for 'Barnum's American Museum', *New York Times*, 5 March 1860, p. 7.
22 Obituary for 'Zip, Barnum's Famous "What is It" Freak', *New York Times*, 25 April 1926, p. 1.
23 Accounts of Zip's career are given in Cook, op. cit., Bernth Lindfors, 'The Hottentot Venus and Other African Attractions in Nineteenth Century England', *Australasian Drama Studies*, vol. 1, no. 2, April 1983, and Frederick Drimmer, *Very Special People: The Struggles, Loves and Triumphs of Human Oddities*, New York, Bantam, 1976. All of these speculate on the question of how much Zip was in control of his own work as a performer.
24 Robert Bogdan, *Freak Show: Presenting Human Oddities for Amusement and Profit*, Chicago, IL, University of Chicago Press, 1988, p. 135.
25 Cook, op. cit., p. 140.
26 Bluford Adams, *E Pluribus Barnum: The Great Showman and the Making of U.S. Popular Culture*, Minneapolis, University of Minnesota Press, 1999, p. 148.
27 Ibid., p. 160.

28 Misia Landau, *Narratives of Human Evolution*, New Haven, CT, Yale University Press, 1991, pp. 10–12.
29 Advertisement for '"What Can They Be?" at the American Museum', 29 September 1860, HTC.
30 'Circus Folk Mourn the Passing of Zip', *New York Times*, 26 April 1926, p. 1.
31 *The New York Clipper*, cited in Adams, op. cit., p. 58.
32 Prichard, op. cit., p. 1.
33 Susan Stewart, *On Longing: Narratives of the Miniature, the Gigantic, the Souvenir, the Collection*, Durham, NC, Duke University Press, 1993, ch. 2.
34 *The Pictorial Times*, undated cutting, JJC.
35 *Aztec Lilliputians, the Gods of Iximaya*, information booklet in the St Martin's Scrapbook, WCA, London.
36 Ibid.
37 Handbill for 'The Earthmen', 22 August 1853, JJC.
38 *Pagan Rites and Ceremonies of the Mayaboon Indians*, undated booklet, JJC.
39 Gustav Jahoda, *Images of Savages: Ancient Roots of Modern Prejudice in Western Culture*, London, Routledge, 1999, p. 132.
40 Ibid., ch. 12.
41 'The Aztec Children', *The Illustrated Magazine of Art*, September 1853, p. 77.
42 Publicity for 'The Aztec Children' as reported in John Conolly's 'Address on the Ethnological Exhibitions of London', London, John Churchill, 1855, p. 13.
43 Ibid., p. 16.
44 Poster for 'The Aztecs and Earthmen at Saville House', TML.
45 Conolly, op. cit., p. 6.
46 Ibid., p. 22.
47 'The Erdermänne, or Earthmen of South Africa', *The Illustrated Magazine of Art*, November 1853, p. 445.
48 *The London Morning Post*, cited in *The Life of the Aztec Children*, information booklet for Barnum's American Museum, New York, Wynkop, Hallenbeck & Thomas, 1860, p. 45, JJC.
49 Nathaniel P. Willis, *Famous Persons and Places*, New York, J. L. Derby, 1855, pp. 435–6.
50 Ibid., p. 439.
51 Ibid.
52 Ibid., p. 441.
53 *The Life of the Aztec Children*, p. 4.
54 Alexander von Humboldt, cited in *The Life of the Aztec Children*, p. 4.
55 Ibid., p. 10.
56 Ibid., p. 40.
57 Ibid., p. 46.
58 Ernst Haeckel, Preface (1874) to *The Evolution of Man: A Popular Exposition of the Principal Points of Human Ontogeny*, London, Kegan Paul, Trench & Co., 1883, p. xxiii.
59 Handbill for 'Krao at the Aquarium', Westminster, March 1887, TML.
60 H. Keane, 'Krao, the "Human Monkey"', *Nature*, vol. 27, January 1883, p. 245.
61 *Bell's Life in London*, 6 January 1883, cited in 'Krao at the Aquarium'.

62 Some of Bock's sketches are published together with a report of his discovery of the Krao in *The Illustrated London News*, 27 January 1883, p. 105.
63 Jan Bondeson gives a detailed account of this case and of Krao's history in *The Two-Headed Boy and Other Marvels*, Ithaca, NY, Cornell University Press, 2000, ch. 1.
64 Ibid., pp. 7–8.
65 'The "Hairy Luck Bringers" of Theebaw's Court', *Barnum's Advance Courier*, 16 June 1884, pp. 3–4, HTC.
66 E. B. Tylor, *Researches into the Early History of Mankind and the Development of Civilization*, London, John Murray, 1865, p. 15.
67 Matthew Murtagh and Eugene Watters, *Infinite Variety: Dan Lowry's Music Hall, 1879–97*, London, Gill & Macmillan, 1975, pp. 66–7.
68 *The Times*, 2 January 1883, p. 9.
69 *Land and Water,* 6 January 1883, cited on handbills for 'Krao at the Aquarium', Westminster, WCA.
70 Bondeson, op. cit., p. 20.
71 *The Wonder Book of Freaks and Animals in the Barnum and Bailey Greatest Show on Earth*, London, Walter Hill, 1898, p. 4, TML.

3 PERFORMING ETHNOLOGY

1 Richard Cull, 'Sketch on the Recent Progress of Ethnology', address to the Ethnological Society in May 1855, London, M. Watts, 1855, p. 8.
2 Statement made by the Society's president John Conolly in a review of its proceedings. 'Address to the Ethnological Society of London delivered at the Annual Meeting, 25th. May, 1855', London, W. M. Watts, 1855, p. 4.
3 James G. Paradis includes a useful account of the scientific interests of the early *Punch* writers in 'Satire and Science in Victorian Culture', in Bernard Lightman (ed.), *Victorian Science in Context*, Chicago, IL, University of Chicago Press, 1997, pp. 143–60.
4 *Punch*, 18 September 1841, p. 119.
5 *Punch*, 16 October 1841, p. 157.
6 *Punch*, 17 July 1841, p. 1.
7 Handbill for 'The Botocudos', Leicester Square Scrapbook, WCA. As the Botocudos tour took place twenty years previously (in 1821–2), *Punch* would appear to be commenting on the lasting impression they made as one of the first groups exhibited to display the savage prototype.
8 *Punch*, 31 July 1841, p. 27.
9 Robert Knox, *The Races of Men*, Philadelphia, PA, Lea & Blanchard, 1850, p. 3.
10 George W. Stocking Jr., *Victorian Anthropology*, New York, The Free Press, 1987, p. 48.
11 *The Athenaeum*, 6 December 1845, p. 117.
12 Handbill for 'Bushmen Children at the Egyptian Hall', August 1845, WCA.
13 *The Times*, 19 May 1847, p. 1.
14 *The Illustrated London News*, 12 June 1847, p. 381.
15 Ibid.
16 Charles Dickens, 'The Noble Savage' (1853), in *Selected Journalism, 1850–1870*, London, Penguin, 1997, p. 561.

17 *The Times*, 19 May 1847, p. 7.
18 Barbara Kirshenblatt-Gimlett, 'Objects of Ethnography', in Ivan D. Karp and Steven D. Lavine (eds), *Exhibiting Cultures: The Poetics and Politics of Museum Display*, Washington, DC, Smithsonian Institution Press, 1991, p. 415.
19 William Hazlitt, cited in Toby Cole and Helen Crich Chinoy (eds), *Actors on Acting*, New York, Crown, 1970, p. 327.
20 Advertisement, *The Times*, 16 June 1853, p. 4.
21 *Punch*, 8 October 1853, p. 142.
22 *Punch*, 23 July 1853, p. 38.
23 *The Athenaeum*, 28 May 1853, p. 650; *The Times*, 16 May 1853, p. 8.
24 *The Times*, 18 May 1853, p. 8.
25 Broadside for 'The Zulu Kafirs at St. George's Hall', JJC.
26 *The Athenaeum*, 28 May 1853, p. 650.
27 Unsourced newspaper clipping, 2 August 1853, JJC.
28 Dickens, op. cit., p. 562.
29 E. B. Tylor, *Researches into the Early History of Mankind and the Development of Civilization*, London, John Murray, 1865, p. 39.
30 Ibid., pp. 44 and 77.
31 Ibid., p. 42.
32 *The Athenaeum*, 10 February 1844, pp. 135–6.
33 Michael MacDonald Mooney, Introduction to George Catlin, *Letters and Notes on the North American Indians*, New York, Clarkson N. Potter, 1975, p. 2.
34 Programme for 'Tableaux Vivants of the Red Indians at Catlin's Indian Gallery', 1844, Play Places Box 10, JJC.
35 George Catlin, description of Mandan village, Upper Missouri, in Mooney, op. cit., p. 176.
36 *Punch*, 25 May 1845, p. 225.
37 Phineas Taylor Barnum, *Struggles and Triumphs, or Forty Years' Recollections*, New York, Warren, Johnson & Co, 1872, p. 151.
38 Ibid., p. 152.
39 *The Illustrated London News*, 10 August 1844, p. 85.
40 Ibid., p. 86.
41 *Punch*, 14 June 1845, p. 258.
42 Barnum, op. cit., p. 271.
43 Programme for 'Five African Savages at the American Museum', 7 January 1861, HTC.
44 Tylor, op. cit., p. 2.
45 Charles Rau, cited in Robert Rydell, *All the World's a Fair: Visions of Empire at American International Expositions, 1876–1916*, Chicago, IL, University of Chicago Press, 1984, p. 24.
46 *Barnum's Advance Courier*, 16 June 1884, pp. 2 and 4, HTC.
47 Ibid., p. 3.
48 I have discussed the roles played by the Aboriginal Group in greater detail in Jane Goodall, 'Acting Savage', in Peta Tait (ed.), *Body Show/s*, Amsterdam, Rodopi, 2001. Important documentary research on this group was presented in the exhibition *Captive Lives: Looking for Tambo and his Companions*, curated by Roslyn Poignant for the National Library of Australia, Canberra, 1997.

49 Programme for 'The Greatest Show on Earth at New Haven', HTC.
50 Pascal Ory, *L'Expo Universelle 1889*, Paris, Editions Complexes, 1989, pp. 83–101.
51 Hubert Howe Bancroft, *The Book of the Fair: An Historical and Descriptive Presentation Viewed through the Columbian Exposition at Chicago in 1893*, New York, Bounty, 1894, p. 36.
52 Frederick Ward Putnam, draft of speech made to the Chicago Committee of Liberal Arts on 21 September 1891, cited in Curtis M. Hinsley, 'The World as Market Place: Commodification of the Exotic at the World's Columbian Exposition, Chicago 1893', in Karp and Lavine, op. cit., p. 347.
53 *Chicago Sunday Herald*, 12 September 1893, cited in Hinsley, op. cit., p. 348.
54 Hinsley, op. cit., p. 351.
55 Sol Bloom, cited in Rydell, op. cit., p. 62.
56 'Fire in the Dahomey Village', *Chicago Tribune*, 8 June 1893, p. 9.
57 'Samoan Warriors Do a War Dance', *Chicago Daily Tribune*, 2 June 1893, p. 1.
58 'Night Scenes on the Midway', *Chicago Sunday Tribune*, 4 June 1893, p. 1.
59 Adam Forepaugh, 'The Progress of Civilization', information booklet for *Forepaugh's Wild West*, 1888 (unpaginated), HTC.
60 'Tattersall's Mimic Warriors Veterans of the Zulu War', *Chicago Sunday Tribune*, 11 June 1893, p. 14.
61 Publicity for 'Farini's Zulus at the London Aquarium' (1879), cited in Shane Peacock, *The Great Farini: The High-wire Life of William Hunt*, Toronto, Viking, 1995, p. 253.
62 Advertisement for 'Ferocious Zulus' in *Barnum's Advance Courier,* 1883, p. 3, HTC.
63 Imre Kiralfy, *America*, London, Routledge, 1893, pp. 13–14 and 34.
64 Posters for 'The Rocky Mountain and Prairie Exhibition', reproduced in Greg Martin and R. L. Wilson, *Buffalo Bill's Wild West: An American Legend*, London, Greenhill Books, 1998, p. 44.
65 L. G. Moses, *Wild West Shows and the Images of American Indians, 1883–1933*, Albuquerque, NM, University of New Mexico Press, 1996, pp. 34–5.
66 Ibid., p. 7.
67 Ibid., p. 11.
68 *Buffalo Bill's Wild West*, information booklet,1898, p. 23, HTC.
69 Commissioner Hiram Price, *Annual Report of the Commissioner of Indian Affairs, 1881*, cited in Moses, op. cit., p. 61.
70 Thomas Jefferson Morgan, cited in Moses, op. cit., p. 78.

4   VARIETIES

1 Charles Darwin, *The Origin of Species*, 1st edn (1859), London, Penguin, 1968, p. 319.
2 Charles Darwin, *The Origin of Species*, 6th edn (1872), New York, Modern Library, 1998, p. 41.
3 Francis Darwin (ed.), *The Autobiography of Charles Darwin and Selected Letters*, New York, Dover Press, 1958, p. 21.
4 Ibid., p. 6.
5 Ibid.

6 Phineas Taylor Barnum, *Struggles and Triumphs, or Forty Years' Recollections*, New York, Warren, Johnson & Co, 1872, p. 534.

7 Charles Darwin, *The Origin of Species*, 6th edn, p. 60.

8 Ibid., p. 89.

9 Ibid., p. 145.

10 *Punch*, July 1849, p. 188.

11 Charles Darwin, *The Descent of Man* (1871), Chicago, Encyclopaedia Britannica, 1986, p. 340.

12 Rosemarie M. Bank, *Theatre Culture in America, 1825–1860*, Cambridge, Cambridge University Press, 1997, pp. 42–3.

13 George Odell, *Annals of the New York Stage*, vol. IV (1834–43), New York, Columbia University Press, 1928, p. 666.

14 Barnum, op. cit., pp. 142–3.

15 Odell, op. cit., p. 418.

16 Ibid., p. 507.

17 Charles Macklin, 'The Art and Duty of the Actor' (1799), in Toby Cole and Helen Crich Chinoy (eds), *Actors on Acting*, New York, Crown, 1970, p. 121.

18 Shearer West, *The Image of the Actor*, London, Pinter, 1991, ch. 5.

19 Anne Mathews, *Memoirs of Charles Mathews, Comedian*, vol. 1, London, Richard Bentley, 1838. The epithet appears on the title page, where Mathews is also described as 'Proteus for shape, and mocking bird for tongue'.

20 Anne Mathews, *Memoirs of Charles Mathews*, vol. 3, p. 60.

21 Unsourced comments of Mathews, cited in ibid., pp. 181–2.

22 Ibid., p. 114.

23 Ibid., pp. 262–3.

24 The *heterotopia* is Foucault's term for a space that never belongs in any particular location, being an overlay of many places and spaces from disparate geographical and social zones. His examples include the museum, the library and the fairground (Michel Foucault, 'Of Other Spaces', *Diacritics*, spring 1986).

25 Edwin G. Burroughs and Mike Wallace, *Gotham, A History of New York City to 1898*, New York, Oxford University Press, 1999, pp. 478–9.

26 Herbert Spencer, *An Autobiography*, London, Williams & Norgate, 1904, vol. 2, p. 10.

27 'Mr. Mathews' Trip to America' (1821), script reprinted in Richard L. Klepac, *Mr. Mathews At Home*, London, The Society for Theatre Research, 1979, pp. 98–120.

28 George A. Thompson Jr., *A Documentary History of the African Theatre*, Chapel Hill, Northwestern University Press, 1998, p. 14.

29 Klepac, op. cit., pp. 106–7.

30 'Sketches of Mr. Mathews' Celebrated Trip to America', extract reproduced as Document 46 in Thompson, op. cit., p. 120.

31 See accounts from the *New York Daily Advertiser*, 2 December 1825, and the *New York National Advocate*, 23 December 1825, in Thompson, op. cit., pp. 160–2.

32 James Hewlett, letter to the *National Advocate*, 8 May 1824, Document 61 in Thompson, op. cit., pp. 147–8.

33 Eric Lott tells Aldridge's side of the story in *Love and Theft*, New York, Oxford University Press, 1993, pp. 45–6. The relevant documents are published in Thompson, op. cit., pp. 210–12.

34 Jonas Barish, *The Antitheatrical Prejudice*, Berkeley, University of California Press, 1981, p. 128.

35 Mathews, op. cit., p. 414.

36 Advertisement for 'Niblo's Garden', *New York Tribune*, 8 July 1856, reproduced in John Purdy Blair, *Productions at Niblo's Garden Theatre, 1849–1862*, Ph.D. dissertation for the University of Georgia (1982), Ann Arbor, MI, University Microfilms International, 1984, p. 185.

37 Playbills for 'Grace Egerton at the Egyptian Hall', undated, JJC.

38 Playbills for 'Alfred Burnett' (1874), 'Howard Liston' (1878), 'Frank Lincoln' (1882) and 'Fleming Norton' (1883) at the Egyptian Hall, undated, JJC.

39 Henry Mayhew and John Binny, *The Criminal Prisons of London*, London, Charles Griffin, 1862, pp. 4–5.

40 Anne Humphreys, *Travels into the Poor Man's Country: The Work of Henry Mayhew*, Athens, University of Georgia Press, 1977.

41 As Richard Moody points out, Harrigan's Irishness was somewhat exaggerated. His father was actually from Newfoundland and he had to look at least two generations back for Irish forebears (Richard Moody, *Ned Harrigan: From Corlear's Hook to Herald Square*, Chicago, IL, Nelson-Hall, 1980, p. 11).

42 Interview with Edward Harrigan (1894), cited in 'Edward Harrigan's Career', obituary article published in *The New York Dramatic Mirror*, 14 June 1911.

43 Interview with Edward Harrigan, *The New York Dramatic Mirror*, 7 March 1891.

44 Handbill for 'Ernst Schultz at The Egyptian Hall', December 1866, in the Enthoven Collection, TML.

45 *The Times*, 27 February 1867.

46 Playbill for the Théâtre Comique, undated, sequenced with other playbills for 1871 in Charles C. Moreau, 'Negro Minstrelsy in New York', scrapbook, HTC.

47 A brief account of Vousden's career is given in Eugene Watters and Matthew Murtagh, *Infinite Variety, Dan Lowry's Music Hall, 1879–97*, London, Gill & Macmillan, 1975, p. 27.

48 Charles Darwin, *The Voyage of the Beagle*, London, Penguin, 1989, p. 173.

49 Robert FitzRoy, *Narrative of the Surveying Voyages of* HMS Adventure *and* Beagle (1839), cited in Michael Taussig, *Mimesis and Alterity*, London, Routledge, 1993, p. 76.

50 Taussig, op. cit., pp. 81 and 79.

51 Ibid., p. 77.

52 Ralph Ellison, 'Change the Joke and Slip the Yoke' (1958), in *Shadow and Act*, New York, Vintage Books, 1995, p. 49.

53 Ibid., p. 51.

54 Robert C. Toll, 'Showbiz in Blackface: The Evolution of the Minstrel Show as a Theatrical Form', in Myron Matlaw (ed.), *American Popular Entertainment: Proceedings of the 1977 Conference on the History of American Popular Entertainment*, London, Greenwood Press, 1979, p. 23.

55 An especially valuable analysis here is Eric Lott's *Love and Theft: Blackface Minstrelsy and the American Working Class*, New York, Oxford University Press, 1993.

56 Eric Lott considers most of these issues in *Love and Theft*. Other studies offering significant contextual views include Robert Toll, *Blacking Up: The Minstrel Show in Nineteenth Century America*, New York, Oxford University Press, 1974; Alexander Saxton, *The Rise and Fall of the White Republic: Class Politics and Mass Culture in Nineteenth Century America*, London, Verso, 1990; Annemarie Bean, James Hatch and Brooks McNamara (eds), *Inside the Minstrel Mask*, Hanover, Wesleyan University Press, 1996; W. T. Lamon Jr., *Raising Cain: Blackface Performance from Jim Crow to Hip Hop*, Cambridge, MA, Harvard University Press, 1998.

57 Lott, op. cit., p. 6.

58 These summaries are drawn from handbills in the HTC.

59 Taussig, op. cit., p. 78.

60 Programme for 'Juba, the Greatest Dancer of the World' (1845), HTC.

61 Charles Dickens, *American Notes* (1842), Harmondsworth, Penguin, 1972, p. 43.

62 Charles Dickens, 'The Noble Savage' (1853), in *Selected Journalism, 1850–1870*, London, Penguin, 1997, p. 560.

63 Playbill for the American Museum, 19 July 1853, HTC.

64 'Ole Virginny Break Down' (1841), in Hans Nathan, *Dan Emmett and the Rise of Early Negro Minstrelsy*, Norman, University of Oklahoma Press, 1962, p. 53.

65 Bean, Hatch and McNamara, op. cit., p. 13.

66 'Jim Crow' songsheet published by J. Duncombe, JJC.

67 Ibid.

68 Christy's minstrels performed '16,000 Years Ago' at various venues in New York between 1859 and 1866. Bob Hart performed his Darwinian stump speeches at the Globe Theatre and the Théâtre Comique, and with Emerson's minstrels. William Arlington's 'Darwinian Theory' was performed with the California minstrels in 1875 and Emerson's in 1877. Details from programmes in the HTC.

69 W. H. McDougall, 'Heroes of the Burnt Cork', undated newspaper clipping in Charles Moreau, 'Negro Minstrelsy in New York' (1891), scrapbook, HTC.

70 Ronald R. Numbers, *Darwinism Comes to America*, Cambridge, MA, Harvard University Press, 1998, ch. 1.

71 Sigmund Freud, 'Group Psychology and the Analysis of the Ego', The Pelican Freud Library, vol. 12, trans. James Strachey, *Civilization, Society and Religion*, Harmondsworth, Penguin, 1985, p. 100.

72 Ibid., p. 148.

73 Sigmund Freud, 'Civilization and its Discontents', The Pelican Freud Library, vol. 12, trans. James Strachey, *Civilization, Society and Religion*, Harmondsworth, Penguin, 1985, p. 260.

74 Ibid., p. 274.

75 Programme for 'The Chicago Troubadors at St. James's Hall', London, JJC.

76 Over seventy etiquette manuals were published in New York between 1830 and 1860 (Rosemarie K. Bank, *Theatre Culture in America, 1825–1860*, Cambridge, Cambridge University Press, 1997, p. 107).

77 The 'Shaking Quaker Burlesque' was performed by the Ethiopian Serenaders (1850) and Bryant's (1857). Black Shakers appear on programmes for the Virginia Minstrels (1850), the Ethiopian Serenaders (1851), Pierce's (1850) and Bryant's (1874). The Exempt Shakers appeared with Campbell's (1863) and Bryant's (1865).

78 'The Coloured Opera Troupe', *The Illustrated London News*, 13 November 1858, p. 455.

79 Freud, 'Civilization and its Discontents', p. 267.

80 For more detailed discussion of minstrel dances, see Nathan, op. cit., ch. 5.

81 Odell, op. cit., p. 115.

82 Robert C. Allen, *Horrible Prettiness: Burlesque and American Culture*, Chapel Hill, Northwestern University Press, 1991, pp. 17–18.

83 *New York Times*, 1 October 1871.

84 *New York Times*, 27 September 1868, p. 4.

85 'The Burlesque Madness', *New York Times*, 5 February 1869, p. 5.

86 Ibid.

87 William Dean Howells, 'The New Taste in Theatricals', *Atlantic Monthly*, May 1969, p. 640.

88 Ibid.

89 George Foster, *New York by Gaslight* (1850), ed. Stuart M. Blumin, Berkeley, University of California Press, 1990, pp. 78–9.

90 Richard Grant White, 'The Age of Burlesque', cited in Allen, op. cit., p. 25.

91 Henry Morley, 'Journal of a London Playgoer' (1866), in Michael Booth (ed.), *English Plays of the Nineteenth Century*, Oxford, Oxford University Press, 1976, vol. 5, p. 471.

92 *The Athenaeum*, 14 January 1871, in Booth, op. cit., p. 471.

93 Mike Hawkins, *Social Darwinism in European and American Thought: Nature as Model and Nature as Threat, 1860–1945*, Cambridge, Cambridge University Press, 1997, p. 18.

5   LOWLY ORIGINS

1 Charles Darwin, *The Descent of Man*, Chicago, Encyclopaedia Britannica and the University of Chicago, p. 597.

2 Ibid., p. 318.

3 Ibid., p. 323.

4 Ibid., p. 589.

5 Ibid., p. 583.

6 Ibid., p. 578.

7 Ibid.

8 Ibid., p. 567.

9 Ibid., p. 580.

10 Ibid., p. 585.

11 Edwin G. Burrows and Mike Wallace, *Gotham: A History of New York to 1898*, New York, Oxford University Press, 1999, p. 804.

12 George Foster, *New York by Gaslight* (1850), ed. Stuart M. Blumin, Berkeley, University of California Press, 1990, pp. 94–5.

13 Review in *The Morning Post*, 3 June 1843, cited in Bruce Seymour, *Lola Montez, A Life*, New Haven, CT, Yale University Press, 1996, p. 34.

14 William Dean Howells, 'The New Taste in Theatricals', *Atlantic Monthly*, May 1969, p. 638.

NOTES

15 Ada Isaacs Menken, 'My Heritage', reprinted in Wolf Mankowitz, *Mazeppa: the Lives, Loves and Legends of Adah Isaacs Menken*, London, Blond & Briggs, 1982. Mankowitz's stylish biography remains the most comprehensively researched account of Menken's career.

16 The term 'new free female species' is used by Mankowitz, op. cit., p. 174.

17 Review of Mazeppa in *The Liverpool Albion*, cited in Mankowitz, op. cit., p. 149.

18 Baroness Von Hutten, *The Courtesan: The Life of Cora Pearl*, London, Peter Davies, 1933, p. 69. Copy held in the TML.

19 Cora Pearl, *Mémoires*, Paris, Jules Lévy, 1886, pp. 16–26. Copy held in the British Library.

20 Sacheverell Sitwell, *La Vie Parisienne*, London, Faber & Faber, undated, p. 36.

21 Ibid., p. 37.

22 For an account of Halévy's political views see Eric C. Hansen, *Ludovic Halévy: A Study of Frivolity and Fatalism in Nineteenth-century France*, Lanham, University Press of America, 1987, chs 3–5.

23 Ludovic Halévy and Henri Meilhac, *La Belle Hélène*, libretto, Paris, Heugel, 1864, act III, scene 5, unpaginated. Translation is my own.

24 Carl Vogt, *Lectures on Man*, lecture III, London, Longman, Green & Roberts, 1864, p. 82.

25 Emile Zola, *Oeuvres complètes*, cited in Frederick Brown, *Zola: A Life*, London, Macmillan, 1995, pp. 176–7.

26 Emile Zola, *La Fortune des Rougon*, Dossier, Paris, Presses Pocket, 1991, p. 394.

27 Emile Zola, *Nana* (1879), trans. George Holden, London, Penguin, 1972, p. 452.

28 Ibid., p. 311.

29 Ibid, p. 364.

30 Pearl, op. cit., p. 302.

31 Ibid., p. 355.

32 Alexander Faris, *Jacques Offenbach*, London, Faber & Faber, 1980, p. 39.

33 Emile Zola, 'Le Bien Publique' (15 May 1876), in Henri Mitterand (ed.), *Oeuvres complètes*, Paris, Cercle du Livre Précieux, 1969, vol. 9, pp. 503–4.

34 For a detailed account of Zola's environmental research, see Brown, op. cit.

35 Zola, *Nana*, p. 30.

36 Ibid., p. 33.

37 Ibid., p. 99.

38 Ibid., p. 147.

39 Ibid., p. 230.

40 Brown, op. cit., p. 189.

41 Zola, 'Contemporary Novelists' (1878), cited in Brown, op. cit., p. 411.

42 Zola, *Nana*, p. 384.

43 Sitwell, op. cit., p. 39.

44 Zola (1869), cited in Brown, op. cit., p. 177.

45 *The Times*, 26 November 1810, p. 3.

46 *Journal des Dames et des Modes*, 12 February 1815, cited in Bernth Lindfors, 'The Hottentot Venus and Other African Attractions in Nineteenth Century England', *Australasian Drama Studies*, vol. 1, no. 2, April 1983, p. 88.

47 T. Denean Sharpley-Whiting, *Black Venus: Sexualised Savages, Primal Fears, and Primitive Narratives in French*, Durham, NC, Duke University Press, 1999, pp. 77–8.

48 Emile Zola, 'Le Naturalisme au Théâtre', in Henri Mitterand (ed.), *Oeuvres complètes*, Paris, Cercle du Livre Précieux, 1967, vol. 2, p. 344.

49 Ibid., pp. 313–14.

50 Ibid., pp. 290–1.

51 George Henry Lewes, *On Actors and the Art of Acting* (1875), New York, Grove Press, 1957, pp. 6 and 8.

52 Ibid., p. 27.

53 Ibid., p. 90.

54 Ibid., p. 108.

55 Ibid., p. 104.

56 Ibid., p. 93.

57 Zola, 'Le Naturalisme', p. 322.

58 Ibid., p. 338.

59 Ibid., p. 357.

60 Joseph R. Roach, *The Player's Passion: Studies in the Science of Acting*, London and Toronto, Associated University Presses, 1985, p. 54.

61 Ibid., pp. 86–9.

62 Ibid., p. 100.

63 Ibid.

64 Denis Diderot, 'Paradoxe Sur le Comédien' (1773), ed. Ernest Dupuy, Geneva, Slatkine Reprints, 1968, p. 99.

65 Ibid., p. 107.

66 Ibid., p. 108.

67 Ibid., p. 129.

68 Ibid., p. 56.

69 Herbert Spencer, *The Principles of Sociology*, London, Williams & Norgate, 1893 edn, vol. 1, p. 55.

70 Diderot, op. cit., p. 178.

71 Lewes, op. cit., p. 17.

72 Ibid., p. 16.

73 Ibid., p. 19.

74 Ibid., p. 17.

75 Toby Cole and Helen Crich Chinoy (eds), *Actors on Acting*, New York, Crown, 1970, p. 339.

76 Nina Auerbach, *Private Theatricals: The Lives of the Victorians*, Cambridge, MA: Harvard University Press, 1990, pp. 76–7.

77 James Rees, *The Life of Edwin Forrest with Personal Reminiscences and Recollections*, Philadelphia, PA, Peterson & Brothers, 1874, p. 374.

78 Ibid., p. 211.

79 Lewes, op. cit., p. 71.

80 Bram Stoker, *Personal Reminiscences of Henry Irving*, London, Heinemann, 1906, p. 128.

81 Mary Midgley, *Beast and Man*, London, Routledge, 1996, p. 35.

82 Stoker, op. cit., p. 10.

83 Ibid.

84 Charles Darwin, *The Expression of Emotion in Man and Animals* (1872), ed. Paul Ekman, London, HarperCollins, 1998, pp. 234–7.

85 Ibid., pp. 182–3.
86 Henry Maudsley, cited in Darwin, *Expression*, p. 241.
87 Darwin, *Expression*, p. 359.
88 Ibid., p. 360.
89 Lewes, op. cit., p. 88.
90 Darwin, *Expression*, p. 352.
91 Joseph R. Roach, 'Darwin's Passion: The Language of Expression on Nature's Stage', *Discourse*, vol. 13, no. 1, fall–winter 1990–1, p. 49.
92 Ibid., p. 53.
93 Unnamed writer cited in Marius Goring's Foreward to David Mayer (ed.), *Henry Irving and The Bells*, Manchester, Manchester University Press, 1980, p. xv.
94 William Archer, 'Masks or Faces? A Study in the Psychology of Acting' (1880), in Cole and Crich Chinoy, op. cit., p. 369.
95 Ibid., p. 368.
96 André Antoine cited in Jean Chiotha, *André Antoine*, Cambridge, Cambridge University Press, 1991, p. 3.
97 Ibid., p. 35.
98 André Antoine, *Memoires of the Théâtre Libre,* trans. Marvin A. Carlson, ed. H. D. Albright, Florida, University of Miami Press, 1964, p. 35.
99 Oscar Métenier, 'Les Voyous au Théâtre' (1891), cited in Daniel Gerould, 'Oscar Métenier and Comédie Rosse', *The Drama Review*, vol. 28, no. 1, spring 1984, p. 17.
100 Frantisek Deak, 'The Grand Guignol', *The Drama Review*, vol. 18, no. 1, March 1974, p. 35.
101 Pierre Citti, 'Le Drame au Grand Guignol des Origines à 1914', *Europe*, November–December 1987, p. 90.
102 Peter J. Hutchings, *The Criminal Spectre in Law, Literature and Aesthetics*, London, Routledge, 2001.
103 Frederick Courtney Selous cited in Mike Hawkins, *Social Darwinism in European and American Thought: Nature as Model and Nature as Threat, 1860–1945*, Cambridge, Cambridge University Press, 1997, p. 205.
104 F. Rivière and F. Witkop, *Le Grand Guignol*, Paris, Veyrier, 1979, p. 23.
105 Albert Sorel, Preface to André de Lorde's 'Théâtre d'Epouvante', in Camillo Antona-Traversi, *L'Histoire du Grand Guignol*, Paris, Librairie Théâtrale, 1933, p. 12.
106 Victor Emeljanow, 'Grand Guignol and the Orchestration of Violence', *Themes in Drama*, no. 13, 1991, p. 159.
107 Rivière and Witkop, op. cit., p. 24.
108 A translation of de Lorde's play is published as *The System of Dr. Goudron and Professor Plume*, in Mel Gordon (ed.), *The Grand Guignol: Theatre of Fear and Terror*, New York, Da Capo Press, 1997, pp. 119–41.
109 André de Lorde, cited in Traversi, op. cit., p. 28.

6   NATURAL VIGOUR

1 Hermann von Helmholtz, 'On the Interaction of Natural Forces', cited in Anson Rabinbach, *The Human Motor: Energy, Fatigue and the Origins of Modernity*, Berkeley, University of California Press, 1992, p. 61.

2   Hermann von Helmholtz, cited in Howard E. Gruber, *Darwin on Man: Darwin's Early and Unpublished Notebooks, with a Psychological Study of Scientific Creativity*, trans. Paul H. Barrett, London, Wildwood House, 1974, p. 210.

3   Georges Leclerc, comte de Buffon, cited in Gustav Jahoda, *Images of Savages: Ancient Roots of Modern Prejudice in Western Culture*, London, Routledge, 1999, p. 20.

4   Benedict Morel, *Traité des Dégénerescences physiques, intellectuelles et morales de l'Espèce humaine et des Causes qui produisent les Variétés maladives*, Paris, 1857, p. 5.

5   Arthur Gobineau, letter to Alexis de Tocqueville, 20 March 1856, cited in Arthur Herman, *The Idea of Decline in Western History*, New York, Free Press, 1997, p. 66.

6   George Miller Beard, *A Practical Treatise on Nervous Exhaustion*, London, H. K. Lewes, 1890, p. 245.

7   Henry Irving, 'The Art of Acting' (1885), in Toby Cole and Helen Crich Chinoy (eds), *Actors on Acting*, New York, Crown, 1970, p. 355.

8   Robert Louis Stevenson, *Dr. Jekyll and Mr. Hyde*, London, New English Library, 1974, p. 103.

9   Bram Stoker, *Dracula* (1897), ed. Glennis Byron, Ontario, Broadview Press, 1998, p. 396.

10 Cesare Lombroso, 'Criminal Man', passage reproduced as Appendix F in Stoker, op. cit., p. 468.

11 Stephen D. Arata, 'The Occidental Tourist: Dracula and the Anxiety of Reverse Colonization', *Victorian Studies*, summer 1990, p. 623.

12 Bram Dijkstra, *Idols of Perversity: Fantasies of Feminine Evil in Fin-de-siècle Culture*, New York, Oxford University Press, 1986, p. 160.

13 Elaine Showalter, *Sexual Anarchy: Gender and Culture at the Fin de Siècle*, New York, Viking Penguin, 1990.

14 Bram Stoker, cited in Showalter, op. cit., p. 8.

15 Albert Smith, *The Natural History of the Ballet Girl*, London, D. Bogue, 1847, p. 12.

16 Ibid., p. 84.

17 Ibid., p. 16. Andrew Crosse claimed to have made a successful experiment in spontaneous generation in his private laboratory in 1836.

18 Ibid, p. 55.

19 Théophile Gautier, cited in Sally Banes, *Dancing Women: Female Bodies on Stage*, London, Routledge, 1998, p. 14.

20 Jules Janin, 'Selected Criticism' (1832), trans. John V. Chapman, in Lyn Garafola (ed.), *Rethinking the Sylph: New Perspectives on the Romantic Ballet*, Hanover, Wesleyan University Press, 1997, pp. 213–14.

21 Théophile Gautier, cited in Ivor Guest, *The Ballet of the Second Empire*, Middletown, Wesleyan University Press, 1974, p. 158.

22 Felicia McCarren, *Dance Pathologies: Performance, Poetics, Medicine*, Stanford, CA, Stanford University Press, 1998, p. 106.

23 Natalia Makarova, *A Dance Autobiography*, New York, Alfred A. Knopf, 1979, p. 129.

24 Théophile Gautier, cited in Ivor Guest, *Fanny Elssler*, London, Adam & Charles Black, 1970, p. 86.

25 McCarren, op. cit., p. 12.

26 Lynn Garafola, 'The Travesty Dancer in Nineteenth-Century Ballet', *Dance Research Journal*, vol. 18, no. 1, 1985–6, p. 36.

27 Sam Ward, letter to Henry Wadsworth Longfellow, cited in Guest, *Fanny Elssler*, p. 147.

28 Phineas Taylor Barnum, *Struggles and Triumphs, or Forty Years' Recollections*, New York, Warren, Johnson & Co, 1872, p. 108; Philip B. Kunhardt Jr., Philip B. Kunhardt III and Peter W. Kunhardt, *P. T. Barnum, America's Greatest Showman: An Illustrated Biography*, New York, Alfred A. Knopf, 1995, pp. 30–1.

29 Banes, op. cit., p. 14.

30 Ibid., p. 27.

31 Handbill for 'The American Museum', 6 January 1845, HTC.

32 'The London Music Halls', *The Era*, 2 January 1870, p. 13.

33 Advertisement, *The Illustrated London News*, 25 March 1871, p. 302.

34 Unsourced press clippings in scrapbook collection on Ella Zoyara, HTC.

35 Ibid.

36 Thomas Bailey Aldrich, extract from short story cited in scrapbook collection on Ella Zoyara, HTC. Aldrich used Zoyara as the model for a fictional character who takes in a string of male admirers with his perfect command of stage femininity.

37 See Shane Peacock, *The Great Farini: the High-wire Life of William Hunt*, Toronto, Viking, 1995, pp. 188–9.

38 'An Extraordinary Performance', *The Era*, 15 January 1871, p. 12.

39 'Lulu at the Holborn Amphitheatre', *The Era*, 12 February 1871, p. 11.

40 Cited in Peacock, op. cit., p. 211.

41 Ibid., p. 199.

42 Frank Wedekind, *Diary of an Erotic Life*, trans. W. E. Yuill, ed. Gerhard Hay, Oxford, Blackwell, 1990, p. 226.

43 Jennifer Ham, 'Taming the Beast: Animality in Wedekind and Nietzsche', in Jennifer Ham and Matthew Senior (eds), *Animal Acts: Configuring the Human in Western History*, London, Routledge, 1997, p. 146.

44 Frank Wedekind, *Earth Spirit* in *The Lulu Plays and Other Sex Tragedies*, trans. Stephen Spender, London, John Clader, 1977, p. 9.

45 Ibid., p. 11.

46 Ibid., p. 75.

47 Tilly Wedekind, *Lulu, Die Rolle meines Lebens*, Munich, Rutten & Loenig Verlag, 1969, p. 39.

48 Bertolt Brecht, 'Memoir of Frank Wedekind', trans. and ed. John Willett, *Brecht on Theatre*, London, Methuen, 1974, p. 3.

49 Sol Gittleman, *Frank Wedekind*, New York, Frederick Ungar, 1969, p. 1.

50 Frank Wedekind, *Pandora's Box* in *The Lulu Plays and Other Sex Tragedies*, trans. Stephen Spender, London, John Calder, 1977, p. 117.

51 Ibid, p. 126.

52 Ibid., p. 127.

53 Frank Wedekind, 'Zirkusgedanken', in *Frank Wedekind, Prosa*, Berlin, Aufbau Verlag, 1969.

54 Friedrich Nietzsche, *The Birth of Tragedy*, trans. Ronald Speirs, Cambridge, Cambridge University Press, 1999, p. 120.

55 Friedrich Nietzsche, *Twilight of the Idols*, trans. R. J. Hollingdale, Harmondsworth, Penguin, 1968, p. 94.

56 Ibid., p. 90.
57 Nietzsche, *The Birth of Tragedy*, p. 21.
58 J. K. Huysmans, *Against Nature*, trans. Robert Baldick, Harmondsworth, Penguin, 1959, p. 65.
59 Ibid.
60 Ibid., p. 170.
61 Ibid., p. 173.
62 Ibid., p. 65.
63 Stuart Merrill, 'Some Unpublished Recollections of Oscar Wilde', in E. H. Mikhail (ed.), *Oscar Wilde: Interviews and Recollections*, London, Macmillan, 1979, vol. 2, p. 470.
64 Gustave Flaubert, 'Herodias', in *Tales from Flaubert*, trans. George Burnham Ives, New York, Putnam, 1905, p. 202.
65 McCarren, op. cit., pp. 145 and 153.
66 Richard Ellmann, *Oscar Wilde*, London, Penguin, 1987, pp. 350–1 and 323.
67 Henry James, cited in Arthur Gold and Robert Fizdale, *The Divine Sarah*, New York, Knopf, 1991, p. 151.
68 Lytton Strachey, cited in Michael Holroyd, *Lytton Strachey: A Critical Biography*, London, Heinemann, 1967, vol. 1, p. 370.
69 Jules Lemaître, cited in Maurice Baring, *Sarah Bernhardt*, London, Peter Davies, 1933, p. 88.
70 Ibid., p. 122.
71 Ibid., p. 117.
72 Oscar Wilde, letter to Leonard Smithers, 2 September 1900, in Rupert Hart-Davis (ed.), *The Letters of Oscar Wilde*, London, Rupert Hart-Davis, 1962, p. 834.
73 Ellen Terry, cited in Baring, op. cit., p. 25.
74 Flaubert, op. cit., p. 199.
75 Oscar Wilde, *Salomé*, Harmondsworth, Penguin, 1974, p. 322.
76 Ibid., p. 340.
77 Oscar Wilde, 'Commonplace Book', in Phillip E. Smith II and Michael S. Helfland (eds), *Oscar Wilde's Oxford Notebooks: A Portrait of a Mind in the Making*, Oxford, Oxford University Press, 1898, p. 140. Smith and Helfland's Introduction to these early writings provides a valuable account of the intellectual milieu in which Wilde's ideas were being formed.
78 Wilde, *Salomé*, p. 339.
79 Oscar Wilde, 'The Decay of Lying', in *De Profundis and Other Writings*, Harmondsworth, Penguin, 1976, p. 57.
80 Ibid., p. 72.
81 Wilde, 'Commonplace Book', p. 125.
82 Showalter, op. cit., p. 145.
83 Wilde, notebook kept at Oxford, Smith and Helfland, op. cit., p. 164.
84 William Tydeman and Steven Price, *Wilde: Salomé*, Cambridge, Cambridge University Press, 1996, p. 15.
85 Ibid., p. 21.
86 Max Nordau, *Degeneration* (1892), Lincoln, University of Nebraska Press, 1968, p. 12.
87 Ibid., p. 1.
88 Ibid., p. 540.

89 Miriam R. Levin, *When the Eiffel Tower Was New*, Massachusetts, Mount Holyoke College Art Museum, undated, p. 22.

90 Hachette Guide, cited in Philippe Jullian, *The Triumph of Art Nouveau: Paris Exhibition 1900*, London, Phaidon, 1974, p. 83.

91 Unsourced citation in ibid., p. 39.

92 Paul Morand, '1900', in *Oeuvres*, Paris, Flammarion, 1981, pp. 351–2.

93 J. E. Crawford Flitch, *Modern Dancing and Dancers*, London, Grant Richards, 1912, p. 86. Copy held in the Enthoven collection, TML.

94 Description of Fuller by her friend Gab, cited in Loie Fuller, *Fifteen Years of a Dancer's Life*, London, Herbert Jenkins, 1913, p. 265.

95 Stéphane Mallarmé, *Oeuvres complètes*, Paris, Pleiade, 1945, p. 308.

96 Nordau, op. cit., pp. 11 and 27.

97 'A Chat with Miss Loie Fuller', *The Sketch*, 12 April 1893, p. 642.

98 Fuller, op. cit., p. 132.

99 Ibid., p. 71.

100 A manuscript book entitled 'Lecture on Radium' containing these notes was listed in Bonham's Auction Catalogue for 1995, a copy of which is held in the TML.

101 Programme for the *Folies Bergère*, 24 March 1893, Enthoven Collection, TML.

102 Rhonda K. Garelick, 'Electric Salomé: Loie Fuller at the Exposition Universelle of 1900', in J. Ellen Gainor (ed.), *Imperialism and Theatre*, London, Routledge, 1995, p. 95.

103 'La Loie and her Artistic Advertisements', *The Poster*, February 1899, p. 69.

104 Jacques Rivière, *Le Sacre du Printemps*, trans. Miriam Lassman in Lincoln Kirstein, *Nijinsky Dancing*, London, Thames & Hudson, 1975, p. 168.

105 Suzanne Gapps, a postgraduate student at the University of Western Sydney, is conducting a witty and insightful analysis of the imaging of Darwin on the internet.

BIBLIOGRAPHY

Adams, Bluford, *E Pluribus Barnum: The Great Showman and the Making of U.S. Popular Culture*, Minneapolis, University of Minnesota Press, 1999.

Allen, Robert C., *Horrible Prettiness: Burlesque and American Culture*, Chapel Hill, NC, Northwestern University Press, 1991.

Altick, Richard, *The Shows of London*, Cambridge, MA, Harvard University Press, 1978.

Antoine, André, *Memoires of the Théâtre Libre*, trans. Marvin A. Carlson, ed. H. D. Albright, Florida, University of Miami Press, 1964.

Antona-Traversi, Camillo, *L'historie du Grand Guignol*, Paris, Librairie Théâtrale, 1933.

Arata, Stephen D., 'The Occidental Tourist: Dracula and the Anxiety of Reverse Colonization', *Victorian Studies* (1990), 621–45.

Auerbach, Nina, *Private Theatricals: The Lives of the Victorians*, Cambridge, MA, Harvard University Press, 1990.

Aztec Lilliputians, The Gods of Iximaya, information booklet for the London visit of the Aztec children, 1853–5, undated.

Bacon, Francis, *The Advancement of Learning*, ed. G. W. Kitchen, London, J. M. Dent, 1861.

Bancroft, Hubert Howe, *The Book of the Fair: An Historical and Descriptive Presentation Viewed through the Columbian Exposition at Chicago in 1893*, New York, Bounty, 1894.

Banes, Sally, *Dancing Women: Female Bodies on Stage*, London, Routledge, 1998.

Bank, Rosemarie M., *Theatre Culture in America, 1825–1860*, Cambridge, Cambridge University Press, 1997.

Baring, Maurice, *Sarah Bernhardt*, London, Peter Davies, 1933.

Barnum, Phineas Taylor, *The Humbugs of the World*, London, John Camden Hotten, 1866.

——*Struggles and Triumphs, or Forty Years' Recollections*, New York, Warren, Johnson & Co, 1872.

——*Barnum and Bailey's Handbook of Natural History*, 1888.

Bean, Annemarie, James Hatch and Brooks McNamara, eds, *Inside the Minstrel Mask*, Hanover, Wesleyan University Press, 1996.

Beard, George Miller, *A Practical Treatise on Nervous Exhaustion*, London, H. K. Lewes, 1890.

Bennett, Tony, *The Birth of the Museum*, London, Routledge, 1995.

Betts, John Richard, 'P. T. Barnum and the Popularisation of Natural History', *Journal of the History of Ideas* 20 (1959), 53–68.

Blair, John Purdy Jr., *Productions at Niblo's Garden, 1849–1862*, Ph.D. thesis for the University of Georgia, Ann Arbor, University Microfilms International, 1984.

Bogdan, Robert, *Freak Show: Presenting Human Oddities for Amusement and Profit*, Chicago, IL, University of Chicago Press, 1988.

Bondeson, Jan, *The Feejee Mermaid and Other Essays in Natural and Unnatural History*, Ithaca, NY, Cornell University Press, 1999.

——*The Two-Headed Boy and Other Marvels*, Ithaca, NY, Cornell University Press, 2000.

Booth, Michael, ed., *English Plays of the Nineteenth Century*, Vol. 5, Oxford, Oxford University Press, 1976.

Bostock, E. H., *Menageries, Circuses and Theatres*, New York, Blom, 1972.

Brecht, Bertolt, *Brecht on Theatre*, ed. John Willett, London, Methuen, 1974.

Brigham, David R., *Public Culture in the Early Republic: Peale's Museum and its Audience*, Washington, DC, Smithsonian Institute Press, 1995.

Brown, Frederick, *Zola: A Life*, London, Macmillan, 1995.

Buffalo Bill's Wild West, information booklet, 1898.

Burroughs, Edwin G. and Mike Wallace, *Gotham, A History of New York City to 1898*, New York, Oxford University Press, 1999.

Catlin, George, *Letters and Notes on the North American Indians*, New York, Clarkson N. Potter, 1975.

Chiotha, Jean, *André Antoine*, Cambridge, Cambridge University Press, 1991.

Citti, Pierre, 'Le Drame au Grand Guignol des Origines à 1914', *Europe* 703–4 (1987), 90–6.

Cole, Toby and Helen Crich Chinoy, eds, *Actors on Acting*, New York, Crown, 1970.

Coleridge, Samuel Taylor, *Biographia Literaria*, ed. George Watson, London, Everyman, 1967.

Conolly, John, *Address on the Ethnological Exhibitions of London*, London, John Churchill, 1855.

——*Address to the Ethnological Society of London delivered at the Annual Meeting, 25th. May, 1855*, London, W. M. Watts, 1855.

Cook, James R. Jr. 'Of Men, Missing Links, and Nondescripts: The Strange Career of P. T. Barnum's "What is it?" Exhibition', in *Freakery: Cultural Spectacles of the Extraordinary Body*, ed. Rosemary Garland Thomson, New York, New York University Press, 1996, pp. 139–57.

Crawford Flitch, J. E., *Modern Dancing and Dancers*, London, Grant Richards, 1971.

Cull, Richard, *Sketch on the Recent Progress of Ethnology*, Address to the Ethnological Society in May 1855, London, M. Watts, 1855.

Darwin, Charles, *The Autobiography of Charles Darwin and Selected Letters*, ed. Francis Darwin, New York, Dover, 1958.

——*The Origin of Species*, 1st edn, London, Penguin, 1968.

——*The Descent of Man*, Chicago, IL, Encyclopaedia Britannica, 1986.

——*The Voyage of the Beagle*, London, Penguin, 1989.

——*The Expression of Emotion in Man and Animals*, ed. Paul Ekman, London, HarperCollins, 1998.

——*The Origin of Species*, 6th edn, New York, Modern Library, 1998.

Daston, Lorraine and Katherine Park, *Wonders and the Order of Nature, 1150–1750*, New York, Zone Books, 1998.

Deak, Frantisek, 'The Grand Guignol', *The Drama Review* 18 (1974), 34–44.

Desmond, Adrian, *The Politics of Evolution: Morphology, Medicine and Reform in Radical London*, Chicago, IL, Chicago University Press, 1989.

——*Huxley*, London, Penguin, 1997.

Dickens, Charles, *American Notes*, Harmondsworth, Penguin, 1972.

——*Hard Times*, London, Penguin, 1995.

——*Selected Journalism, 1850–1870*, London, Penguin, 1997.

Diderot, Denis, *Paradoxe Sur le Comédien*, ed. Ernest Dupuy, Geneva, Slatkine Reprints, 1968.

Dijkstra, Bram, *Idols of Perversity: Fantasies of Feminine Evil in Fin-de-siècle Culture*, New York, Oxford University Press, 1986.

Drimmer, Frederick, *Very Special People: The Struggles, Loves and Triumphs of Human Oddities*, New York, Bantam, 1976.

Eagle, Ron and Tice L. Miller, eds, *The American Stage: Social and Economic Issues from the Colonial Period to the Present*, Cambridge, Cambridge University Press, 1993.

Ellison, Ralph, *Shadow and Act*, New York, Vintage Books, 1995.

Ellmann, Richard, *Oscar Wilde*, London, Penguin, 1987.

Emeljanow, Victor, 'Grand Guignol and the Orchestration of Violence', *Themes in Drama* 13 (1991), 151–63.

Evelyn, John, *John Evelyn's Diary*, ed. Philip Francis, London, Folio, 1963.

Findlen, Paula, *Possessing Nature: Museums, Collecting and Scientific Culture in Early Modern Italy*, Berkeley, University of California Press, 1994.

Flaubert, Gustave, *Tales from Flaubert*, trans. George Burnham Ives, New York, Putnam, 1905.

Foster, George, *New York by Gaslight*, ed. Stuart M. Blumin, Berkeley, University of California Press, 1990.

Foucault, Michel, 'Of Other Species', *Diacritics*, (spring 1986), 22–7.

——*The Order of Things*, London, Routledge, 1991.

Fox, Robert, 'Report on Two Cases of Monstrosity', *The Lancet* (21 December 1839), 471–2.

Freud, Sigmund, *Introductory Lectures on Psychoanalysis*, The Pelican Freud Library, Vol. I, trans. James Strachey, Harmondsworth, Pelican, 1984.

——*Civilization, Society and Religion*, The Pelican Freud Library, Vol. XII, trans. James Strachey, Harmondsworth, Penguin, 1985.

Fuller, Loie, *Fifteen Years of a Dancer's Life*, London, Herbert Jenkins, 1913.

Garafola, Lyn, 'The Travesty Dancer in Nineteenth-Century Ballet', *Dance Research Journal* 18 (1985–6), 35–40.

——*Rethinking the Sylph: New Perspectives on the Romantic Ballet*, Hanover, Wesleyan University Press, 1997.

Gardens and Parks of the Zoological Society of London Delineated, London, Thomas Tegg, 1830.

Garelick, Rhonda K., 'Electric Salomé: Loie Fuller at the Exposition Universelle of 1900', in *Imperialism and Theatre*, ed. J. Ellen Gainor, London, Routledge, 1995, pp. 85–103.

Gerould, Daniel, 'Oscar Métenier and Comédie Rosse', *The Drama Review* 28 (1984), 15–28.

Gittleman, Sol, *Frank Wedekind*, New York, Frederick Ungar, 1969.

Gold, Arthur and Robert Fizdale, *The Divine Sarah*, New York, Knopf, 1991.

Goodall, Jane R., 'Acting Savage', in *Body Show/s*, ed. Peta Tait, Amsterdam, Riobi, 2001, pp. 14–28.

Gordon, Mel, ed., *The Grand Guignol: Theatre of Fear and Terror*, New York, Da Capo Press, 1997.

Gould, Stephen Jay, *The Mismeasure of Man*, London, Penguin, 1981.

Gruber, Howard E., *Darwin on Man: Darwin's Early and Unpublished Notebooks, with a Psychological Study of Scientific Creativity*, trans. Paul H. Barrett, London, Wildwood House, 1974.

Guest, Ivor, *Fanny Elssler*, London, Adam & Charles Black, 1970.

——*The Ballet of the Second Empire*, Middletown, Wesleyan University Press, 1974.

Gunther, Albert E., *History of the Collections Contained in the Natural History Departments of the British Museum, 1856–1895*, London, Longmans, 1912.

——*A Century of Zoology at the British Museum Through the Lives of Two Keepers, 1815–1914*, London, Dawson & Sons, 1975.

Gunther, R. T., *Early Science in Oxford Volume III: The Biological Sciences and the Biological Collections*, Oxford, Oxford University Press, 1925.

Haeckel, Ernst, *The Evolution of Man: A Popular Exposition of the Principal Points of Human Ontogeny*, London, Kegan Paul, Trench & Co, 1883.

Halévy, Ludovic and Henri Meilhac, *La Belle Hélène*, Paris, Heugel, 1864.

Ham, Jennifer and Matthew Senior, eds, *Animal Acts: Configuring the Human in Western History*, London, Routledge, 1997.

Hansen, Eric C., *Ludovic Halévy: A Study of Frivolity and Fatalism in Nineteenth Century France*, Lanham, University Press of America, 1987.

Harris, Neil, *Humbug: The Art of P. T. Barnum*, Boston, Little Brown & Co, 1973.

Hawkins, Mike, *Social Darwinism in European and American Thought: Nature as Model and Nature as Threat, 1860–1945*, Cambridge, Cambridge University Press, 1997.

Herman, Arthur, *The Idea of Decline in Western History*, New York, Free Press, 1997.

Holroyd, Michael, *Lytton Strachey: A Critical Biography*, London, Heinemann, 1967.

Hooper-Greenhill, Eileen, *Museums and the Shaping of Knowledge*, London, Routledge, 1992.

Howells, William Dean, 'The New Taste in Theatricals', *Atlantic Monthly* (May 1969), 635–44.

Humphreys, Anne, *Travels into the Poor Man's Country: The Work of Henry Mayhew*, Athens, University of Georgia Press, 1977.

Hutchings, Peter J., *The Criminal Spectre in Law, Literature and Aesthetics*, London, Routledge, 2001.

Huysmans, Joris Karl, *Against Nature*, trans. Robert Baldick, Harmondsworth, Penguin, 1959.

Jahoda, Gustav, *Images of Savages: Ancient Roots of Modern Prejudice in Western Culture*, London, Routledge, 1999.

James, Henry, *A Small Boy and Others*, London, Macmillan, 1913.

Jay, Ricky, *Learned Pigs and Fireproof Women*, New York, Warner Books, 1986.

Jullian, Philippe, *The Triumph of Art Nouveau: Paris Exhibition 1900*, London, Phaidon, 1974.

Karp, Ivan and Steven D. Lavine. *Exhibiting Cultures: The Poetics and Politics of Museum Display*, Washington, DC, Smithsonian Institution Press, 1991.

Keane, H., 'Krao, the "Human Monkey"', *Nature* 27 (1883), 245–6.

Kiralfy, Imre, *America*, London, Routledge, 1893.

Klepac, Richard L., *Mr. Mathews At Home*, London, The Society for Theatre Research, 1979.

Knox, Robert, *The Races of Men*, Philadelphia, Lea & Blanchard, 1850.

Kunhardt, Philip B. Jr., Philip B. Kunhardt III and Peter W. Kunhardt, *P. T. Barnum, America's Greatest Showman: An Illustrated Biography*, New York, Alfred A. Knopf, 1995.

Lamon, W. T. Jr., *Raising Cain: Blackface Performance from Jim Crow to Hip Hop*, Cambridge, MA, Harvard University Press, 1998.

Landau, Misia, *Narratives of Human Evolution*, New Haven, CT, Yale University Press, 1991.

Leibnitz, Gottfried, *Leibnitz Selections*, ed. Philip P. Wiener, New York, Charles Scribner & Sons, 1951.

Levin, Miriam R., *When the Eiffel Tower Was New*, Massachusetts, Mount Holyoke College Art Museum, undated.

Lewes, George Henry, *On Actors and the Art of Acting*, New York, Grove Press, 1957.

The Life of the Aztec Children, information booklet for the Aztecs under Barnum's management, 1860.

Lindfors, Bernth, 'The Hottentot Venus and Other African Attractions in Nineteenth Century England', *Australasian Drama Studies* 1 (1983), 83–104.

Linnaeus, Carolus, *Systema Naturae*, trans. M. S. J. Engel-Lederboer, Amsterdam, Nieuwkoop & B. de Graaf, 1964.

Lorimer, Douglas A., *Colour, Class and the Victorians: English Attitudes to the Negro in the Mid-Nineteenth Century*, Leicester, Leicester University Press, 1978.

Lott, Eric, *Love and Theft*, New York, Oxford University Press, 1993.

Lurieu, Jules Joseph Gabriel de, *Jocko ou le singe du Brésil*, Paris, Chez Quoy, 1825.

McCarren, Felicia, *Dance Pathologies: Performance, Poetics, Medicine*, Stanford, CA, Stanford University Press, 1998.

Makarova, Natalia, *A Dance Autobiography*, New York, Alfred A. Knopf, 1979.

Mallarmé, Stéphane, *Oeuvres Complètes*, Paris, Pleiade, 1945.

Mankowitz, Wolf, *Mazeppa: The Lives, Loves and Legends of Adah Isaacs Menken*, London, Blond & Briggs, 1982.

Martin, Greg and R. L. Wilson, *Buffalo Bill's Wild West: An American Legend*, London, Greenhill Books, 1998.

Mathews, Anne, *Memoirs of Charles Mathews, Comedian*, 3 vols, London, Richard Bentley, 1838.

Mayer, David, ed., *Henry Irving and The Bells*, Manchester, Manchester University Press, 1980.

Mayhew, Henry and John Binny, *The Criminal Prisons of London*, London, Charles Griffin, 1862.

MacGregor, Arthur, ed., *Tradescant's Rarities*, Oxford, Clarendon Press, 1983.

Midgley, Mary, *Beast and Man*, London, Routledge, 1996.

Mikhail, E. H., ed., *Oscar Wilde: Interviews and Recollections*, London, Macmillan, 1979.

Miller, Lilliam B., ed., *The Selected Papers of Charles Willson Peale and his Family*, New Haven, CT, Yale University Press, 1983.

Moody, Richard, *Ned Harrigan: From Corlear's Hook to Herald Square*, Chicago, IL, Nelson-Hall, 1980.

Morand, Paul, *Oeuvres*, Paris, Flammarion, 1981.

Morel, Benedict, *Traité des Dégénerescences physiques, intellectuelles et morales de l'Espèce humaine et des Causes qui produisent les Variétés maladives*, Paris, 1857.

Morley, Henry, *Memoirs of Bartholomew Fair*, London, Chatto & Windus, 1880.

Moses, L. G., *Wild West Shows and the Images of American Indians, 1883–1933*, Albuquerque, University of New Mexico Press, 1996.

Moyal, Ann, *Platypus*, Sydney, Allen & Unwin, 2001.

Murttagh, Matthew and Eugene Watters, *Infinite Variety: Dan Lowry's Music Hall, 1879–97*, London, Gill & Macmillan, 1975.

Nathan, Hans, *Dan Emmett and the Rise of Early Negro Minstrelsy*, Norman, University of Oklahoma Press, 1962.

Nietzsche, Friedrich, *Twilight of the Idols*, trans. R. J. Hollingdale, Harmondsworth, Penguin, 1968.

——*The Birth of Tragedy*, trans. Ronald Speirs, Cambridge, Cambridge University Press, 1999.

Nordau, Max, *Degeneration*, Lincoln, University of Nebraska Press, 1968.

North, John, 'A Lecture on Monstrosities, Part One', *The Lancet* (7 March 1840), 857–61.

——'A Lecture on Monstrosities, Part Two', *The Lancet* (14 March 1840), 913–18.

Numbers, Ronald R., *Darwinism Comes to America*, Cambridge, MA, Harvard University Press, 1998.

Odell, George, *Annals of the New York Stage*, Vol. IV (1834–43), New York, Columbia University Press, 1928.

Ory, Pascal, *L'Expo Universelle 1889*, Paris, Editions Complexes, 1989.

Paradis, James G., 'Satire and Science in Victorian Culture', in *Victorian Science in Context*, ed. Bernard Lightman, Chicago, IL, University of Chicago Press, 1997, pp. 143–75.

Peacock, Shane, *The Great Farini: The High-wire Life of William Hunt*, Toronto, Viking, 1995.

Pearl, Cora, *Mémoires*, Paris, Jules Lévy, 1886.

The Penny Cyclopaedia of The Society for the Diffusion of Useful Knowledge, London, Charles Knight, 1839.

Prichard, James Cowles, *The Natural History of Man*, London, Schulze, 1843.

The Progress of Civilization, information booklet for 'Forepaugh's Wild West', 1888.

Rabinbach, Anson, *The Human Motor: Energy, Fatigue and the Origins of Modernity*, Berkeley, University of California Press, 1992.

Rees, James, *The Life of Edwin Forrest with Personal Reminiscences and Recollections*, Philadelphia, PA, Peterson & Brothers, 1874.

Richardson, Edgar P., Brooke Hindle and Lillian B. Miller, eds, *Charles Willson Peale and his World*, New York, Harry N. Abrams, 1983.

Ritvo, Harriet, *The Platypus and the Mermaid and Other Figments of the Classifying Imagination*, Cambridge, MA, Harvard University Press, 1997.

Rivière, F. and F. Witkop, *Le Grand Guignol*, Paris, Veyrier, 1979.

Rivière, Jacques, 'Le Sacre du Printemps', trans. Miriam Lassman, in *Nijinsky Dancing*, Lincoln Kirstein, London, Thames & Hudson, 1975, 164–8.

Roach, Joseph R., *The Player's Passion: Studies in the Science of Acting*, London and Toronto, Associated University Presses, 1985.

——'Darwin's Passion: The Language of Expression on Nature's Stage', *Discourse* 13 (1990–1), 39–60.

Rydell, Robert W., *All the World's a Fair: Visions of Empire at the American International Expositions, 1876–1916*, Chicago, IL, University of Chicago Press, 1984.

Saxon, A. H., *P. T. Barnum, The Legend and the Man*, New York, Columbia University Press, 1989.

Saxton, Alexander, *The Rise and Fall of the White Republic: Class Politics and Mass Culture in Nineteenth Century America*, London, Verso, 1990.

Sellers, Charles Coleman, *Charles Willson Peale*, New York, Charles Scribner & Sons, 1969.

Seymour, Bruce, *Lola Montez, A Life*, New Haven, CT, Yale University Press, 1996.

Sharpley-Whiting, T. Denean, *Black Venus: Sexualised Savages, Primal Fears, and Primitive Narratives in French*, Durham, NC, Duke University Press, 1999.

Showalter, Elaine, *Sexual Anarchy: Gender and Culture at the Fin de Siècle*, New York, Viking Penguin, 1990.

Sitwell, Sacheverell, *La Vie Parisienne*, London, Faber & Faber, undated.

Smith, Albert, *The Natural History of the Ballet Girl*, London, D. Brogue, 1847.

Smith, Philip E. II and Michael S. Helfland, eds, *Oscar Wilde's Oxford Notebooks: A Portrait of a Mind in the Making*, Oxford, Oxford University Press, 1898.

Spencer, Herbert, *The Principles of Sociology*, London, Williams & Norgate, 1893 edn, 2 vols.

——*An Autobiography*, London, Williams & Norgate, 1904, 2 vols.

Sprat, Thomas, *The History of the Royal Society of London for the Improving of Natural Knowledge*, London, J. Martyn, 1667.

Stallybrass, Peter and Allon White, *The Politics and Poetics of Transgression*, New York, Cornell University Press, 1986.

Stearn, William T., *The Natural History Museum at South Kensington: A History of the British Museum (Natural History), 1753–1980*, London, Heinemann, 1981.

Stevenson, Robert Louis, *Dr. Jekyll and Mr. Hyde*, London, New English Library, 1974.

Stewart, Susan, *On Longing: Narratives of the Miniature, the Gigantic, the Souvenir, the Collection*, Durham, NC, Duke University Press, 1993.

Stocking, George W. Jr., *Victorian Anthropology*, New York, The Free Press, 1987.

Stoker, Bram, *Personal Reminiscences of Henry Irving*, London, Heinemann, 1906.

——*Dracula*, ed. Glennis Byron, Ontario, Broadview Press, 1998.

Taussig, Michael, *Mimesis and Alterity*, London, Routledge, 1993.

Thompson, George A. Jr., *A Documentary History of the African Theatre*, Nebraska, Northwestern University Press, 1998.

Toll, Robert, *Blacking Up: The Minstrel Show in Nineteenth Century America*, New York, Oxford University Press, 1974.

——'Showbiz in Blackface: The Evolution of the Minstrel Show as a Theatrical Form', in *American Popular Entertainment: Proceedings of the 1977 Conference on the History of American Popular Entertainment*, ed. Myron Matlaw, London, Greenwood Press, 1979, 21–32.

Tydeman, William and Steven Price, *Wilde: Salomé*, Cambridge, Cambridge University Press, 1996.

Tylor, E. B., *Researches into the Early History of Mankind and the Development of Civilization*, London, John Murray, 1865.

Vogt, Carl, *Lectures on Man*, London, Longman, Green & Roberts, 1864.

Von Hutten, Baroness, *The Courtesan: The Life of Cora Pearl*, London, Peter Davies, 1933.

Wedekind, Frank, *Prosa*, Berlin, Aufbau-Verlag, 1969.

——*Earth Spirit* in *The Lulu Plays and Other Sex Tragedies*, trans. Stephen Spender, London, John Calder, 1977.

——*Diary of an Erotic Life*, trans. W. E. Yuill, ed. Gerhard Hay, Oxford, Blackwell, 1990.

Wedekind, Tilly, *Lulu, Die Rolle meines Lebens*, Munich, Rutten & Loenig Verlag, 1969.

West, Shearer, *The Image of the Actor*, London, Pinter, 1991.

Whitaker, Katie, 'The Culture of Curiosity', in *Cultures of Natural History*, ed. N. Jardine, J. A. Secord and E. C. Spary, Cambridge, Cambridge University Press, 1996, pp. 75–90.

Whitehead, P. J. P., 'Museums in the History of Zoology', *Museums Journal* 70 (1970), 50–7.

Wilde, Oscar, *The Letters of Oscar Wilde*, ed. Rupert Hart-Davis, London, Rupert Hart-Davis, 1962.

——*De Profundis and Other Writings*, Harmondsworth, Penguin, 1976.

——*Salomé*, Harmondsworth, Penguin, 1974.

Willis, Nathaniel P., *Famous Persons and Places*, New York, J. L. Derby, 1855.

The Wonder Book of Freaks and Animals in the Barnum and Bailey Greatest Show on Earth, London, Walter Hill & Co, 1898.

Wordsworth, William, *The Prelude*, ed. J. Wordsworth, M. H. Abrams and S. Gill, New York, W. W. Norton, 1979.

Zola, Emile, *Nana*, trans. George Holden, London, Penguin, 1972.

——*La Fortune des Rougon*, Dossier, Paris, Presses Pocket, 1991.

——*Oeuvres Complètes*, ed. Henri Mitterand, Paris, Cercle du Livre Précieux, 1967–9.

Zuckerman, S., ed., *The Zoological Society of London, 1826–1976 and Beyond: Proceedings of the 150th Anniversary Symposium of the Zoological Society of London*, London, Academic Press, 1976.

INDEX

251

colonialism: tensions of racial
difference 134–5
colonisation: and culture of natural
history 46; redefinition of 9;
reflected in animal-taming 200–1;
reverse narrative in *Dracula* 188
Coloured Opera Troupe 140–1
comic acting: Hart and Harrigan
128–9; traditions 116, *see also*
impersonation
comic lectures: Valentine 115–16, 124
comic songs: Mathews 119, 121–2
commerce: and show business 92–3,
94, 111
communication: through theatre and
performance 5
Congress of Rough Riders of the World
(show) 96, 107–8
Conolly, John 69, 71, 75
Cony and Blanchard 52
Cooke, James W. 57
Coon, Zip 57, 137–8
Copernicus, Nicolaus 9
Cosmorama: African exhibition **88**
Cossacks 98, 105
Covent Garden 31
creation: Biblical accounts 47; Chapin's
sermon 25
Cross, Edward 208
Crow, Jim: prototypes 137–8
Crystal Palace: Great Exhibition
(1851) 99–100
cultural anxieties 8–9, 189; provoked
by blackface and burlesque 147–8;
of whiteness in America 134
cultural forms: high/low debates 147,
148
curiosities 22, 28, 34, 147, *see also*
cabinets of curiosity
Cuvier, Georges 3, 42, 59, 67, 166,
174

dance and dancers: Elssler 192–4;
featured in minstrel shows 141;
Juba's performances 135–6; Loie
Fuller 213–17, 214; movement
towards natural forms 218; Salomé's
210–11; seen as social threat 185;
symbolism of the body 205, *see also*
ballet; Salomé

Darwin, Charles Robert 1, 6, 9, 21,
59, 168, 170, 173, 182, 194; age of
3, 219–20; concern with varieties
112–13, 113–14, 149; *The Descent of
Man* 4, 74, 149–50, 160; *The
Expression of the Emotions* 174–5,
176–7, 178, 179–80; influence and
status 97, 137, 219–20;
neurasthenia 187; *The Origin of
Species* 4, 9, 13, 52, 54, 73–4, 112,
138, 149; on sexual selection 150–1;
theories used in 'missing link' shows
75, 79; theory of natural selection
44, 74, 107, 112, 113–14, 148,
150, 152, 186, 187–8, 218; *The
Voyage of the Beagle* 131–2, 149, *see
also* social Darwinism
Darwin, Erasmus 3
Darwin and the General Reader
(Ellegard) 4, 5
Daston, Lorraine: *Wonders and the Order
of Nature* (with Park) 14–15, 25
Daumard, Adeline 164
Davenport, Jean 125
De Profundis (Wilde) 211
decadence 212, 219; Loie Fuller 216,
217; and neurasthenic sensibilities
208–9; theatres of 8
'Deformito-mania': *Punch* cartoon 18,
19
Degeneration (Nordau) 211–12, 216
delineation 115–16, 132; cross-racial
123; and ethnological research
126–7; female types 125; Harrigan
128–9; Mathews and influence 120,
124, 132, *see also* minstrelsy
demi-mondaines 147, 154, 158
The Descent of Man (Darwin) 4, 74,
149–50, 160
Diaghilev, Sergei 218
Diamond, John 194
Dickens, Charles: *Hard Times* 42; on
Juba's performance 136; on savages
84, 87–8
Diderot, Denis 3, 169–70, 171, 175
difference *see* gender difference; racial
difference; racial diversity; variety
Dijkstra, Bram 6, 189
Dionysos: Nietzsche's idea of 204–5
Dixey *see* Carncross and Dixey

INDEX